GO!
with Microsoft®

PowerPoint 2007

Brief

Shelley Gaskin and Alicia Vargas

PEARSON

Prentice
Hall

Upper Saddle River, New Jersey

This book is dedicated to my students, who inspire me every day, and to my husband, Fred Gaskin.
—Shelley Gaskin

This book is dedicated with all my love to my husband Vic, who makes everything possible;
and to my children Victor, Phil, and Emmy, who are an unending source of inspiration
and who make everything worthwhile.
—Alicia Vargas

Library of Congress Cataloging-in-Publication Data

Gaskin, Shelley.
　Go! with PowerPoint 2007 : brief / Shelley Gaskin and Alicia Vargas.
　　p. cm.
　Includes index.
　ISBN 0-13-513041-7
　1. Presentation graphics software. 2. Microsoft PowerPoint (Computer file) I. Vargas, Alicia.
II. Title.
　T385.G3788 2007
　005.5'8--dc22

2007011747

Vice President and Publisher: Natalie E. Anderson
Associate VP/Executive Acquisitions Editor, Print: Stephanie Wall
Executive Acquisitions Editor, Media: Richard Keaveny
Product Development Manager: Eileen Bien Calabro
Senior Editorial Project Manager: Laura Burgess
Development Editor: Ginny Munroe
Editorial Assistants: Becky Knauer, Lora Cimiluca
Executive Producer: Lisa Strite
Content Development Manager: Cathi Profitko
Senior Media Project Manager: Steve Gagliostro
Production Media Project Manager: Lorena Cerisano
Director of Marketing: Margaret Waples
Senior Marketing Manager: Jason Sakos
Marketing Assistants: Angela Frey, Kathryn Ferranti
Senior Sales Associate: Rebecca Scott

Managing Editor: Lynda J. Castillo
Manufacturing Production Project Manager: Wanda Rockwell
Production Editor: GGS Book Services
Photo Researcher: GGS Book Services
Manufacturing Buyer: Natacha Moore
Production/Editorial Assistant: Sandra K. Bernales
Design Director: Maria Lange
Art Director/Interior Design: Blair Brown
Cover Photo: Courtesy of Getty Images, Inc./Marvin Mattelson
Composition: GGS Book Services
Project Management: GGS Book Services
Cover Printer: Phoenix Color
Printer/Binder: RR Donnelley/Willard

Microsoft, Windows, Word, PowerPoint, Outlook, FrontPage, Visual Basic, MSN, The Microsoft Network, and/or other Microsoft products referenced herein are either trademarks or registered trademarks of Microsoft Corporation in the U.S.A. and other countries. Screen shots and icons reprinted with permission from the Microsoft Corporation. This book is not sponsored or endorsed by or affiliated with Microsoft Corporation.

Credits and acknowledgments borrowed from other sources and reproduced, with permission, in this textbook are as follows or on the appropriate page within the text.

　Page 2: Rough Guides Dorling Kindersley; page 80: AGE Fotostock America, Inc.; and page 162: The Stock Connection.

10 9 8 7 6 5 4 3 2
ISBN 0-13-513041-7

Contents in Brief

The *GO!* System Visual Walk-Through xiv

Chapter 1   **Getting Started with Microsoft PowerPoint 2007** 1

Chapter 2   **Designing a PowerPoint Presentation**... 79

Chapter 3   **Enhancing a Presentation with Animation, Tables, and Charts**............................... 161

Glossary G-1

Index I-1

Table of Contents

The *GO!* System Visual
Walk-Through xiv

PowerPoint 2007

Chapter 1 Getting Started with Microsoft PowerPoint 2007 1

PROJECT 1A Expansion   **3**

Objective 1 Open, View, and Save a Presentation   **4**
Activity 1.1 Starting PowerPoint and Identifying Parts of the PowerPoint Window   4
Activity 1.2 Opening a Presentation   5
Activity 1.3 Viewing a Slide Show   8
Activity 1.4 Creating Folders and Saving a Presentation   9

Objective 2 Edit a Presentation   **11**
Activity 1.5 Editing Slide Text   11
Activity 1.6 Inserting a New Slide   12
Activity 1.7 Increasing and Decreasing List Levels   14
Activity 1.8 Checking Spelling   16
Activity 1.9 Editing Text by Using the Thesaurus   18
Activity 1.10 Adding Speaker's Notes to a Presentation   19

Objective 3 Format a Presentation   **20**
Activity 1.11 Changing Font and Font Size   20
Activity 1.12 Applying Font Styles   22
Activity 1.13 Aligning Text and Changing Line Spacing   23
Activity 1.14 Modifying Slide Layout   24
Activity 1.15 Changing the Presentation Theme   25

Objective 4 Create Headers and Footers and Print a Presentation   **27**
Activity 1.16 Creating Headers and Footers   28
Activity 1.17 Previewing and Printing a Presentation and Closing PowerPoint   29

PROJECT 1B Overview   **32**

Objective 5 Create a New Presentation   **33**
Activity 1.18 Starting a New Presentation   33
Activity 1.19 Inserting Slides from an Existing Presentation   36

Objective 6 Use Slide Sorter View   **38**
Activity 1.20 Selecting and Deleting Slides   38
Activity 1.21 Moving Slides   39

Objective 7 Add Pictures to a Presentation   **39**
Activity 1.22 Inserting Clip Art   40
Activity 1.23 Moving and Sizing Images   42
Activity 1.24 Applying a Style to a Picture   44

Objective 8 Use the Microsoft Help System   **45**
Activity 1.25 Accessing PowerPoint Help   46

There's More You Can Do!   47
Summary   48
Key Terms   48
Matching   49
Fill in the Blank   50
Skills Review   51
Mastering PowerPoint   58
Business Running Case   69
Rubric   70
Problem Solving   71
You and *GO!*   76
GO! with Help   76
Group Business Running Case   77

Chapter 2 Designing a PowerPoint Presentation 79

PROJECT 2A Welcome   **81**

Objective 1 Format Slide Elements   **82**
Activity 2.1 Selecting Placeholder Text and Using the Repeat Key   82
Activity 2.2 Changing a Bulleted List to a Numbered List   85
Activity 2.3 Modifying the Bulleted List Style   85
Activity 2.4 Applying WordArt Styles to Text   87
Activity 2.5 Using Format Painter   89

Objective 2 Insert and Format Pictures and Shapes   **90**
Activity 2.6 Inserting a Picture Using a Content Layout   91
Activity 2.7 Changing the Size and Shape of a Picture   92
Activity 2.8 Inserting and Positioning a Text Box   93
Activity 2.9 Inserting, Sizing, and Positioning Shapes   96

Activity 2.10   Adding Text to Shapes   98
Activity 2.11   Applying Shape and Picture Styles   99
Activity 2.12   Duplicating and Aligning Objects   101

Objective 3   Apply Slide Transitions   105
Activity 2.13   Applying Slide Transitions to a Presentation   105

PROJECT 2B   Itinerary   108

Objective 4   Reorganize Presentation Text and Clear Formats   109
Activity 2.14   Moving and Copying Text   109
Activity 2.15   Copying Multiple Selections by Using the Office Clipboard   112
Activity 2.16   Undoing and Redoing Changes   114
Activity 2.17   Clearing Formatting from a Selection   114

Objective 5   Create and Format a SmartArt Graphic   115
Activity 2.18   Creating a SmartArt Diagram by Using a Content Layout   115
Activity 2.19   Adding and Removing Shapes in a Diagram   118
Activity 2.20   Changing the Diagram Type and Size   120
Activity 2.21   Creating a SmartArt Diagram from Bullet Points   123
Activity 2.22   Changing the Color and Style of a Diagram   123

There's More You Can Do!   125
Summary   126
Key Terms   126
Matching   127
Fill in the Blank   128
Skills Review   129
Mastering PowerPoint   136
Business Running Case   150
Rubric   151
Problem Solving   152
You and GO!   158
GO! with Help   158
Group Business Running Case   159

Chapter 3   Enhancing a Presentation with Animation, Tables, and Charts   161

PROJECT 3A   New Homes   163

Objective 1   Customize Slide Backgrounds and Themes   164
Activity 3.1   Applying a Background Style   164
Activity 3.2   Hiding Background Graphics   165

Activity 3.3   Formatting a Slide Background with a Picture   166
Activity 3.4   Applying a Background Fill Color and Resetting a Slide Background   170
Activity 3.5   Modifying Font Themes   171

Objective 2   Animate a Slide Show   172
Activity 3.6   Applying Entrance Effects   172
Activity 3.7   Setting Effect and Timing Options   175
Activity 3.8   Applying Animation to a SmartArt Graphic   179

PROJECT 3B   Developments   181

Objective 3   Create and Modify Tables   182
Activity 3.9   Creating a Table   182
Activity 3.10   Modifying the Layout of a Table   185
Activity 3.11   Modifying a Table Design   188

Objective 4   Create and Modify Charts   190
Activity 3.12   Creating a Column Chart and Applying a Chart Style   190
Activity 3.13   Deleting Chart Data and Changing the Chart Type   195
Activity 3.14   Animating a Chart   197

There's More You Can Do!   199
Summary   200
Key Terms   200
Matching   201
Fill in the Blank   202
Skills Review   203
Mastering PowerPoint   211
Business Running Case   224
Rubric   225
Problem Solving   226
You and GO!   232
GO! with Help   232
Group Business Running Case   233

Glossary **G-1**
Index **I-1**

Letter from the Editor

Dear Instructors and Students,

The primary goal of the *GO!* Series is two-fold. The first goal is to help instructors teach the course they want in less time. The second goal is to provide students with the skills to solve business problems using the computer as a tool, for both themselves and the organization for which they might be employed.

The *GO!* Series was originally created by Series Editor Shelley Gaskin and published with the release of Microsoft Office 2003. Her ideas came from years of using textbooks that didn't meet all the needs of today's diverse classroom and that were too confusing for students. Shelley continues to enhance the series by ensuring we stay true to our vision of developing quality instruction and useful classroom tools.

But we also need your input and ideas.

Over time, the *GO!* Series has evolved based on direct feedback from instructors and students using the series. *We are the publisher that listens.* To publish a textbook that works for you, it's critical that we continue to listen to this feedback. It's important to me to talk with you and hear your stories about using *GO!* Your voice can make a difference.

My hope is that this letter will inspire you to write me an e-mail and share your thoughts on using the *GO!* Series.

Stephanie Wall
Executive Editor, *GO!* Series
stephanie_wall@prenhall.com

GO! System Contributors

We thank the following people for their hard work and support in making the *GO!* System all that it is!

Additional Author Support

Coyle, Diane	Montgomery County Community College
Fry, Susan	Boise State
Townsend, Kris	Spokane Falls Community College
Stroup, Tracey	Amgen Corporation

Instructor Resource Authors

Amer, Beverly	Northern Arizona University	Paterson, Jim	Paradise Valley Community College
Boito, Nancy	Harrisburg Area Community College	Prince, Lisa	Missouri State
Coyle, Diane	Montgomery County Community College	Rodgers, Gwen	Southern Nazarene University
Dawson, Tamara	Southern Nazarene University	Ruymann, Amy	Burlington Community College
Driskel, Loretta	Niagara County Community College	Ryan, Bob	Montgomery County Community College
Elliott, Melissa	Odessa College		
Fry, Susan	Boise State	Smith, Diane	Henry Ford Community College
Geoghan, Debra	Bucks County Community College	Spangler, Candice	Columbus State Community College
Hearn, Barbara	Community College of Philadelphia	Thompson, Joyce	Lehigh Carbon Community College
Jones, Stephanie	South Plains College	Tiffany, Janine	Reading Area Community College
Madsen, Donna	Kirkwood Community College	Watt, Adrienne	Douglas College
Meck, Kari	Harrisburg Area Community College	Weaver, Paul	Bossier Parish Community College
Miller, Cindy	Ivy Tech	Weber, Sandy	Gateway Technical College
Nowakowski, Tony	Buffalo State	Wood, Dawn	
Pace, Phyllis	Queensborough Community College	Weissman, Jonathan	Finger Lakes Community College

Super Reviewers

Brotherton, Cathy	Riverside Community College	Maurer, Trina	Odessa College
Cates, Wally	Central New Mexico Community College	Meck, Kari	Harrisburg Area Community College
		Miller, Cindy	Ivy Tech Community College
Cone, Bill	Northern Arizona University	Nielson, Phil	Salt Lake Community College
Coverdale, John	Riverside Community College	Rodgers, Gwen	Southern Nazarene University
Foster, Nancy	Baker College	Smolenski, Robert	Delaware Community College
Helfand, Terri	Chaffey College	Spangler, Candice	Columbus State Community College
Hibbert, Marilyn	Salt Lake Community College	Thompson, Joyce	Lehigh Carbon Community College
Holliday, Mardi	Community College of Philadelphia	Weber, Sandy	Gateway Technical College
Jerry, Gina	Santa Monica College	Wells, Lorna	Salt Lake Community College
Martin, Carol	Harrisburg Area Community College	Zaboski, Maureen	University of Scranton

Technical Editors

Janice Snyder
Joyce Nielsen
Colette Eisele
Janet Pickard
Mara Zebest
Lindsey Allen
William Daley

Student Reviewers

Allen, John	Asheville-Buncombe Tech Community College	Erickson, Mike	Ball State University
		Gadomski, Amanda	Northern Michigan University
Alexander, Steven	St. Johns River Community College	Gyselinck, Craig	Central Washington University
Alexander, Melissa	Tulsa Community College	Harrison, Margo	Central Washington University
Bolz, Stephanie	Northern Michigan University	Heacox, Kate	Central Washington University
Berner, Ashley	Central Washington University	Hill, Cheretta	Northwestern State University
Boomer, Michelle	Northern Michigan University	Innis, Tim	Tulsa Community College
Busse, Brennan	Northern Michigan University	Jarboe, Aaron	Central Washington University
Butkey, Maura	Central Washington University	Klein, Colleen	Northern Michigan University
Christensen, Kaylie	Northern Michigan University	Moeller, Jeffrey	Northern Michigan University
Connally, Brianna	Central Washington University	Nicholson, Regina	Athens Tech College
Davis, Brandon	Northern Michigan University	Niehaus, Kristina	Northern Michigan University
Davis, Christen	Central Washington University	Nisa, Zaibun	Santa Rosa Community College
Den Boer, Lance	Central Washington University	Nunez, Nohelia	Santa Rosa Community College
Dix, Jessica	Central Washington University	Oak, Samantha	Central Washington University
Moeller, Jeffrey	Northern Michigan University	Oertii, Monica	Central Washington University
Downs, Elizabeth	Central Washington University	Palenshus, Juliet	Central Washington University

Pohl, Amanda — Northern Michigan University
Presnell, Randy — Central Washington University
Ritner, April — Northern Michigan University
Rodriguez, Flavia — Northwestern State University
Roberts, Corey — Tulsa Community College
Rossi, Jessica Ann — Central Washington University
Shafapay, Natasha — Central Washington University

Shanahan, Megan — Northern Michigan University
Teska, Erika — Hawaii Pacific University
Traub, Amy — Northern Michigan University
Underwood, Katie — Central Washington University
Walters, Kim — Central Washington University
Wilson, Kelsie — Central Washington University
Wilson, Amanda — Green River Community College

Series Reviewers

Abraham, Reni — Houston Community College
Agatston, Ann — Agatston Consulting Technical College
Alexander, Melody — Ball Sate University
Alejandro, Manuel — Southwest Texas Junior College
Ali, Farha — Lander University
Amici, Penny — Harrisburg Area Community College
Anderson, Patty A. — Lake City Community College
Andrews, Wilma — Virginia Commonwealth College, Nebraska University
Anik, Mazhar — Tiffin University
Armstrong, Gary — Shippensburg University
Atkins, Bonnie — Delaware Technical Community College
Bachand, LaDonna — Santa Rosa Community College
Bagui, Sikha — University of West Florida
Beecroft, Anita — Kwantlen University College
Bell, Paula — Lock Haven College
Belton, Linda — Springfield Tech. Community College
Bennett, Judith — Sam Houston State University
Bhatia, Sai — Riverside Community College
Bishop, Frances — DeVry Institute—Alpharetta (ATL)
Blaszkiewicz, Holly — Ivy Tech Community College/Region 1
Branigan, Dave — DeVry University
Bray, Patricia — Allegany College of Maryland
Brotherton, Cathy — Riverside Community College
Buehler, Lesley — Ohlone College
Buell, C — Central Oregon Community College
Byars, Pat — Brookhaven College
Byrd, Lynn — Delta State University, Cleveland, Mississippi
Cacace, Richard N. — Pensacola Junior College
Cadenhead, Charles — Brookhaven College
Calhoun, Ric — Gordon College
Cameron, Eric — Passaic Community College
Carriker, Sandra — North Shore Community College
Cannamore, Madie — Kennedy King
Carreon, Cleda — Indiana University—Purdue University, Indianapolis
Chaffin, Catherine — Shawnee State University
Chauvin, Marg — Palm Beach Community College, Boca Raton
Challa, Chandrashekar — Virginia State University
Chamlou, Afsaneh — NOVA Alexandria
Chapman, Pam — Wabaunsee Community College
Christensen, Dan — Iowa Western Community College
Clay, Betty — Southeastern Oklahoma State University
Collins, Linda D. — Mesa Community College
Conroy-Link, Janet — Holy Family College
Cosgrove, Janet — Northwestern CT Community
Courtney, Kevin — Hillsborough Community College
Cox, Rollie — Madison Area Technical College
Crawford, Hiram — Olive Harvey College

Crawford, Thomasina — Miami-Dade College, Kendall Campus
Credico, Grace — Lethbridge Community College
Crenshaw, Richard — Miami Dade Community College, North
Crespo, Beverly — Mt. San Antonio College
Crossley, Connie — Cincinnati State Technical Community College
Curik, Mary — Central New Mexico Community College
De Arazoza, Ralph — Miami Dade Community College
Danno, John — DeVry University/Keller Graduate School
Davis, Phillip — Del Mar College
DeHerrera, Laurie — Pikes Peak Community College
Delk, Dr. K. Kay — Seminole Community College
Doroshow, Mike — Eastfield College
Douglas, Gretchen — SUNYCortland
Dove, Carol — Community College of Allegheny
Driskel, Loretta — Niagara Community College
Duckwiler, Carol — Wabaunsee Community College
Duncan, Mimi — University of Missouri-St. Louis
Duthie, Judy — Green River Community College
Duvall, Annette — Central New Mexico Community College
Ecklund, Paula — Duke University
Eng, Bernice — Brookdale Community College
Evans, Billie — Vance-Granville Community College
Feuerbach, Lisa — Ivy Tech East Chicago
Fisher, Fred — Florida State University
Foster, Penny L. — Anne Arundel Community College
Foszcz, Russ — McHenry County College
Fry, Susan — Boise State University
Fustos, Janos — Metro State
Gallup, Jeanette — Blinn College
Gelb, Janet — Grossmont College
Gentry, Barb — Parkland College
Gerace, Karin — St. Angela Merici School
Gerace, Tom — Tulane University
Ghajar, Homa — Oklahoma State University
Gifford, Steve — Northwest Iowa Community College
Glazer, Ellen — Broward Community College
Gordon, Robert — Hofstra University
Gramlich, Steven — Pasco-Hernando Community College
Graviett, Nancy M. — St. Charles Community College, St. Peters, Missouri
Greene, Rich — Community College of Allegheny County
Gregoryk, Kerry — Virginia Commonwealth State
Griggs, Debra — Bellevue Community College
Grimm, Carol — Palm Beach Community College
Hahn, Norm — Thomas Nelson Community College
Hammerschlag, Dr. Bill — Brookhaven College
Hansen, Michelle — Davenport University
Hayden, Nancy — Indiana University—Purdue University, Indianapolis

Hayes, Theresa	Broward Community College
Helfand, Terri	Chaffey College
Helms, Liz	Columbus State Community College
Hernandez, Leticia	TCI College of Technology
Hibbert, Marilyn	Salt Lake Community College
Hoffman, Joan	Milwaukee Area Technical College
Hogan, Pat	Cape Fear Community College
Holland, Susan	Southeast Community College
Hopson, Bonnie	Athens Technical College
Horvath, Carrie	Albertus Magnus College
Horwitz, Steve	Community College of Philadelphia
Hotta, Barbara	Leeward Community College
Howard, Bunny	St. Johns River Community
Howard, Chris	DeVry University
Huckabay, Jamie	Austin Community College
Hudgins, Susan	East Central University
Hulett, Michelle J.	Missouri State University
Hunt, Darla A.	Morehead State University, Morehead, Kentucky
Hunt, Laura	Tulsa Community College
Jacob, Sherry	Jefferson Community College
Jacobs, Duane	Salt Lake Community College
Jauken, Barb	Southeastern Community
Johnson, Kathy	Wright College
Johnson, Mary	Kingwood College
Johnson, Mary	Mt. San Antonio College
Jones, Stacey	Benedict College
Jones, Warren	University of Alabama, Birmingham
Jordan, Cheryl	San Juan College
Kapoor, Bhushan	California State University, Fullerton
Kasai, Susumu	Salt Lake Community College
Kates, Hazel	Miami Dade Community College, Kendall
Keen, Debby	University of Kentucky
Keeter, Sandy	Seminole Community College
Kern-Blystone, Dorothy Jean	Bowling Green State
Keskin, Ilknur	The University of South Dakota
Kirk, Colleen	Mercy College
Kleckner, Michelle	Elon University
Kliston, Linda	Broward Community College, North Campus
Kochis, Dennis	Suffolk County Community College
Kramer, Ed	Northern Virginia Community College
Laird, Jeff	Northeast State Community College
Lamoureaux, Jackie	Central New Mexico Community College
Lange, David	Grand Valley State
LaPointe, Deb	Central New Mexico Community College
Larson, Donna	Louisville Technical Institute
Laspina, Kathy	Vance-Granville Community College
Le Grand, Dr. Kate	Broward Community College
Lenhart, Sheryl	Terra Community College
Letavec, Chris	University of Cincinnati
Liefert, Jane	Everett Community College
Lindaman, Linda	Black Hawk Community College
Lindberg, Martha	Minnesota State University
Lightner, Renee	Broward Community College
Lindberg, Martha	Minnesota State University
Linge, Richard	Arizona Western College
Logan, Mary G.	Delgado Community College
Loizeaux, Barbara	Westchester Community College
Lopez, Don	Clovis-State Center Community College District

Lord, Alexandria	Asheville Buncombe Tech
Lowe, Rita	Harold Washington College
Low, Willy Hui	Joliet Junior College
Lucas, Vickie	Broward Community College
Lynam, Linda	Central Missouri State University
Lyon, Lynne	Durham College
Lyon, Pat Rajski	Tomball College
MacKinnon, Ruth	Georgia Southern University
Macon, Lisa	Valencia Community College, West Campus
Machuca, Wayne	College of the Sequoias
Madison, Dana	Clarion University
Maguire, Trish	Eastern New Mexico University
Malkan, Rajiv	Montgomery College
Manning, David	Northern Kentucky University
Marcus, Jacquie	Niagara Community College
Marghitu, Daniela	Auburn University
Marks, Suzanne	Bellevue Community College
Marquez, Juanita	El Centro College
Marquez, Juan	Mesa Community College
Martyn, Margie	Baldwin-Wallace College
Marucco, Toni	Lincoln Land Community College
Mason, Lynn	Lubbock Christian University
Matutis, Audrone	Houston Community College
Matkin, Marie	University of Lethbridge
McCain, Evelynn	Boise State University
McCannon, Melinda	Gordon College
McCarthy, Marguerite	Northwestern Business College
McCaskill, Matt L.	Brevard Community College
McClellan, Carolyn	Tidewater Community College
McClure, Darlean	College of Sequoias
McCrory, Sue A.	Missouri State University
McCue, Stacy	Harrisburg Area Community College
McEntire-Orbach, Teresa	Middlesex County College
McLeod, Todd	Fresno City College
McManus, Illyana	Grossmont College
McPherson, Dori	Schoolcraft College
Meiklejohn, Nancy	Pikes Peak Community College
Menking, Rick	Hardin-Simmons University
Meredith, Mary	University of Louisiana at Lafayette
Mermelstein, Lisa	Baruch College
Metos, Linda	Salt Lake Community College
Meurer, Daniel	University of Cincinnati
Meyer, Marian	Central New Mexico Community College
Miller, Cindy	Ivy Tech Community College, Lafayette, Indiana
Mitchell, Susan	Davenport University
Mohle, Dennis	Fresno Community College
Monk, Ellen	University of Delaware
Moore, Rodney	Holland College
Morris, Mike	Southeastern Oklahoma State University
Morris, Nancy	Hudson Valley Community College
Moseler, Dan	Harrisburg Area Community College
Nabors, Brent	Reedley College, Clovis Center
Nadas, Erika	Wright College
Nadelman, Cindi	New England College
Nademlynsky, Lisa	Johnson & Wales University
Ncube, Cathy	University of West Florida
Nagengast, Joseph	Florida Career College
Newsome, Eloise	Northern Virginia Community College Woodbridge
Nicholls, Doreen	Mohawk Valley Community College
Nunan, Karen	Northeast State Technical Community College

Odegard, Teri	Edmonds Community College	Sterling, Janet	Houston Community College
Ogle, Gregory	North Community College	Stoughton, Catherine	Laramie County Community College
Orr, Dr. Claudia	Northern Michigan University South	Sullivan, Angela	Joliet Junior College
Otieno, Derek	DeVry University	Szurek, Joseph	University of Pittsburgh at Greensburg
Otton, Diana Hill	Chesapeake College		
Oxendale, Lucia	West Virginia Institute of Technology	Tarver, Mary Beth	Northwestern State University
		Taylor, Michael	Seattle Central Community College
Paiano, Frank	Southwestern College	Thangiah, Sam	Slippery Rock University
Patrick, Tanya	Clackamas Community College	Thompson-Sellers, Ingrid	Georgia Perimeter College
Peairs, Deb	Clark State Community College	Tomasi, Erik	Baruch College
Prince, Lisa	Missouri State University-Springfield Campus	Toreson, Karen	Shoreline Community College
		Trifiletti, John J.	Florida Community College at Jacksonville
Proietti, Kathleen	Northern Essex Community College		
Pusins, Delores	HCCC	Trivedi, Charulata	Quinsigamond Community College, Woodbridge
Raghuraman, Ram	Joliet Junior College		
Reasoner, Ted Allen	Indiana University—Purdue	Tucker, William	Austin Community College
Reeves, Karen	High Point University	Turgeon, Cheryl	Asnuntuck Community College
Remillard, Debbie	New Hampshire Technical Institute	Turpen, Linda	Central New Mexico Community College
Rhue, Shelly	DeVry University		
Richards, Karen	Maplewoods Community College	Upshaw, Susan	Del Mar College
Richardson, Mary	Albany Technical College	Unruh, Angela	Central Washington University
Rodgers, Gwen	Southern Nazarene University	Vanderhoof, Dr. Glenna	Missouri State University-Springfield Campus
Roselli, Diane	Harrisburg Area Community College		
Ross, Dianne	University of Louisiana in Lafayette	Vargas, Tony	El Paso Community College
Rousseau, Mary	Broward Community College, South	Vicars, Mitzi	Hampton University
Samson, Dolly	Hawaii Pacific University	Villarreal, Kathleen	Fresno
Sams, Todd	University of Cincinnati	Vitrano, Mary Ellen	Palm Beach Community College
Sandoval, Everett	Reedley College	Volker, Bonita	Tidewater Community College
Sardone, Nancy	Seton Hall University	Wahila, Lori (Mindy)	Tompkins Cortland Community College
Scafide, Jean	Mississippi Gulf Coast Community College		
		Waswick, Kim	Southeast Community College, Nebraska
Scheeren, Judy	Westmoreland County Community College		
		Wavle, Sharon	Tompkins Cortland Community College
Schneider, Sol	Sam Houston State University		
Scroggins, Michael	Southwest Missouri State University	Webb, Nancy	City College of San Francisco
Sever, Suzanne	Northwest Arkansas Community College	Wells, Barbara E.	Central Carolina Technical College
		Wells, Lorna	Salt Lake Community College
Sheridan, Rick	California State University-Chico	Welsh, Jean	Lansing Community College Nebraska
Silvers, Pamela	Asheville Buncombe Tech		
Singer, Steven A.	University of Hawai'i, Kapi'olani Community College	White, Bruce	Quinnipiac University
		Willer, Ann	Solano Community College
Sinha, Atin	Albany State University	Williams, Mark	Lane Community College
Skolnick, Martin	Florida Atlantic University	Wilson, Kit	Red River College
Smith, T. Michael	Austin Community College	Wilson, Roger	Fairmont State University
Smith, Tammy	Tompkins Cortland Community Collge	Wimberly, Leanne	International Academy of Design and Technology
Smolenski, Bob	Delaware County Community College	Worthington, Paula	Northern Virginia Community College
Spangler, Candice	Columbus State		
Stedham, Vicki	St. Petersburg College, Clearwater	Yauney, Annette	Herkimer County Community College
Stefanelli, Greg	Carroll Community College		
Steiner, Ester	New Mexico State University	Yip, Thomas	Passaic Community College
Stenlund, Neal	Northern Virginia Community College, Alexandria	Zavala, Ben	Webster Tech
		Zlotow, Mary Ann	College of DuPage
St. John, Steve	Tulsa Community College	Zudeck, Steve	Broward Community College, North

About the Authors

Shelley Gaskin, Series Editor, is a professor of business and computer technology at Pasadena City College in Pasadena, California. She holds a master's degree in business education from Northern Illinois University and a doctorate in adult and community education from Ball State University. Dr. Gaskin has 15 years of experience in the computer industry with several Fortune 500 companies and has developed and written training materials for custom systems applications in both the public and private sector. She is also the author of books on Microsoft Outlook and word processing.

Alicia Vargas is a faculty member in Business Information Technology at Pasadena City College. She holds a master's and a bachelor's degree in business education from California State University, Los Angeles, and has authored several textbooks and training manuals on Microsoft Word, Microsoft Excel, and Microsoft PowerPoint.

Visual Walk-Through of the *GO!* System

The *GO!* System is designed for ease of implementation on the instructor side and ease of understanding on the student. It has been completely developed based on professor and student feedback.

The *GO!* System is divided into three categories that reflect how you might organize your course— **Prepare**, **Teach**, and **Assess**.

Prepare

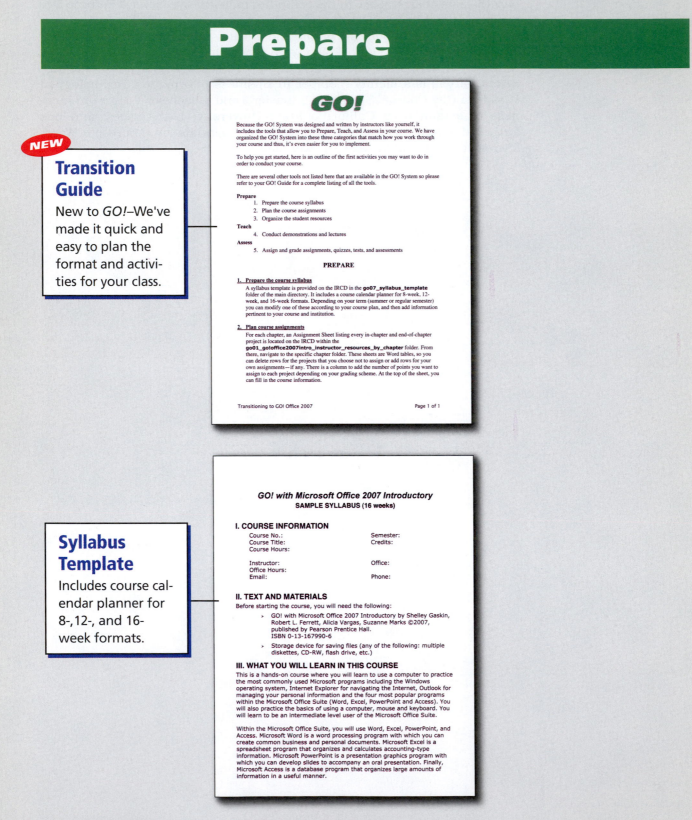

NEW

Transition Guide

New to *GO!*—We've made it quick and easy to plan the format and activities for your class.

Syllabus Template

Includes course calendar planner for 8-,12-, and 16-week formats.

Assignment Sheet

One per chapter. Lists all possible assignments; add to and delete from this simple Word table according to your course plan.

GO! with Microsoft Office 2007 Introductory

Assignment Sheet for GO! with Microsoft Office 2007 Introductory
Chapter 5

Instructor Name: _____
Course Information: _____

Do This (✔ when done)	Then Hand In This — Check each Project for the elements listed on the Assignment Tag. Attach the Tag to your Project.	Submit Printed Formulas	By This Date	Possible Points	Your Points
Study the text and perform the steps for Activities 5.1 – 5.11	Project 5A Application Letter				
Study the text and perform the steps for Activities 5.12 – 5.23	Project 5B Company Overview				
End-of-Chapter Assessments					
Complete the Matching and Fill-in-the-Blank questions	As directed by your instructor				
Complete Project 5C	Project 5C Receipt Letter				
Complete Project 5D	Project 5D Marketing				
Complete Project 5E	Project 5E School Tour				
Complete Project 5F	Project 5F Scouting Trip				
Complete Project 5G	Project 5G Contract				
Complete Project 5H	Project 5H Invitation				
Complete Project 5I	Project 5I Fax Cover				
Complete Project 5J	Project 5J Business Running Case				
Complete Project 5K	Project 5K Services				
Complete Project 5L	Project 5L Survey Form				
Complete Project 5M	Project 5M Press Release				

Copyright © 2008 Pearson Prentice Hall   Page 1 of 1

File Guide to the GO! Supplements

Tabular listing of all supplements and their file names.

GO! with Microsoft Office Office 2003
Supplements File Guide - Assess & Grade

(table of supplement file names)

NEW

Assignment Planning Guide

Description of GO! assignments with recommendations based on class size, delivery mode, and student needs. Includes examples from fellow instructors.

GO! with Microsoft Office 2007 Introductory
Assignment Planning Guide

Planning the Course Assignments

For each chapter in GO!, an Assignment Sheet listing every in-chapter and end-of-chapter project is located on the IRCD. These sheets are Word tables, so you can delete rows for the projects that you will not assign, and then add rows for any of your own assignments that you may have developed. There is a column to add the number of points you want to assign to each project—depending on your grading scheme. At the top of the sheet, you can fill in your course information.

Additionally, for each chapter, student Assignment Tags are provided for every project (including Problem Solving projects)—also located on the IRCD. These are small scoring checklists on which you can check off errors made by the student, and with which the student can verify that all project elements are complete. For campus classes, the student can attach the tags to his or her paper submissions. For online classes, many GO! instructors have the student include these with the electronic submission.

Deciding What to Assign

Front Portion of the Chapter—Instructional Projects: The projects in the front portion of the chapter, which are listed on the first page of each chapter, are the instructional projects. Most instructors assign all of these projects, because this is where the student receives the instruction and engages in the active learning.

End-of-Chapter—Practice and Critical Thinking Projects: In the back portion of the chapter (the gray pages), you can assign on a prescriptive basis; that is, for students who were challenged by the instructional projects, you might assign one or more projects from the two *Skills Reviews,* which provide maximum prompting and a thorough review of the entire chapter. For students who have previous software knowledge and who completed the instructional projects easily, you might assign only the *Mastery Projects.*

You can also assign prescriptively by Objective, because each end-of-chapter project indicates the Objectives covered. So you might assign, on a student-by-student basis, only the projects that cover the Objectives with which the student seemed to have difficulty in the instructional projects.

The five Problem Solving projects and the You and GO! project are the authentic assessments that pull together the student's learning. Here the student is presented with a "messy real-life situation" and then uses his or her knowledge and skill to solve a problem, produce a product, give a presentation, or demonstrate a procedure. You might assign one or more of the Problem

GO! Assignment Planning Guide   Page 1 of 1

Student Data Files

Music School Records discovers, launches, and and develops the careers of young artists in classical, jazz, and contemporary music. Our philosophy is to not only shape, distribute, and sell a music product, but to help artists create a career that can lats a lifetime. too often in the music industry, artists are forced to fit their music to a trend that is short-lived. Music School Records doesn't just follow trends, we take a long-term view of the music industry and help our artists develop a style and repertiore that is fluid and flexible and that will appeal to audiences for years and even decades.

The music industry is constantly changing, but over the last decade the changes have been enormous. New forms of entertainment such as DVDs, video games, and the Internet mean there are more competition for the leisure dollar in the market. New technologies give consomers more options for buying and listening to music, and they are demaning high quality recordings. Young consomers are comfortable with technology and want the music they love when and where they want it, no matter where they are or what they are doing.

Music School Records embraces new technologies and the sophisticated market of young music lovers. We believe that providing high quality recordings of truly talented artists make for more discerning listeners who will cherish the gift of music for the rest of their lives. The expertise of Music School Records includes:

- Insight into our target market and the ability to reach the desired audience
- The ability to access all current sources of music income
- A management team with years of experience in music commerce
- Innovative business strategies and artist development plans
- Investment in technology infrastructure for high quality recordings and business services
- Initiative and proactive management of artist careers

Online Study Guide for Students

Interactive objective-style questions based on chapter content.

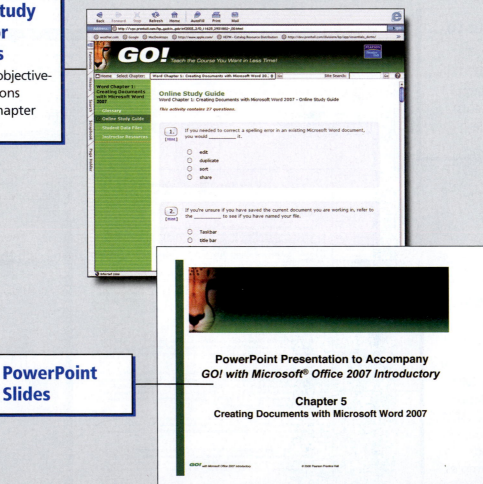

PowerPoint Slides

Teach

Student Textbook

Learning Objectives and Student Outcomes

Objectives are clustered around projects that result in student outcomes. They help students learn how to solve problems, not just learn software features.

Project-Based Instruction

Students do not practice features of the application; they create real projects that they will need in the real world. Projects are color coded for easy reference and are named to reflect skills the students will be practicing.

A and B Projects

Each chapter contains two instructional projects—A and B.

Each chapter opens with a story that sets the stage for the projects the student will create; the instruction does not force the student to pretend to be someone or make up a scenario.

Each chapter has an introductory paragraph that briefs students on what is important.

Visual Summary

Shows students upfront what their projects will look like when they are done.

Objective

The skills the student will learn are clearly stated at the beginning of each project and color coded to match projects listed on the chapter opener page.

Project Summary

Stated clearly and quickly in one paragraph.

NEW

File Guide

Clearly shows students which files are needed for the project and the names they will use to save their documents.

Teachable Moment

Expository text is woven into the steps—at the moment students need to know it—not chunked together in a block of text that will go unread.

NEW

Screen Shots

Larger screen shots.

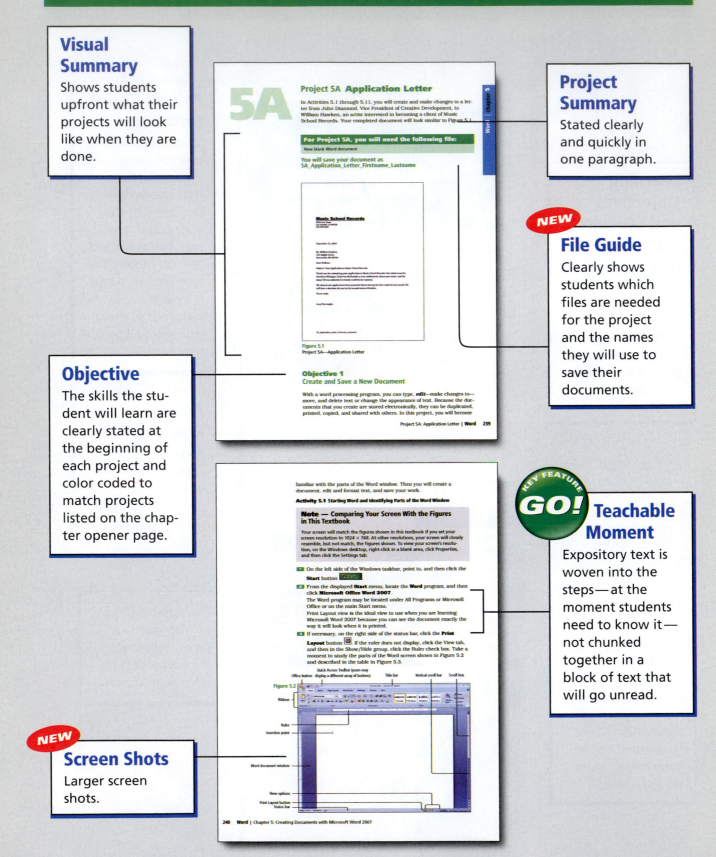

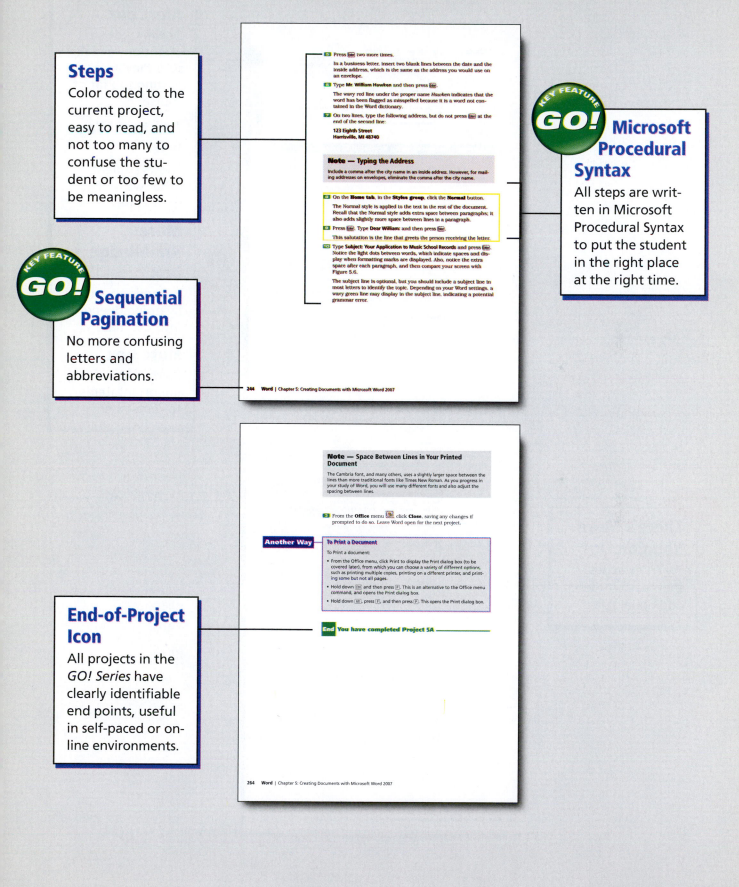

Steps

Color coded to the current project, easy to read, and not too many to confuse the student or too few to be meaningless.

Sequential Pagination

No more confusing letters and abbreviations.

Microsoft Procedural Syntax

All steps are written in Microsoft Procedural Syntax to put the student in the right place at the right time.

End-of-Project Icon

All projects in the *GO! Series* have clearly identifiable end points, useful in self-paced or on-line environments.

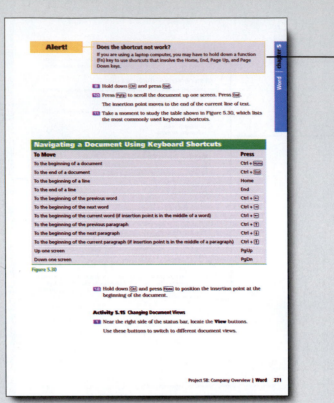

Alert box
Draws students' attention to make sure they aren't getting too far off course.

Another Way box
Shows students other ways of doing tasks.

More Knowledge box
Expands on a topic by going deeper into the material.

Note box
Points out important items to remember.

NEW

There's More You Can Do!
Try IT! exercises that teach students additional skills.

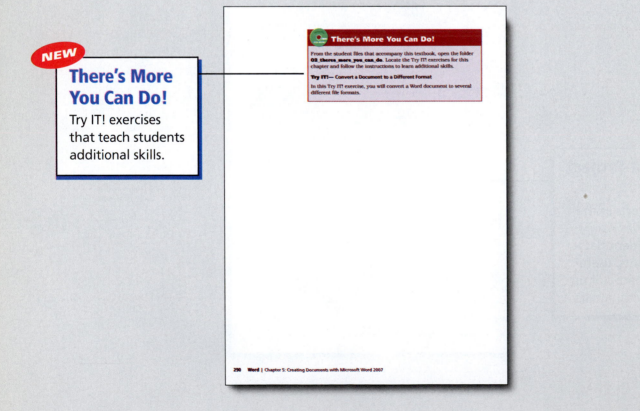

End-of-Chapter Material

Take your pick! Content-based or Outcomes-based projects to choose from. Below is a table outlining the various types of projects that fit into these two categories.

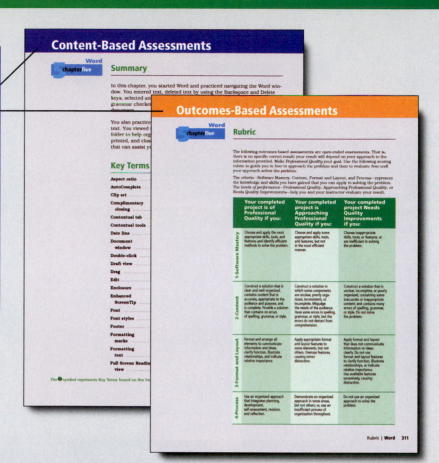

Content-Based Assessments
(Defined solutions with solution files provided for grading)

Project Letter	Name	Objectives Covered
N/A	Summary and Key Terms	
N/A	Multiple Choice	
N/A	Fill-in-the-blank	
C	Skills Review	Covers A Objectives
D	Skills Review	Covers B Objectives
E	Mastering Excel	Covers A Objectives
F	Mastering Excel	Covers B Objectives
G	Mastering Excel	Covers any combination of A and B Objectives
H	Mastering Excel	Covers any combination of A and B Objectives
I	Mastering Excel	Covers all A and B Objectives
J	Business Running Case	Covers all A and B Objectives

Outcomes-Based Assessments
(Open solutions that require a rubric for grading)

Project Letter	Name	Objectives Covered
N/A	Rubric	
K	Problem Solving	Covers as many Objectives from A and B as possible
L	Problem Solving	Covers as many Objectives from A and B as possible.
M	Problem Solving	Covers as many Objectives from A and B as possible.
N	Problem Solving	Covers as many Objectives from A and B as possible.
O	Problem Solving	Covers as many Objectives from A and B as possible.
P	You and GO!	Covers as many Objectives from A and B as possible
Q	GO! Help	Not tied to specific objectives
R	* Group Business Running Case	Covers A and B Objectives

* This project is provided only with the *GO! with Microsoft Office 2007 Introductory* book.

Objectives List

Most projects in the end-of-chapter section begin with a list of the objectives covered.

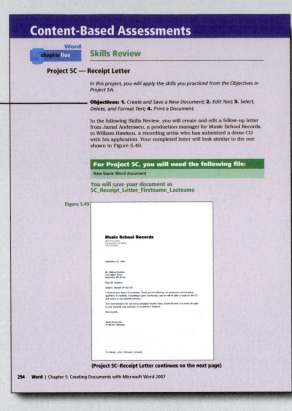

Content-Based Assessments

Word chapter five **Skills Review**

Project 5C — Receipt Letter

In this project, you will apply the skills you practiced from the Objectives in Project 5A.

Objectives: 1. Create and Save a New Document; **2.** Edit Text; **3.** Select, Delete, and Format Text; **4.** Print a Document.

In the following Skills Review, you will create and edit a follow-up letter from Jamal Anderssen, a production manager for Music School Records, to William Hawken, a recording artist who has submitted a demo CD with his application. Your completed letter will look similar to the one shown in Figure 5.49.

For Project 5C, you will need the following file:

New blank Word document

You will save your document as
5C_Receipt_Letter_Firstname_Lastname

Figure 5.49

(Project 5C–Receipt Letter continues on the next page)

294   Word | Chapter 5: Creating Documents with Microsoft Word 2007

Content-Based Assessments

Word chapter five **Skills Review**

(Project 5C–Receipt Letter continued)

14. Save the changes you have made to your document. Press Ctrl + A to select the entire document. On the **Home tab**, in the **Font group**, click the **Font button arrow**. Scroll as necessary, and watch Live Preview change the document font as you point to different font names. Click to choose **Tahoma**. Recall that you can type T in the Font box to move quickly to the fonts beginning with that letter. Click anywhere in the document to cancel the selection.

15. Select the entire first line of text—*Music School Records*. On the Mini toolbar, click the **Font button arrow**, and then click **Arial Black**. With the Mini toolbar still displayed, click the **Font Size button arrow**, and then click **20**. With the Mini toolbar still displayed, click the **Bold** button.

16. Select the second, third, and fourth lines of text, beginning with *2620 Vine Street* and ending with the telephone number. On the Mini toolbar, click the **Font button arrow**, and then click **Arial**. With the Mini toolbar still displayed, click the **Font Size button arrow**, and then click **10**. With the Mini toolbar still displayed, click the **Italic** button.

17. In the paragraph beginning *Your demonstration*, select the text *Music School Records*. On the Mini toolbar, click the **Italic** button, and then click anywhere to deselect the text.

18. Click the **Insert tab**. In the **Header & Footer group**, click the **Footer** button,

and then click **Edit Footer**. On the **Design tab**, in the **Insert group**, click the **Quick Parts** button, and then click **Field**. In the **Field** dialog box, under **Field names**, scroll down and click to choose **FileName**, and then click **OK**. Double-click anywhere in the document to leave the footer area.

19. Click the **Page Layout tab**. In the **Page Setup group**, click the **Margins** button to display the Margins gallery. At the bottom of the **Margins gallery**, click **Custom Margins** to display the **Page Setup** dialog box. Near the top of the **Page Setup** dialog box, click the **Layout tab**. Under **Page**, click the **Vertical alignment arrow**, click **Center**, and then click **OK**.

20. From the **Office** menu, point to the **Print arrow**, and then click **Print Preview** to make a final check of your letter. Follow your instructor's directions for submitting this file. Check your *Chapter Assignment Sheet* or *Course Syllabus* or consult your instructor to determine if you are to submit your assignments on paper or electronically. To submit electronically, go to Step 22, and then follow the instructions provided by your instructor.

21. On the **Print Preview tab**, in the **Print group**, click the **Print** button. Collect your printout from the printer and submit it as directed.

22. From the **Office** menu, click **Exit Word**, saving any changes if prompted to do so.

End You have completed Project 5C

296   Word | Chapter 5: Creating Documents with Microsoft Word 2007

End of Each Project Clearly Marked

Clearly identified end points help separate the end-of-chapter projects.

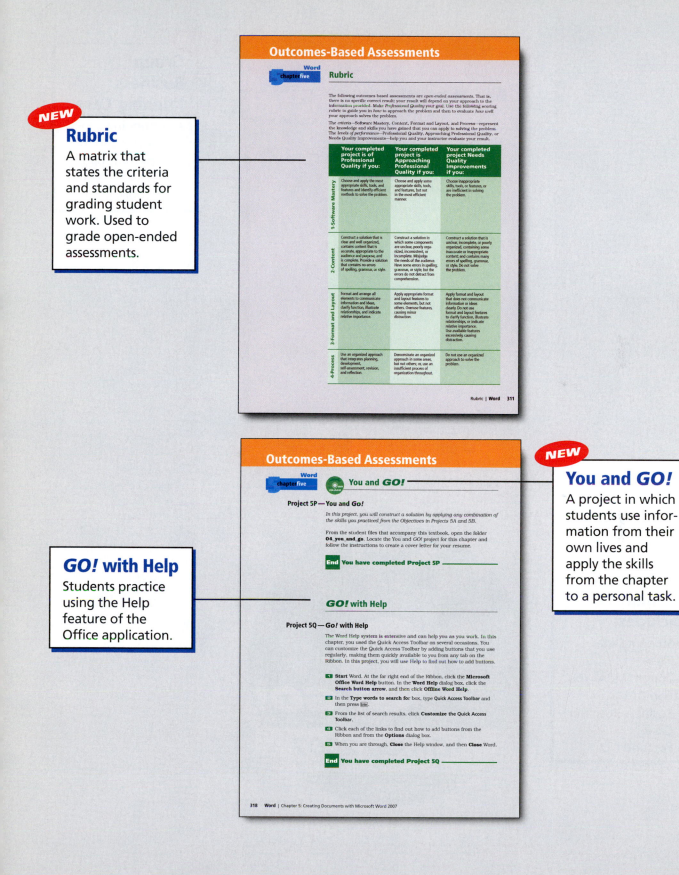

NEW

Rubric

A matrix that states the criteria and standards for grading student work. Used to grade open-ended assessments.

GO! with Help

Students practice using the Help feature of the Office application.

NEW

You and *GO!*

A project in which students use information from their own lives and apply the skills from the chapter to a personal task.

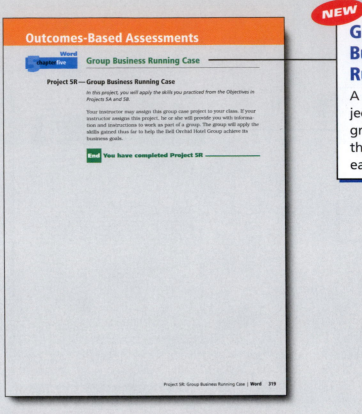

Group Business Running Case

A continuing project developed for groups that spans the chapters within each application.

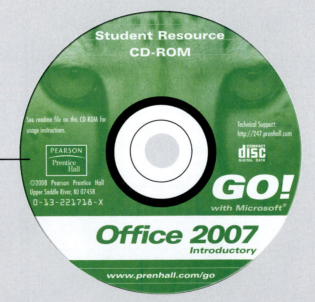

Student CD includes:
- Student Data Files
- There's More You Can Do!
- Business Running Case
- You and *GO!*

Companion Web site

An interactive Web site to further student leaning.

Online Study Guide

Interactive objective-style questions to help students study.

Teach (continued)

Annotated Instructor Edition

The Annotated Instructor Edition contains a full version of the student textbook that includes tips, supplement references, and pointers on teaching with the *GO!* instructional system.

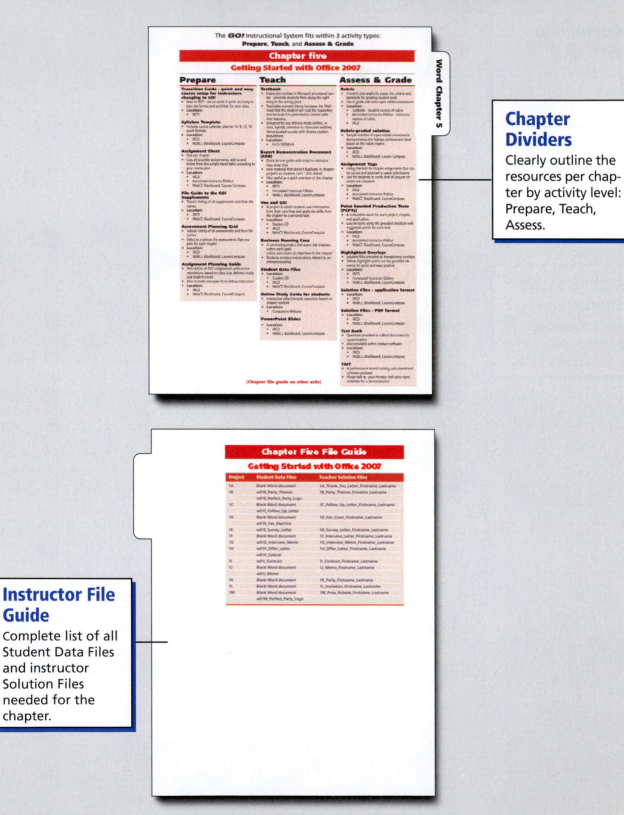

Chapter Dividers

Clearly outline the resources per chapter by activity level: Prepare, Teach, Assess.

Instructor File Guide

Complete list of all Student Data Files and instructor Solution Files needed for the chapter.

Helpful Hints, Teaching Tips, Expand the Project

References correspond to what is being taught in the student textbook.

NEW

Full-Size Textbook Pages

An instructor copy of the textbook with traditional Instructor Manual content incorporated.

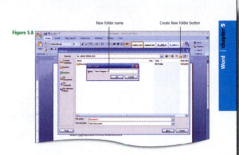

Figure 5.8

New folder name   Create New Folder button

Teaching Tip

Saving files with spaces in the file name is an acceptable practice in Microsoft Word, but if students need to submit files electronically, they will need to use an underscore instead of a space in the file name.

Teaching Tip

It is important to give meaningful names to files and folders. One should be able to guess the purpose of a file or folder without looking inside it.

Expand the Project

Provide students with a few examples of files and ask them to suggest how to name them. What would you name the file and folder for the following examples?
• Homework from chemistry lab class today
• Résumé for an internship job at Jones, Inc.
• Letter to your congressional representative
• List of potential employers

More Knowledge

Renaming a Folder

You can also rename existing folders. To rename a folder, right-click the folder in the Save As dialog box, click Rename from the shortcut menu, and then type a new folder name. This procedure also works in My Computer or Windows Explorer. You can follow the same procedure to rename an individual file, as long as you do not modify the file extension.

5 In the lower portion of the **Save As** dialog box, locate the **File name** box. If necessary, select or delete the existing text, and then in the **File name** box, using your own first and last names, type **5A_Application_Letter_Firstname_Lastname** being sure to include the underscore—⇧ Shift + ⎵ —instead of spaces between words, as shown in Figure 5.9.

Throughout this textbook, you will be instructed to save your files using the file name followed by your first and last names. Check with your instructor to see if there is some other file-naming arrangement for your course.

The Microsoft Windows operating system recognizes file names with spaces. However, some Internet file transfer programs do not. To facilitate sending your files over the Internet, using a course-management system, in this textbook you will be instructed to save files using an underscore instead of a space. The underscore key is the shift of the ⎵ key—on most keyboards located two keys to the left of ← Bksp.

Project 5A: Application Letter | **Word** 247

End-of-Chapter Concepts Assessments

contain the answers for quick reference.

Content-Based Assessments

Word
chapter five   **Matching**

Match each term in the second column with its correct definition in the first column. Write the letter of the term on the blank line in front of the correct definition.

C **1.** The location in the Word window, indicated by a blinking vertical line, where text will be inserted when you start to type.

F **2.** In the Word window, the location of the Minimize, Maximize/Restore Down, and Close buttons.

O **3.** A button that represents the command to reveal nonprinting characters.

K **4.** The action that takes place when the insertion point reaches the right margin and automatically moves down and to the left margin of the next line.

B **5.** The process of setting the overall appearance of the text within the document.

G **6.** To hold down the left mouse button and move the mouse pointer over text to select it.

H **7.** A set of ...
and sh...

A Draft
B Drag
C Font
D Footer
E Formatting
F Insertion point
G Keyboard shortcut
H Live preview
I Point
J Sans serif
K Serif
L Shortcut menu
M Show/Hide ¶

Content-Based Assessments

Word
chapter five   **Fill in the Blank**

Write the correct word in the space provided.

1. Microsoft Word 2007 is a word **Right** program that you can use to perform tasks such as writing a memo, a report, or a letter.

2. Located at the bottom of the Word window, the bar that provides information such as page number and word count is referred to as the **Space** bar.

3. Within the scroll bar, dragging the **Double Click** downward causes the document on your screen to move up.

4. A toolbar above the Ribbon and to the right of the Office button, which can be customized by adding frequently used buttons, is called the **Blank Blank Blank** (QAT).

5. Characters that display on the screen to show the location of paragraph marks, tabs, and spaces but that do not print are called **Space** marks.

6. If you point to a button on the Ribbon, a **Help** displays the name of the button.

7. A purple dotted line under an address or a date indicating that the information could be placed into another Office program such as Outlook is a **URL**.

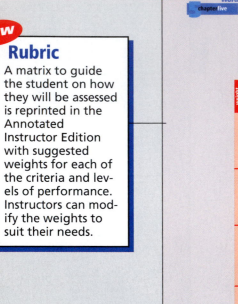

NEW

Rubric

A matrix to guide the student on how they will be assessed is reprinted in the Annotated Instructor Edition with suggested weights for each of the criteria and levels of performance. Instructors can modify the weights to suit their needs.

Assess

Assignment Tags

Scoring checklist for assignments. **NEW** Now also available for Problem-Solving projects.

Highlighted Overlays

Solution files provided as transparency overlays. Yellow highlights point out the gradable elements for quick and easy grading.

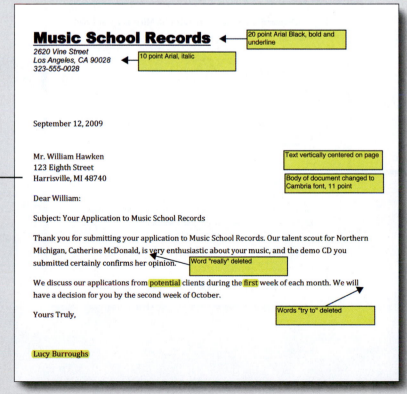

GO! with Microsoft® Office 2007

Assignment Tags for GO! with Office 2007
Word Chapter 5

Name:		Project:	5A
Professor:		Course:	
Task	**Points**	**Your Score**	
Center text vertically on page	2		
Delete the word "really"	1		
Delete the words "try to"	1		
Replace "last" with "first"	1		
Insert the word "potential"	1		
Replace "John W. Diamond" with "Lucy Burrows"	2		
Change entire document to the Cambria font	2		
Change the first line of text to Arial Black 20 pt. font	2		
Bold the first line of text	2		
Change the 2nd through 4th lines to Arial 10 pt.	2		
Italicize the 2nd through 4th lines of text	2		
Correct/Add footer as instructed	2		
Circled information is incorrect or formatted incorrectly			
Total Points	**20**	**0**	

Name:		Project:	5B
Professor:		Course:	
Task	**Points**	**Your Score**	
Insert the file w05B_Music_School_Records	4		
Insert the Music Logo	4		
Remove duplicate "and"	2		
Change spelling and grammar errors (4)	8		
Correct/Add footer as instructed	2		
Circled information is incorrect or formatted incorrectly			
Total Points	**20**	**0**	

Name:		Project:	5C
Professor:		Course:	
Task	**Points**	**Your Score**	
Add four line letterhead	2		
Insert today's date	1		
Add address block, subject line, and greeting	2		
Add two-paragraph body of letter	2		
Add closing, name, and title	2		
In subject line, capitalize "receipt"	1		
Change "standards" to "guidelines"	1		
Insert "quite"	1		
Insert "all"	1		
Change the first line of text to Arial Black 20 pt. font	2		
Bold the first line of text	1		
Change the 2nd through 4th lines to Arial 10 pt.	1		
Italicize the 2nd through 4th lines of text	1		
Correct/add footer as instructed	2		
Circled information is incorrect or formatted incorrectly			
Total Points	**20**	**0**	

Name:		Project:	5D
Professor:		Course:	
Task	**Points**	**Your Score**	
Insert the file w05D_Marketing	4		
Bold the first two title lines	2		
Correct spelling of "Marketting"	2		
Correct spelling of "geners"	2		
Correct all misspellings of "allready"	2		
Correct grammar error "are" to "is"	2		
Insert the Piano image	4		
Correct/add footer as instructed	2		
Circled information is incorrect or formatted incorrectly			
Total Points	**20**	**0**	

Music School Records ← 20 point Arial Black, bold and underline

2620 Vine Street
Los Angeles, CA 90028 ← 10 point Arial, italic
323-555-0028

September 12, 2009

Mr. William Hawken
123 Eighth Street
Harrisville, MI 48740

Text vertically centered on page

Body of document changed to Cambria font, 11 point

Dear William:

Subject: Your Application to Music School Records

Thank you for submitting your application to Music School Records. Our talent scout for Northern Michigan, Catherine McDonald, is very enthusiastic about your music, and the demo CD you submitted certainly confirms her opinion.

Word "really" deleted

We discuss our applications from **potential** clients during the **first** week of each month. We will have a decision for you by the second week of October.

Yours Truly,

Words "try to" deleted

Lucy Burroughs

Point-Counted Production Tests (PCPTs)

A cumulative exam for each **project**, **chapter**, and **application**. Easy to score using the provided checklist with suggested points for each task.

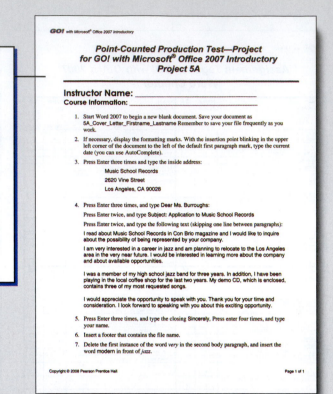

Test Bank

Available as TestGen Software or as a Word document for customization.

Solution Files– Application and PDF format

Music School Records

Music School Records discovers, launches, and develops the careers of young artists in classical, jazz, and contemporary music. Our philosophy is to not only shape, distribute, and sell a music product, but to help artists create a career that can last a lifetime. Too often in the music industry, artists are forced to fit their music to a trend that is short-lived. Music School Records does not just follow trends, we take a long-term view of the music industry and help our artists develop a style and repertoire that is fluid and flexible and that will appeal to audiences for years and even decades.

The music industry is constantly changing, but over the last decade, the changes have been enormous. New forms of entertainment such as DVDs, video games, and the Internet mean there is more competition for the leisure dollar in the market. New technologies give consumers more options for buying and listening to music, and they are demanding high quality recordings. Young consumers are comfortable with technology and want the music they love when and where they want it, no matter where they are or what they are doing.

Music School Records embraces new technologies and the sophisticated market of young music lovers. We believe that providing high quality recordings of truly talented artists make for more discerning listeners who will cherish the gift of music for the rest of their lives. The expertise of Music School Records includes:

- Insight into our target market and the ability to reach the desired audience
- The ability to access all current sources of music income
- A management team with years of experience in music commerce
- Innovative business strategies and artist development plans
- Investment in technology infrastructure for high quality recordings and business services

pagexxxix_top.docx

Online Assessment and Training

my**it**lab is Prentice Hall's new performance-based solution that allows you to easily deliver outcomes-based courses on Microsoft Office 2007, with customized training and defensible assessment. Key features of my**it**lab include:

A *true* "system" approach: my**it**lab content is the same as in your textbook.
Project-based *and* skills-based: Students complete real-life assignments.
Advanced reporting *and* gradebook: These include student click stream data.
***No* installation required:** my**it**lab is completely Web-based. You just need an Internet connection, small plug-in, and Adobe Flash Player.

Ask your Prentice Hall sales representative for a demonstration or visit:

www.prenhall.com/myitlab

chapter one

Getting Started with Microsoft PowerPoint 2007

OBJECTIVES

At the end of this chapter you will be able to:

1. Open, View, and Save a Presentation
2. Edit a Presentation
3. Format a Presentation
4. Create Headers and Footers and Print a Presentation

OUTCOMES

Mastering these objectives will enable you to:

PROJECT 1A
Open, Edit, Save, and Print a Presentation

5. Create a New Presentation
6. Use Slide Sorter View
7. Add Pictures to a Presentation
8. Use the Microsoft Help System

PROJECT 1B
Create and Format a Presentation

Skyline Bakery and Cafe

Skyline Bakery and Cafe is a chain of casual dining restaurants and bakeries based in Boston. Each restaurant has its own in-house bakery, which produces a wide variety of high-quality specialty breads, breakfast sweets, and desserts. Breads and sweets are sold by counter service along with coffee drinks, gourmet teas, fresh juices, and sodas. The full-service restaurant area features a menu of sandwiches, salads, soups, and light entrees. Fresh, high-quality ingredients and a professional and courteous staff are the hallmarks of every Skyline Bakery and Cafe.

Getting Started with Microsoft Office PowerPoint 2007

Presentation skills are among the most important skills you will ever learn. Good presentation skills enhance all of your communications—written, electronic, and interpersonal. In our technology-enhanced world of e-mail and wireless phones, communicating ideas clearly and concisely is a critical personal skill. Microsoft Office PowerPoint 2007 is a presentation graphics software program used to create electronic slide presentations and black-and-white or color overhead transparencies that you can use to effectively present information to your audience.

Project 1A **Expansion**

In Activities 1.1 through 1.17, you will edit and format a presentation that Lucinda dePaolo, Chief Financial Officer, has created that details the Skyline Bakery and Cafe's expansion plan. Your completed presentation will look similar to Figure 1.1.

For Project 1A, you will need the following file:

p1A_Expansion

You will save your presentation as
1A_Expansion_Firstname_Lastname

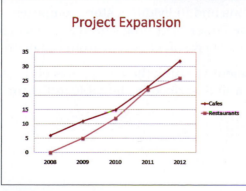

Figure 1.1
Project 1A—Expansion

Objective 1
Open, View, and Save a Presentation

Microsoft Office PowerPoint is a ***presentation graphics software*** program that you can use to effectively present information to your audience. The purpose of any presentation is to influence your audience. Whether you are presenting a new product to coworkers, making a speech at a conference, or expressing your opinion to your city council, you want to make a good impression and give your audience a reason to agree with your point of view. The way in which your audience reacts to your message depends on the information you present and how you present yourself. In the following activities, you will start Microsoft Office PowerPoint 2007, become familiar with the PowerPoint window, and then open, edit, and save an existing PowerPoint presentation.

Activity 1.1 Starting PowerPoint and Identifying Parts of the PowerPoint Window

In this activity, you will start PowerPoint and identify the parts of the PowerPoint window.

Note — Comparing Your Screen with the Figures in This Textbook

Your screen will match the figures shown in this textbook if you set your screen resolution to 1,024 × 768. At other resolutions, your screen will closely resemble, but not match, the figures shown. To view your screen's resolution, on the Windows desktop, right-click in a blank area, click Properties, and then click the Settings tab.

1 On the left side of the Windows taskbar, point to, and then click, the **Start** button.

2 From the displayed **Start** menu, locate the **PowerPoint** program, and then click **Microsoft Office PowerPoint 2007**.

Organizations and individuals store computer programs in a variety of ways. The PowerPoint program may be located under All Programs, or Microsoft Office, or from the main Start menu.

3 Take a moment to study the main parts of the screen as shown in Figure 1.2 and described in the table in Figure 1.3.

Figure 1.2

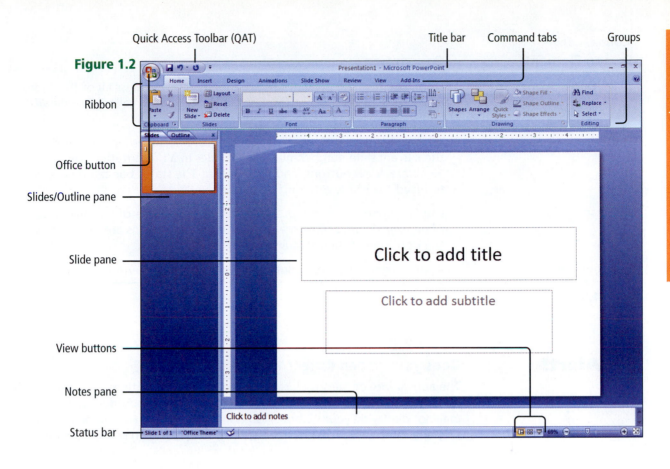

Labels around figure: Quick Access Toolbar (QAT) · Title bar · Command tabs · Groups · Ribbon · Office button · Slides/Outline pane · Slide pane · View buttons · Notes pane · Status bar

Click to add title

Click to add subtitle

Click to add notes

Microsoft PowerPoint Screen Elements

Screen Element	Description
Command tab	Displays the commands most relevant for a particular task area, such as inserting, designing, and animating.
Group	Related command buttons associated with the selected command tab.
Notes pane	Displays below the Slide pane and allows you to type notes regarding the active slide.
Office button	Displays a list of commands related to things you can do with a presentation, such as opening, saving, printing, or sharing.
Quick Access Toolbar (QAT)	Displays buttons to perform frequently used commands with a single click. Frequently used commands in PowerPoint include Save, Undo, and Repeat. For commands that you use frequently, you can add additional buttons to the Quick Access Toolbar.
Ribbon	Organizes commands on tabs, and then groups the commands by topic for performing related presentation tasks.
Slide pane	Displays a large image of the active slide.

(Continued)

Screen Element	Description
Slides/Outline pane	Displays either the presentation outline (Outline tab) or all of the slides in the presentation in the form of miniature images called *thumbnails* (Slides tab).
Status bar	A horizontal bar at the bottom of the presentation window that displays the current slide number, number of slides in a presentation, Design Template, View buttons, and Zoom slider. The status bar can be customized to include other information.
Title bar	Displays the name of the presentation and the name of the program. The Minimize, Maximize/Restore Down, and Close buttons are grouped on the right side of the title bar.
View buttons	A set of commands that control the look of the presentation window.

Figure 1.3

Alert!

Does your screen differ?

The appearance of the screen can vary, depending on settings that were established when the program was installed. For example, the Add-Ins tab may or may not display on your Ribbon. Additionally, the Quick Access Toolbar can display any combination of buttons, and may occupy its own row on the Ribbon.

Activity 1.2 Opening a Presentation

To open a presentation that has already been created in PowerPoint, use the Office button. As you work on a presentation, save your changes frequently.

1 In the upper left corner of the PowerPoint window, click the **Office** button , and then click **Open** to display the Open dialog box.

2 In the **Open** dialog box, at the right edge of the **Look in** box, click the **Look in arrow** to view a list of the drives available on your system, as shown in Figure 1.4.

Your list of available drives may differ.

Your list of available drives will differ   Look in arrow

Figure 1.4

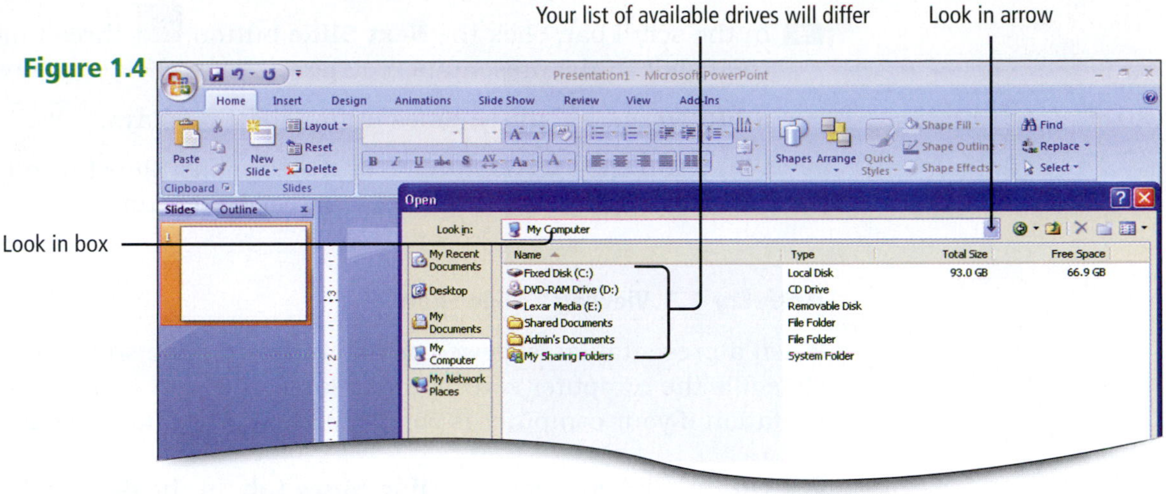

Look in box

3 Navigate to the location where the student files for this textbook are stored. Click **p1A_Expansion**, and then click the **Open** button or press Enter to display Slide 1 of the presentation in the PowerPoint window.

PowerPoint displays the file name of the presentation in the title bar at the top of the screen.

4 Look at the **Slides/Outline pane** on the left side of the window and notice that the presentation contains four slides. Additionally, at the right side of the window, a scroll bar displays a scroll box and up and down pointing arrows for navigating through your presentation.

Below the scroll bar, the Previous Slide 🔼 and Next Slide 🔽 buttons display. See Figure 1.5.

Figure 1.5

Scroll box

Slides/Outline pane

Scroll bar

Previous Slide button

Next Slide button

Skyline Bakery and Cafe

Expansion Plans

5 In the scroll bar, click the **Next Slide** button ⬇ three times so that each slide in the presentation displays. Then click the **Previous Slide** button ⬆ three times until Slide 1 displays.

When you click the Next Slide or the Previous Slide button, you can scroll through your presentation one slide at a time.

Activity 1.3 Viewing a Slide Show

When a presentation is viewed as an electronic slide show, the entire slide fills the computer screen, and a large audience can view your presentation if your computer is connected to a projection system.

1 On the Ribbon, click the **Slide Show tab**. In the **Start Slide Show group**, click the **From Beginning** button.

The first slide fills the entire screen and animation effects display the picture, and then the title and subtitle. *Animation effects* introduce individual slide elements one element at a time. These effects add interest to your slides and draw attention to important features.

Another Way ── **To Start a Slide Show**

On the right side of the status bar, from the View buttons, click the Slide Show button. You can also display the first slide that you want to show, and then press F5.

2 Click the left mouse button or press Spacebar to advance to the second slide, noticing the transition as Slide 1 moves off the screen and Slide 2 displays. An animation effect stretches the graphic images across the screen from left to right.

Transitions refer to the way that a slide appears or disappears during an onscreen slide show. For example, when one slide leaves the screen, it may fade or dissolve into another slide.

3 Click the left mouse button or press Spacebar and notice that the third slide displays and the slide title drops onto the screen from the top of the slide and a picture appears from the lower right corner. Click again or press Spacebar and notice that the first bullet point displays. Continue to click or press Spacebar until each bullet point displays on the slide and the next slide—*Project Expansion*—displays.

4 Click or press Spacebar to display the chart, and then click or press Spacebar one more time to display a black slide.

After the last slide in a presentation, a *black slide* with the text *End of slide show, click to exit.* displays. A black slide is inserted at the end of every slide show to indicate that the presentation is over.

5 On the black slide, click the left mouse button to exit the slide show and return to Slide 1.

Activity 1.4 Creating Folders and Saving a Presentation

In the same way that you use file folders to organize your paper documents, Windows uses a hierarchy of electronic folders to keep your electronic files organized. When you save a presentation file, the Windows operating system stores your presentation permanently on a storage medium. Changes that you make to existing presentations, such as changing text or typing in new text, are not permanently saved until you perform a Save operation.

1 In the upper left corner of the PowerPoint window, click the **Office** button ![office], and then click **Save As** to display the **Save As** dialog box.

2 In the **Save As** dialog box, at the right edge of the **Save in** box, click the **Save in arrow** to view a list of the drives available to you, as shown in Figure 1.6.

Your list of available drives will differ   Save in arrow

Figure 1.6

Save in box

3 Navigate to the drive on which you will be storing your folders and projects for this chapter—for example, a USB flash drive that you have connected, a shared drive on a network, or the drive designated by your instructor or lab coordinator.

4 In the **Save As** dialog box, on the toolbar, click the **Create New Folder** button ![folder]. In the displayed **New Folder** dialog box, in the **Name** box, type **PowerPoint Chapter 1** as shown in Figure 1.7, and then click **OK**.

The new folder name displays in the Save in box, indicating that the folder is open and ready to store your presentation.

Figure 1.7

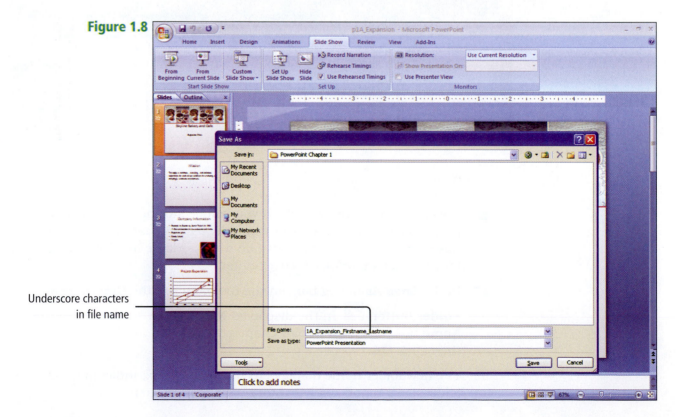

Create New Folder button ——

New folder name ——

5 In the lower portion of the **Save As** dialog box, locate the **File name** box. If necessary, select or delete the existing text, and then in the **File name** box, using your own first and last names, type **1A_Expansion_Firstname_Lastname** as shown in Figure 1.8.

Throughout this textbook, you will be instructed to save your files, using the file name followed by your first and last names. Check with your instructor to see if there is some other file-naming arrangement for your course.

The Microsoft Windows operating system recognizes file names with spaces. However, some Internet file transfer programs do not. To facilitate sending your files over the Internet if you are using a course management system, in this textbook you will be instructed to save files by using an underscore instead of a space.

Figure 1.8

Underscore characters
in file name ——

6 In the lower portion of the **Save As** dialog box, click the **Save** button, or press Enter.

Your presentation is saved on the storage device that you selected, and it is contained in the *PowerPoint Chapter 1* folder with the new file name. The new file name also displays in the title bar.

Objective 2
Edit a Presentation

In **Normal view**, the PowerPoint window is divided into three areas—the Slide pane, the Slides/Outline pane, and the Notes pane. When you make changes to the presentation in the Slides/Outline pane, the changes are reflected immediately in the Slide pane. Likewise, when you make changes in the Slide pane, the changes are reflected in the Slides/Outline pane.

Activity 1.5 Editing Slide Text

Editing is the process of adding, deleting, or changing the contents of a slide. When you click in the middle of a word or sentence and start typing, the existing text moves to the right to make space for your new keystrokes. In this activity, you will edit text in the Slide pane.

1 In the **Slides/Outline pane**, if necessary, click the **Slides tab** to display the slide thumbnails.

You can use the slide thumbnails to navigate in your presentation. When you click on a slide thumbnail, the slide displays in the Slide pane.

2 In the **Slides/Outline pane**, on the **Slides tab**, click **Slide 2** to display the company's mission statement. Move your pointer into the paragraph that contains the company's mission statement, and then click to the left of the word *experience* as shown in Figure 1.9.

On this slide a red wavy underline indicates that there is a misspelled word. Do not be concerned at this time with the misspelling—you will correct it in a later activity.

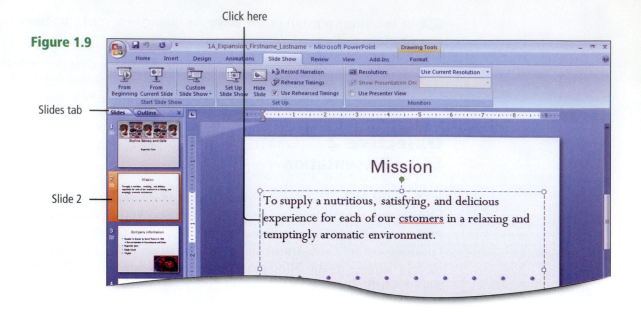

Figure 1.9

Click here

Slides tab

Slide 2

3 Type **meal** and notice that as you type, the existing text moves to the right to accommodate the text that you are inserting. Press [Spacebar] to insert a space between *meal* and *experience*.

After you type the space, the word *meal* moves to the first line of the paragraph because there is enough space in the first line to accommodate the text.

4 In the **Slides/Outline pane**, on the **Slides tab**, click **Slide 3**. In the bulleted list, in the third line, click to the right of the word *plans* and press [Spacebar]. Type **in 2009**

5 On the **Quick Access Toolbar**, click the **Save** button to save the changes you have made to the presentation since your last save operation.

Activity 1.6 Inserting a New Slide

To insert a new slide in a presentation, display the slide that will come before the slide that you want to insert.

1 If necessary, display **Slide 3**. On the Ribbon, click the **Home tab**.

On the Home tab, the Slides group includes the New Slide button. The New Slide button is divided into two parts: the upper part contains the New Slide icon, which inserts a slide without displaying options; the lower part contains the words New Slide and a down-pointing arrow that when clicked, displays a gallery. The **gallery**—a visual representation of a command's options—displays slide layouts. **Layout** refers to the placement and arrangement of the text and graphic elements on a slide.

2 In the **Slides group**, click the lower part of the **New Slide** button to display the gallery.

Alert!

Did you insert a slide without displaying the gallery?

The New Slide button is divided into two parts. If you click the upper part, a new slide is inserted, using the layout of the previous slide. To view the gallery, you must click the lower part of the New Slide button. Do not be concerned if the gallery did not display—the correct type of slide was inserted. Read Step 3, and then continue with Step 4.

3 Point to **Title and Text** as shown in Figure 1.10, and then click to insert a slide with the Title and Text layout. Notice that the new blank slide displays in the Slide pane and in the Slides/Outline pane.

The new slide contains two *placeholders*—one for the slide title and one for content. A placeholder reserves a portion of a slide and serves as a container for text or other content, including pictures, graphics, charts, tables, and diagrams.

Title and Text layout

Figure 1.10

Click New Slide

Gallery

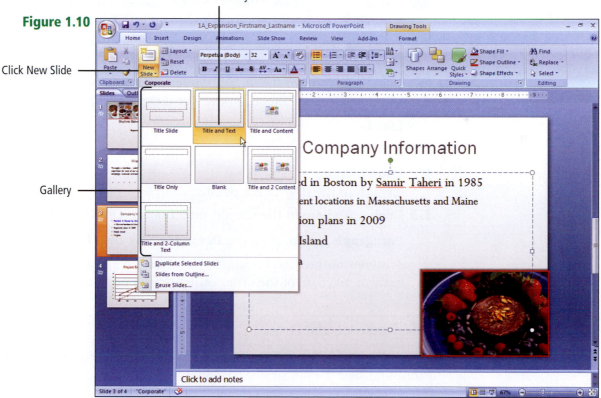

4 In the **Slide pane**, the title placeholder displays the text *Click to add title*. Click in the title placeholder. Type **Expansion Plans** and then click in the *Click to add text* content placeholder.

5 Type **2009** and then press Enter.

6 Type **Rhode Island and Virginia** and then press Enter.

7 Type **2010** and then on the **Quick Access Toolbar**, click the **Save** button [💾] to save your presentation.

Activity 1.7 Increasing and Decreasing List Levels

Text in a PowerPoint presentation is organized according to outline levels, similar to the outline levels you might make for a book report. The highest level on an individual slide is the title. ***Bulleted levels***—outline levels represented by a bullet symbol—are identified in the slides by the indentation and the size of the text. Indented text in a smaller size indicates a lower outline level. It is easy to change the outline level of text to a higher or lower level. For example, you may create a presentation with four bullets on the same level. Then you may decide that one bulleted item relates to one of the other bullets, rather than to the slide title. In this case, a lower outline level should be applied. You can increase the list or indent level of text to apply a *lower* outline level, or decrease the list or indent level of text to apply a *higher* outline level.

1 If necessary, display **Slide 4**, click at the end of the last bullet point—*2010*—and then press Enter to create a new bullet.

2 Press Tab and notice that a lower level bullet point is created. Type **New Hampshire and New Jersey**

3 Click anywhere in the second bullet point—*Rhode Island and Virginia*. On the Ribbon, in the **Paragraph group**, click the **Increase List Level** button [⬆].

A lower outline level is applied to the text.

4 Display **Slide 3**. Notice that the second bullet point is a lower outline level than the first bullet point.

5 Click anywhere in the second bullet point. On the Ribbon, in the **Paragraph group**, click the **Decrease List Level** button [⬇].

A higher outline level is applied so that the second bullet point is equivalent to all of the other bullet points on the slide.

Another Way — **To Decrease List Level**

You can decrease the list level of a bullet point by holding down Shift and pressing Tab.

6 You can change the outline level of more than one bullet point by first selecting all of the text whose outline level you want to change. In the fourth bullet point, position the pointer to the left of *Rhode*, hold down the left mouse button, and then drag to the right and down to select the *Rhode Island* and the *Virginia* bullet points as shown in Figure 1.11. Release the mouse button.

Dragging is the technique of holding down the left mouse button and moving over an area of text so that it is selected. Selected text is indicated when the background changes to a different color than the slide background. When you select text, a ***Mini toolbar*** displays near the selection. The Mini toolbar displays buttons that are commonly used with the selected object, as shown in Figure 1.11. The Mini toolbar is semitransparent unless you move the pointer to it. When you move the pointer away from the Mini toolbar, it disappears. You will learn more about the Mini toolbar in a later activity.

Figure 1.11

Mini toolbar

Both bullet points selected

Note — Demoting and Promoting Text

Increasing and decreasing the list level of a bullet point is sometimes referred to demoting and promoting text.

7 On the **Home** tab, in the **Paragraph group**, click the **Increase List Level** button.

Both bulleted items are demoted to lower levels.

8 Click at the end of the word *Virginia*. Press Enter to create a new bullet, and notice that the new bullet is indented at the same level as *Virginia*.

9 Click the **Decrease List Level** button to promote the new bullet. Type **Awards received this year** and then press Enter.

10 Click the **Increase List Level** button. Type **Golden Bakery** and press Enter. Type **Cuisine Excellence**

11 Compare your slide to Figure 1.12. **Save** your presentation.

Figure 1.12

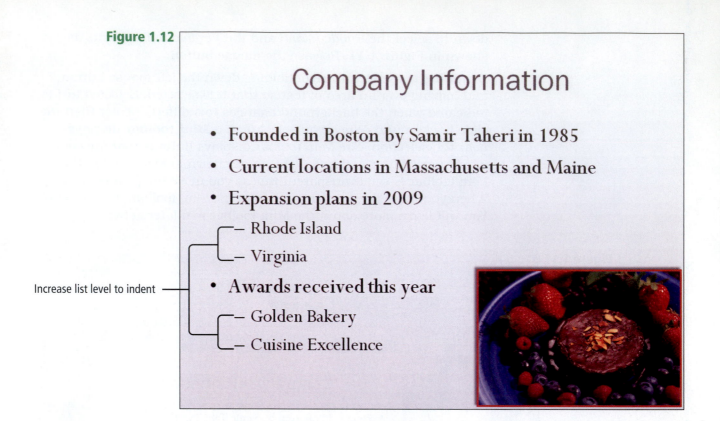

Company Information

- Founded in Boston by Samir Taheri in 1985
- Current locations in Massachusetts and Maine
- Expansion plans in 2009
  - Rhode Island
  - Virginia
- **Awards received this year**
  - Golden Bakery
  - Cuisine Excellence

Increase list level to indent

Activity 1.8 Checking Spelling

As you type, PowerPoint compares your words to those in the PowerPoint dictionary. Words that are not in the PowerPoint dictionary are marked with a wavy red underline. Sometimes these words are correct. For example, a person's name may not be in the dictionary and may be flagged as misspelled even though it is correctly spelled. The red wavy underline does not display when the presentation is viewed as a slide show.

One way to check spelling errors flagged by PowerPoint is to right-click the flagged word or phrase and, from the displayed shortcut menu, select a suitable correction or instruction.

1 Display **Slide 2**. Notice that the word *cstomers* is flagged with a red wavy underline, indicating that it is misspelled.

2 Point to *cstomers* and click the right mouse button to display the ***shortcut menu*** with a suggested solution for correcting the misspelled word, and the Mini toolbar, as shown in Figure 1.13.

A shortcut menu is a context-sensitive menu that displays commands and options relevant to the selected object.

Figure 1.13

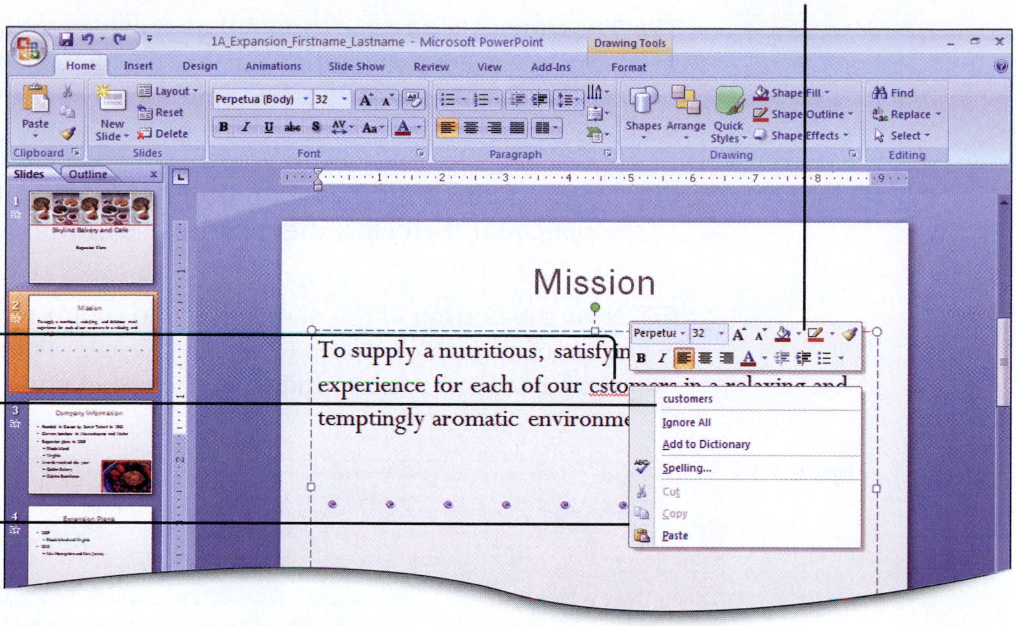

Mini toolbar

Misspelled word

Suggested solution

Shortcut menu

3 From the shortcut menu, click **customers** to correct the spelling of the word.

4 Display **Slide 3** and notice that the name *Samir Taheri* is flagged as misspelled, although it is spelled correctly.

5 Right-click *Samir*, and from the shortcut menu, click **Ignore All** so that every time the name *Samir* displays in the presentation, it will not be flagged as a misspelled word. Repeat this procedure to ignore the flagged word *Taheri*.

More Knowledge

Spelling Correction Options

The Ignore All option is particularly useful when proper nouns are flagged as spelling errors even when they are spelled correctly. If you are using PowerPoint 2007 on a system that you can customize—such as your home computer—you can add frequently used names and proper nouns to the PowerPoint custom dictionary by clicking the Add to Dictionary option from the shortcut menu.

6 Display each slide in the presentation and correct any spelling errors that you may have made when editing the slides.

7 Save 🖫 your presentation.

Another Way — **To Check Spelling**

You can check the spelling of the entire presentation at one time. On the Ribbon, click Review, and then click the Spelling button to display a dialog box that will select each spelling error in your presentation and provide options for correcting it.

Activity 1.9 Editing Text by Using the Thesaurus

The *Thesaurus* is a research tool that provides a list of *synonyms*—words with the same meaning—for text that you select. You can access synonyms by using either the shortcut menu or the Review tab on the Ribbon.

1 Display **Slide 2**. In the first line of the paragraph, point to the word *supply*, and then click the right mouse button to display the shortcut menu.

2 Near the bottom of the shortcut menu, point to **Synonyms** to display a list of suggested words to replace *supply*. Point to **provide** as shown in Figure 1.14, and then click to change *supply* to *provide*.

Figure 1.14

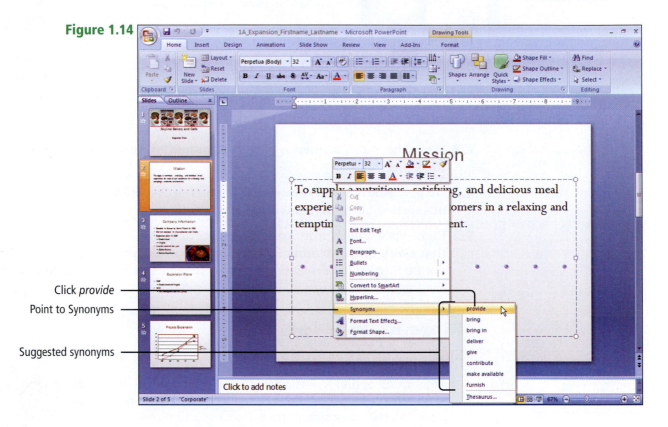

Click *provide*

Point to Synonyms

Suggested synonyms

3 **Save** the presentation.

Another Way — **To Access the Thesaurus**

After you select the word that you want to replace, on the Ribbon, click Review. Click Thesaurus to display the Research task pane, which contains a more comprehensive list of suggested synonyms.

Activity 1.10 Adding Speaker's Notes to a Presentation

Recall that when a presentation is displayed in Normal view, the Notes pane displays below the Slide pane. The Notes pane is used to type speaker's notes that can be printed below a picture of each slide. You can refer to these printouts while making a presentation, thus reminding you of the important points that you want to make while running an electronic slide show.

1 Display **Slide 4**. Look at the PowerPoint window and notice the amount of space that is currently dedicated to each of the three panes—the Slides/Outline pane, the Slide pane, and the Notes pane. Locate the horizontal and vertical borders that separate the three panes.

These narrow borders are used to adjust the size of the panes. If you decide to type speaker notes, you may want to make the Notes pane larger.

2 Point to the border that separates the **Slide pane** from the **Notes pane**. The resize pointer displays as an equal sign with an upward-pointing and a downward-pointing arrow, as shown in Figure 1.15.

Figure 1.15

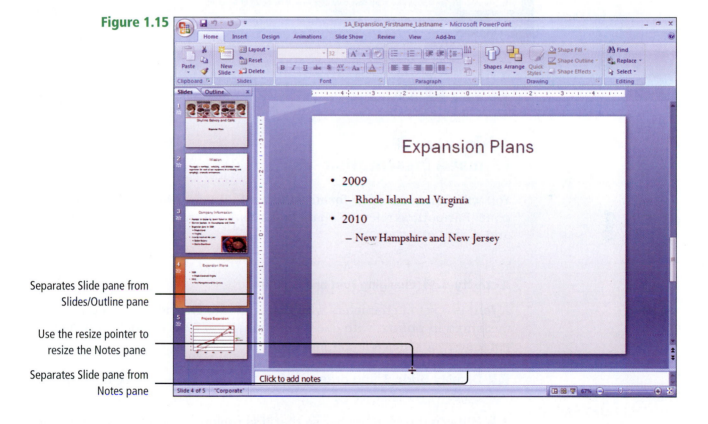

Separates Slide pane from Slides/Outline pane

Use the resize pointer to resize the Notes pane

Separates Slide pane from Notes pane

3 Press and hold down the left mouse button and drag the ⬍ pointer up approximately 1 inch, and then release the left mouse button to resize the pane.

4 With **Slide 4** displayed, click in the **Notes** pane and type **These expansion plans have been approved by the board of directors.** Compare your screen to Figure 1.16.

Figure 1.16

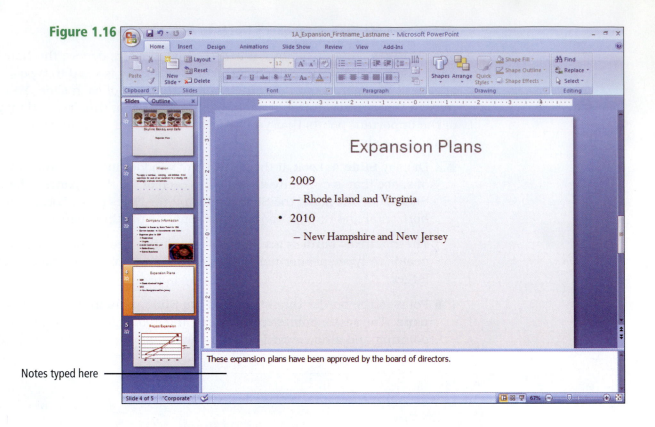

Notes typed here ──────────

These expansion plans have been approved by the board of directors.

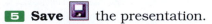

5 **Save** 💾 the presentation.

Objective 3
Format a Presentation

You will do most of your *formatting* work in PowerPoint in the Slide pane. Formatting refers to changing the appearance of the text, layout, and design of a slide.

Activity 1.11 Changing Font and Font Size

A *font* is a set of characters with the same design and shape. Fonts are measured in *points*, with one point equal to 1/72 of an inch. A higher point size indicates a larger font size.

1 Display **Slide 1** and drag to select the title text—*Skyline Bakery and Cafe.*

2 Point to the Mini toolbar so that it is no longer semitransparent, and then click the **Font button arrow** Calibri (Headings) ▾ to display the available fonts, as shown in Figure 1.17.

The two fonts that display at the top of the list are the fonts currently used in the presentation.

Did the Mini toolbar disappear?

When you select text, the Mini toolbar displays. If you move your pointer away from the selection and into the slide area without pointing to the Mini toolbar, it may no longer display. If this happened to you, select the text again, and then point to the Mini toolbar, making sure that you do not point to another area of the slide.

Figure 1.17

Mini toolbar

Font button arrow

Selected text

List of fonts

3 Scroll the displayed list as necessary, and then click **Book Antiqua**.

4 On the Ribbon, if necessary, click the **Home tab**. In the **Font group**, click the **Font Size button arrow** 44 ▾. On the displayed list, click **48**.

5 Select the subtitle text—*Expansion Plans*. On the Ribbon, in the **Font group**, click the **Font button arrow** Calibri (Headings) ▾. In the displayed list, scroll as necessary, and then point to—but do not click—**Arial Black**. Compare your screen with Figure 1.18.

Live Preview is a feature that displays formatting in your presentation so that you can decide whether or not you would like to apply the formatting. In this case, Live Preview displays the selected text in the Arial Black font, even though you did not click the font name. The font will actually change when you click the font name.

Live Preview displays the selection in the selected font

Figure 1.18

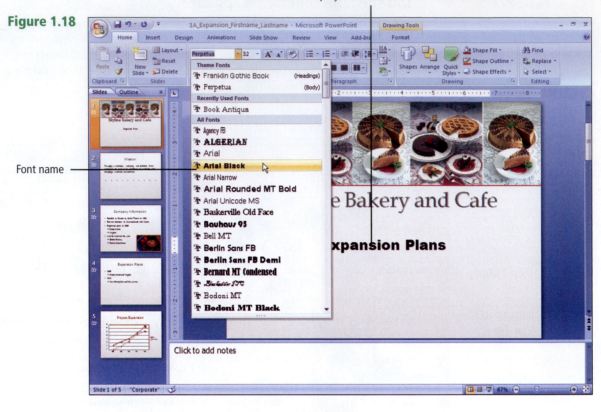

Font name

6 Click **Arial Black**.

7 **Save** ![save icon] the changes you have made to your presentation.

Activity 1.12 Applying Font Styles

Font styles emphasize text and are a visual cue to draw the reader's eye to important text. Font styles include bold, italic, and underline.

1 On **Slide 1**, drag to select the title—*Skyline Bakery and Cafe.* On the

Home tab, in the **Font group**, point to the **Bold** button ![B] as shown in Figure 1.19, and then click to apply bold to the title.

Figure 1.19

PowerPoint | **chapter 1**

Click the Bold button

Selected text

2 Select the subtitle—*Expansion Plans*. On the Mini toolbar, click the **Bold** button $\boxed{B}$, and then click the **Italic** button $\boxed{I}$ to apply both bold and italic to the selection. Notice that on the **Home tab**, in the **Font group**, the **Bold** and **Italic** buttons are selected.

The Bold, Italic, and Underline buttons are *toggle buttons*; that is, you can click the button once to turn it on and click it again to turn it off.

3 With the subtitle still selected, on the **Home tab**, in the **Font group**, click the **Bold** button $\boxed{B}$ to turn off the bold formatting.

4 **Save** $\boxed{}$ your changes.

Another Way

To Apply Font Styles

There are four methods to apply font styles:

- On the Home tab, in the Font group, click the Bold, Italic, or Underline button.
- On the Mini toolbar, click the Bold or Italic button.
- From the keyboard, use the keyboard shortcuts of Ctrl + B for bold, Ctrl + I for italic, or Ctrl + U for underline.
- On the Home tab, in the Font group, click the Dialog Box Launcher to open the Font dialog box, and then click the font styles that you want to apply.

Activity 1.13 Aligning Text and Changing Line Spacing

Text alignment refers to the horizontal placement of text within a placeholder. Text can be aligned left, centered, aligned right, or justified. When text is justified, the left and right margins are even.

1 Display **Slide 2** and click in the paragraph.

2 On the **Home tab**, in the **Paragraph group**, click the **Center** button $\boxed{\equiv}$ to center align the paragraph within the placeholder.

3 In the **Paragraph group**, click the **Line Spacing** button ⯆⯆. In the displayed list, click **1.5** to change from single-spacing between lines to one and a half spaces between lines.

4 **Save** 🖫 your changes.

Activity 1.14 Modifying Slide Layout

Recall that layout refers to the placement and arrangement of the text and graphic elements on a slide. PowerPoint includes a number of pre-defined layouts that you can apply to your slide for the purpose of arranging slide elements. For example, a Title Slide contains two place-holder elements—the title and the subtitle. Additional slide layouts include Title and Content, Title and 2 Content, Comparison, and Picture with Caption. When you design your slides, consider the content that you want to include, and then choose a layout that contains elements that best display the message that you want to convey.

1 Display **Slide 4.**

2 On the **Home tab**, in the **Slides group**, click the **Layout** button to display the **Slide Layout gallery**. The gallery displays an image of each layout and the name of each layout.

3 Point to each layout and notice that a **ScreenTip** also displays the name of the layout.

A ScreenTip is a small box, activated by holding the pointer over a button or other screen object, that displays information about a screen element.

4 Point to **Title and 2-Column Text**—as shown in Figure 1.20—and then click to change the slide layout.

The existing text displays in the placeholder on the left and a blank content placeholder is displayed on the right.

Figure 1.20

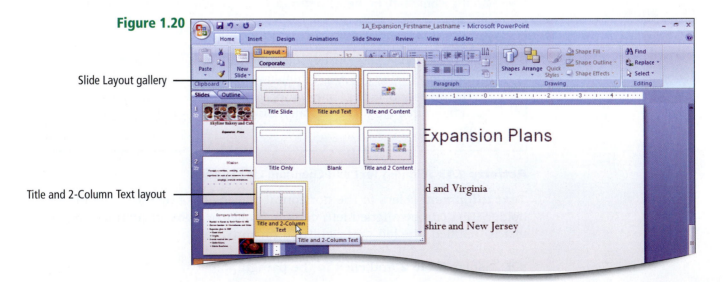

Slide Layout gallery

Title and 2-Column Text layout

5 Click in the placeholder on the right. Type **2011** and then press Enter. Press Tab to increase the list level. Type **West Virginia and Ohio** and then press Enter.

6 Press ⇧Shift + Tab to decrease the list level. Type **2012** and then press Enter. Press Tab to increase the list level. Type **New York and Connecticut**

7 Click outside of the placeholder so that it is not selected, and then compare your slide to Figure 1.21.

8 **Save** 💾 your changes.

Figure 1.21

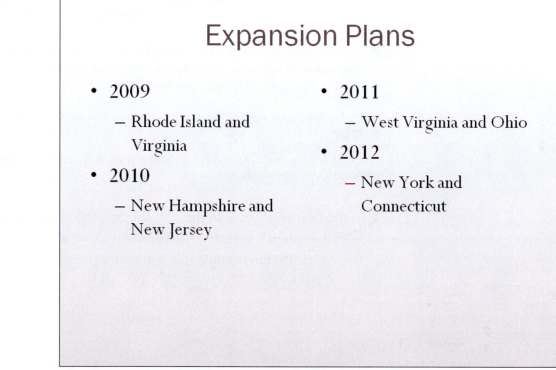

Activity 1.15 **Changing the Presentation Theme**

A **theme** is a set of unified design elements that provides a look for your presentation by using color, fonts, and graphics. The overall *presentation* theme may include background designs, graphics, and objects that can be customized, using one of the three additional types of themes available in PowerPoint 2007. The color themes include sets of colors; the font themes include sets of heading and body text fonts; and the effect themes include sets of effects that can be applied to lines and other objects on your slides. Themes are found on the Design tab.

1 On the Ribbon, click the **Design tab**. In the **Themes group**, to the right of the last displayed theme, point to the **More** button 🔽 as shown in Figure 1.22, and then click to display the **Themes gallery**.

Themes   More button

Figure 1.22

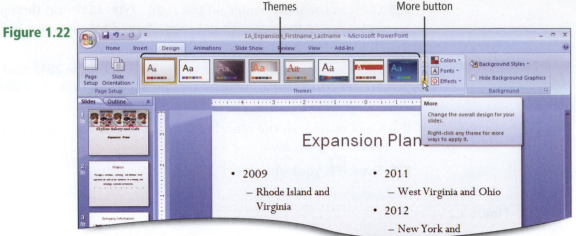

> **2** Under **Built-In**, *point* to several of the themes and notice a ScreenTip displays the name of each theme and that the Live Preview feature displays how each theme will look if applied to your presentation.

Note

The first theme that displays is the Office theme. Subsequent themes are arranged alphabetically.

> **3** In the first row, point to the first theme—the **Office Theme**, as shown in Figure 1.23—and then click to change the theme.
>
> The Office Theme is applied to the entire presentation, and all text, the chart, and accent colors are updated to reflect the change.

Themes

Figure 1.23

Office Theme

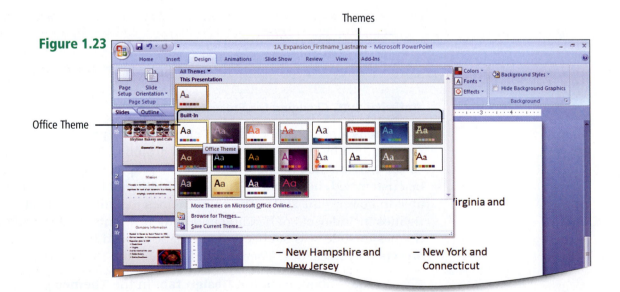

4 In the **Slides/Outline pane**, click to select **Slide 3**, and then press and hold down ⇧Shift and click **Slide 4**. Compare your screen with Figure 1.24.

Both slides are selected as indicated by the contrasting colors that surround the slides in the Slides/Outline pane.

Figure 1.24

Selected slides

5 On the **Design tab**, in the **Themes group**, click the **More** button to display the **Themes gallery**. In the first row, *point* to the fifth theme—**Concourse**—and then click the right mouse button to display the shortcut menu. Click **Apply to Selected Slides**.

The Concourse Theme is applied to Slides 3 and 4.

6 **Save** your presentation.

Objective 4
Create Headers and Footers and Print a Presentation

A **header** is text that prints at the top of each sheet of **slide handouts** or **notes pages**. Slide handouts are printed images of multiple slides on a sheet of paper. Notes pages are printouts that contain the slide image in the top half of the page and notes that you have created in the Notes pane in the lower half of the page.

In addition to headers, you can create **footers**—text that displays at the bottom of every slide or that prints at the bottom of a sheet of slide handouts or notes pages.

Activity 1.16 Creating Headers and Footers

In this activity, you will add a header to the handouts and notes pages that includes the current date and a footer that includes the page number and the file name.

1 Click the **Insert tab**, and then in the **Text group**, click the **Header & Footer** button to display the **Header and Footer** dialog box.

Another Way — **To Display the Header and Footer Dialog Box**

On the Insert tab, in the Text group, you can click either the Date & Time button or the Number button.

2 In the **Header and Footer** dialog box, click the **Notes and Handouts tab**. Under **Include on page**, click to select the **Date and time** check box, and as you do so, watch the Preview box in the lower right corner of the Header and Footer dialog box.

The Preview box indicates the placeholders on the printed Notes and Handouts pages, similar to the way that a slide placeholder reserves a location on a slide for text or other content. The two narrow rectangular boxes at the top of the Preview box indicate placeholders for the header text and date. When you select the Date and time check box, the placeholder in the upper right corner is outlined, indicating the location in which the date will display.

3 If necessary, click the **Update automatically** button so that the current date prints on the notes and handouts each time the presentation is printed.

4 If necessary, click to *clear* the **Header** check box to omit this element. Notice that in the Preview box, the corresponding placeholder is no longer selected.

5 If necessary, click to select the **Page number** and **Footer** check boxes, noticing that when you do so, the insertion point displays in the Footer box. Using your own first and last names, type **1A_ Expansion_Firstname_Lastname** and then compare your dialog box with Figure 1.25.

6 Click **Apply to All**. On the Ribbon, click the **View tab**, and then in the **Presentation Views group**, click the **Handout Master** button. In the lower left corner of the Handout Master, select the file name, right-click, and then in the Mini toolbar, change the **Font Size** to **12**. Click the **View tab**, and then in the **Presentation Views group**, click the **Notes Master** button, and use a similar technique to change the **Font Size** of the file name to **12**. At the right end of the

Ribbon, click **Close Master View**, and then **Save** 🖫 your changes.

Figure 1.25

Notes and Handouts tab   Preview box

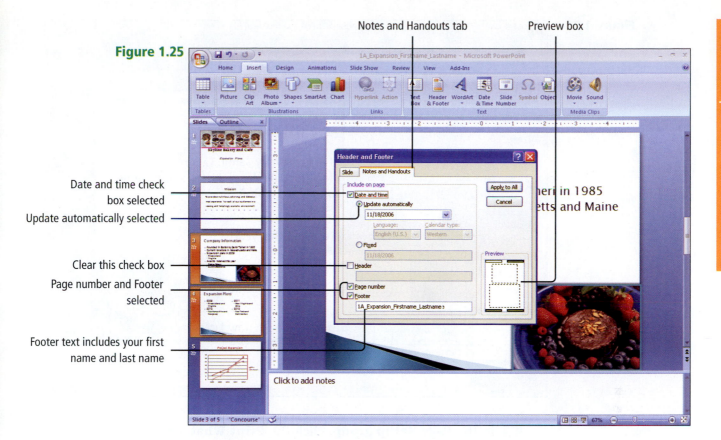

Date and time check box selected

Update automatically selected

Clear this check box

Page number and Footer selected

Footer text includes your first name and last name

More Knowledge

Adding Footers to Slides

You can add footers to slides by using the Slide tab in the Header and Footer dialog box. Headers cannot be added to slides.

Activity 1.17 Previewing and Printing a Presentation and Closing PowerPoint

1 Click the **Office** button , point to the **Print arrow** as shown in Figure 1.26, and then click **Print Preview.**

Print Preview displays your presentation as it will print, based on the options that you choose. In the Print Preview window, you can change the direction on which the paper prints—landscape or portrait—you can choose whether you will print slides, handouts, note pages, or the presentation outline, and you can choose to print your presentation in color, grayscale, or black and white. By default, PowerPoint prints your presentation in grayscale.

Figure 1.26

Office button

Print Preview

Print arrow

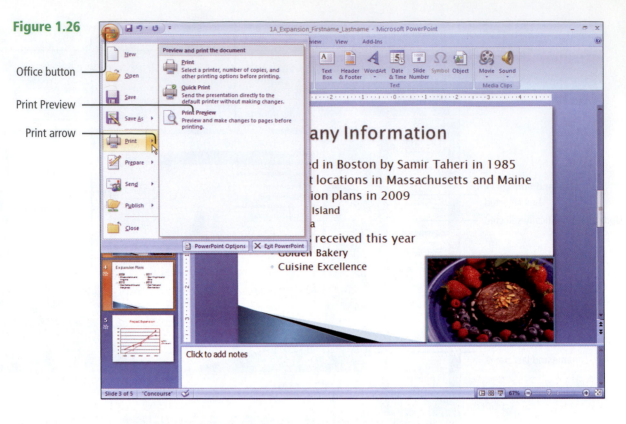

2 In the **Page Setup group**, click the **Print What arrow**, and then click **Handouts (6 Slides Per Page)** as shown in Figure 1.27. Notice that the preview of your printout changes to reflect your selection.

Note — Printing Slide Handouts

Printing a presentation as Slides uses a large amount of ink and toner. Thus, the majority of the projects in this textbook require that you print handouts, not slides.

Figure 1.27

Print What arrow

Click Handouts
(6 Slides Per Page)

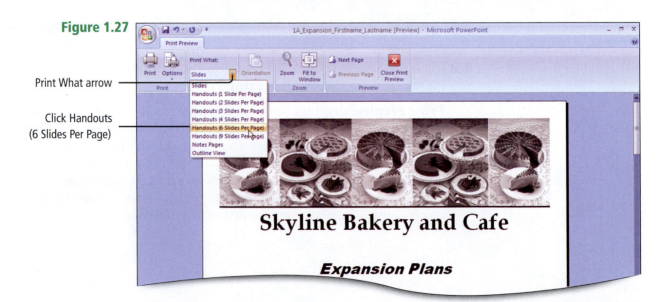

3 Check your *Chapter Assignment Sheet* or *Course Syllabus*, or consult your instructor, to determine if you are to submit your assignments on paper or electronically by using your college's course information management system. To submit electronically, go to Step 8, and then follow the instructions provided by your instructor.

4 In the **Print group**, click the **Print** button, and then in the **Print** dialog box, click **OK** to print your handouts.

5 In the **Page Setup group**, click the **Print What Arrow**, and then click **Notes Pages** to preview the presentation notes for Slide 1.

Recall that you created Notes for Slide 4.

6 At the right side of the **Print Preview** window, drag the scroll box down until **Slide 4** displays.

7 In the **Print group**, click the **Print** button. In the middle of the **Print** dialog box, under **Print range**, click **Current slide**, and then click **OK** to print the Notes pages for Slide 4.

8 Click **Close Print Preview** to close the Print Preview window and return to the presentation.

Another Way — **To Print a Presentation**

Click the Office button, and then click Print to display the Print dialog box. The options that are available in Print Preview can be accessed and modified in the Print dialog box.

9 **Save**  your presentation. On the right edge of the title bar, click the **Close** button X to close the presentation and **Close** PowerPoint.

Note — **Changing Print Options**

When you preview your presentation, check to be sure that the text displays against the slide background. If it does not, on the Print Preview tab in the Print group, click Options. Point to Color/Grayscale, and then click Color or Color (On Black and White Printer).

End **You have completed Project 1A** —————————

Project 1B **Overview**

In Activities 1.18 through 1.25 you will create a presentation that provides details of the Skyline Bakery and Cafe projected expansion. You will add a graphic image to the presentation, insert slides from another PowerPoint presentation, and rearrange and delete slides. Your completed presentation will look similar to Figure 1.28.

For Project 1B, you will need the following files:

p1B_Skyline
p1B_Cake
p1B_Template

You will save your presentation as
1B_Overview_Firstname_Lastname

Figure 1.28
Project 1B—Overview

Objective 5
Create a New Presentation

Microsoft Office PowerPoint 2007 provides a variety of options for starting a new presentation. You can use a ***template*** that is saved on your system or that you access from Microsoft Online. A template is a file that contains the styles in a presentation, including the type and size of bullets and fonts, placeholder sizes and positions, background design and fill color schemes, and theme information. You can also start a blank presentation that has no text, background graphics, or colors that you can then customize yourself.

Activity 1.18 Starting a New Presentation

In this activity, you will create a new presentation based on a template from Microsoft Office Online.

1 **Start** PowerPoint. From the **Office** menu 🔘, click **New** to display the **New Presentation** window. See Figure 1.29.

At the left of the New Presentation window is a list of the Template categories installed on your system or available from Microsoft Office Online. The center section displays either subcategories or thumbnails of the slides in the category that you select. When you click on a template, the right section displays a larger view of the selected template and in some cases, additional information about the template.

New blank presentation

Figure 1.29

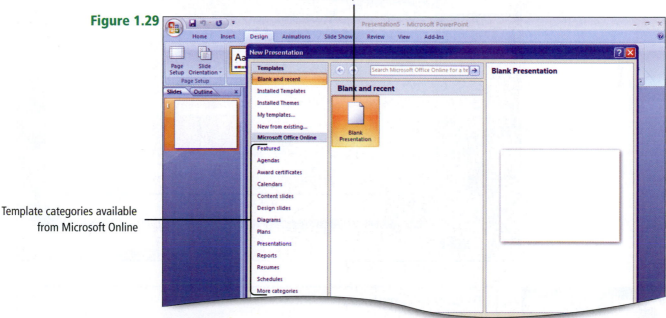

Template categories available from Microsoft Online

2 Under **Templates**, click **Installed Templates**, and then click each displayed template to preview it.

3 In the left panel under **Microsoft Office Online**, click several of the categories. Notice that as you do so, the title of the center panel changes to the name of the category that you have chosen, and in some instances, subcategories display.

Alert!

Are you unable to access the templates from Microsoft Office Online?

If you are unable to access the templates from Microsoft Office Online, the template for this project is available from your student data files. In the New Presentation window, click Cancel to close the New Presentation window. Click the Office button, and then click Open. Navigate to your student files and open the p1B_Template file. Then, skip to Step 6.

4 Under **Microsoft Office Online**, click **Presentations**, and then in the center panel, point to **Other presentations** to display the Link Select pointer 🖑 as shown in Figure 1.30.

Figure 1.30

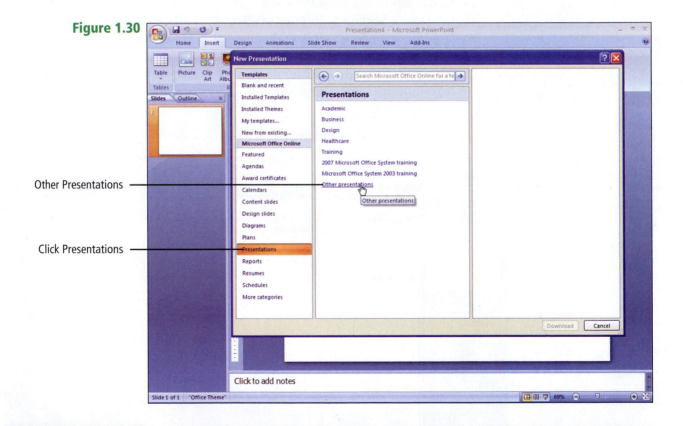

Other Presentations

Click Presentations

Another Way

To Locate Templates

In the New Presentation window, you can search for templates by using key-words. Click the Office button, and then click New. At the top center of the New Presentation Window, type the keyword and then press Enter to view the presentation templates with the keyword that you typed.

5 Click **Other Presentations**. In the center section of the New Presentation window, click **Project overview presentation**, and then in the lower right corner of the window, click **Download** to access the template from Microsoft Office Online.

Alert!

Does a Microsoft window display?

If a window displays regarding the validation of your software, click Continue. If you are unable to download the template, close all message windows and the New Presentation window. Click the Office button, and then click Open. Navigate to your student files, open the p1B_Template file, and then continue with Step 6.

6 If necessary, close any windows that display after the template is downloaded.

The new presentation includes 11 slides with ideas for content when making a project overview presentation. Scroll through the presentation to view the suggested content. Later, you will delete slides that are not relevant to the presentation and you will modify slide text so that the content is specific to this presentation topic.

7 On **Slide 1**, drag to select the text in the title placeholder—*Project Overview*—and then type **Skyline Bakery and Cafe** to replace it. Drag to select the three lines of text in the subtitle placeholder, and then type **Planning for the Future**

8 Display **Slide 2**. Select the text *Ultimate goal of project*, and then type **To develop a culinary presence throughout the East Coast**

9 Select the remaining two bullet points on the slide, and then type to replace them with the text **To expand operations in a manner that maximizes profit while providing outstanding service to customers**

10 Display **Slide 4**. In the bulleted list, select the *Competitors* bullet point and its second-level bullet point—*You may want to allocate one slide per competitor*—and then press Delete. Select *Your strengths relative to competitors*, and then type **Outstanding reputation for quality service** and then press Enter. Type **Nationally recognized chefs**

11 Replace the text *Your weaknesses relative to competitors* with **Inexperience in marketing in new locations**

12 In the scroll bar, click the **Next Slide** button several times until **Slide 11** displays. Select and delete the *Post-mortem* and *Submit questions* bullet points and their subordinate bullet points. Under the *Marketing plan* bullet point, select *Location or contact name/phone*, and then type **Janet Liu/555-9012** Under the *Budget* bullet point, select *Location or contact name/phone*, and then type **Lucinda dePaolo/555-9019**

13 Click the **Office** button , and then click **Save As** to display the **Save As** dialog box. Click the **Save in arrow**, and then navigate to your *PowerPoint Chapter 1* folder.

14 In the **File name** box, delete any existing text, and then using your own first and last names type **1B_Overview_Firstname_Lastname** and then click **Save**.

Activity 1.19 Inserting Slides from an Existing Presentation

Teamwork is an important aspect of all organizations, and presentations are often shared among employees. Another employee may create several slides for a presentation that you are developing. Rather than re-creating the slides, you can insert slides from an existing presentation into the current presentation. In this activity, you will insert slides from an existing presentation into your 1B_Overview presentation.

1 Display **Slide 1**. Click the **Home tab**, and in the **Slides group**, click the **New Slide arrow** to display the **Slide Layout gallery** and additional options for inserting slides as shown in Figure 1.31.

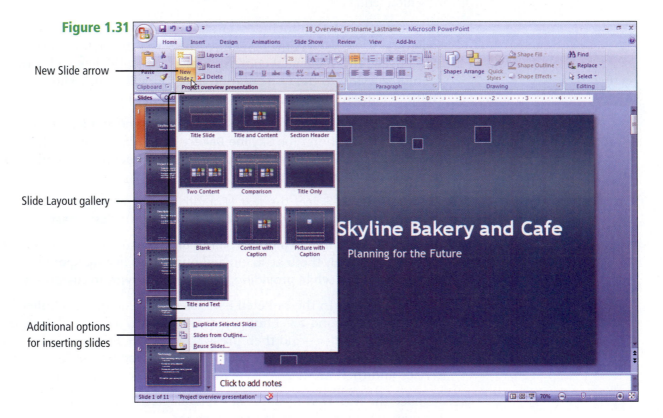

Figure 1.31

New Slide arrow

Slide Layout gallery

Additional options for inserting slides

2 Below the gallery, click **Reuse Slides** to open the **Reuse Slides** task pane on the right side of the PowerPoint window.

A *task pane* enables you to enter options for completing a command.

3 In the **Reuse Slides** task pane, click the **Browse** button, and then click **Browse File**. In the **Browse** dialog box, navigate to where your student files are stored, and then double-click **p1B_ Skyline**.

The slides contained in the p1B_Skyline presentation display in the Reuse Slides task pane. The title of each slide displays to the right of the slide image.

4 In the **Reuse Slides** task pane, point to **Slide 2** and notice that a zoomed image is displayed, as is a ScreenTip with the presentation title and the slide title. See Figure 1.32.

Reuse Slides task pane

Figure 1.32

Zoomed image of slide

5 Click **Slide 2—Mission**—and notice that it is inserted into the current presentation after Slide 1.

The theme of the current presentation is applied to the slide that you inserted. If you want to retain the theme and other formatting from the slide that you insert, you can click to select the *Keep source formatting* check box at the bottom of the Reuse Slides task pane.

More Knowledge
Inserting All Slides

You can insert all of the slides from an existing presentation into the current presentation at one time. In the Reuse Slides task pane, right-click one of the slides that you want to insert, and then click Insert All Slides.

6 In your **1B_Overview** presentation, in the **Slides/Outline pane**, scroll the slide thumbnails to display **Slide 11**. Click **Slide 11** to display it in the **Slide** pane. In the **Reuse Slides** task pane, click **Slide 3—Company Information**, and then click **Slide 4—Expansion Plans** to insert both slides after Slide 11.

Your presentation contains 14 slides.

7 In the **Reuse Slides** task pane, click the **Close** button ☒. **Save** 🖫 your presentation.

Note — Inserting Slides

You can insert slides in any order into your presentation. Just remember to display the slide that will precede the slide that you want to insert.

Objective 6
Use Slide Sorter View

Slide Sorter view displays all of the slides in your presentation in miniature. You can use Slide Sorter view to rearrange and delete slides, to apply formatting to multiple slides, and to get an overall impression of your presentation.

Activity 1.20 Selecting and Deleting Slides

To select more than one slide, click the first slide that you want to select, press and hold down ⇧Shift or Ctrl, and then click another slide. Using ⇧Shift enables you to select a group of slides that are adjacent. Using Ctrl enables you to select a group of slides that are nonadjacent (*not* next to each other). When multiple slides are selected, you can move or delete them as a group. These techniques can also be used when slide miniatures are displayed on the Slides tab.

1 Recall that the View buttons are located on the status bar in the lower right corner of the PowerPoint window. Locate the **View** buttons, and then click the **Slide Sorter** button to display all of the slide thumbnails. Alternatively, on the Ribbon, click the View tab, and then in the Presentation Views group, click Slide Sorter.

2 Click **Slide 4** and notice that a thick outline surrounds the slide, indicating that it is selected. On your keyboard, press Delete to delete the slide.

3 Click **Slide 5**, and then hold down ⇧Shift and click **Slide 10** so that slides 5 through 10 are selected. Compare your screen to Figure 1.33.

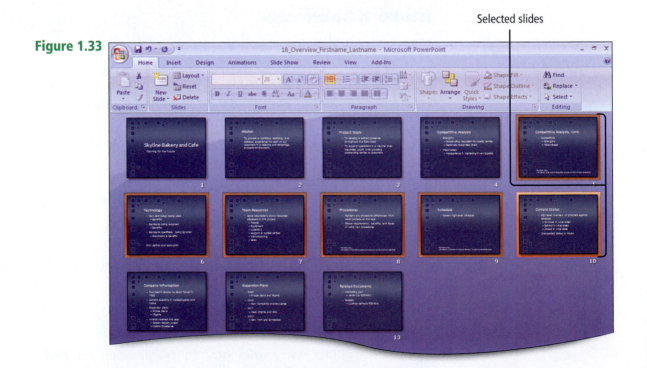

Selected slides

Figure 1.33

4 Press ⌈Delete⌉ to delete the selected slides.

Your presentation contains seven slides.

5 **Save** 🖫 your changes.

Activity 1.21 Moving Slides

1 Click **Slide 5** to select it.

2 While pointing to **Slide 5**, press and hold down the left mouse button, and then drag the slide to the left until the displayed vertical bar is positioned to the left of **Slide 2**, as shown in Figure 1.34. Release the left mouse button.

The slide that you moved becomes Slide 2.

Selected slide

Figure 1.34

Vertical bar positioned between Slides 1 and 2 to move slide to this position

3 Select **Slide 6**. Using the same technique that you used in Step 2, drag to position the slide between **Slides 4** and **5**.

4 In the status bar, click the **Normal** button 🔲. **Save** 🖫 your presentation.

Objective 7
Add Pictures to a Presentation

Images can be inserted into a presentation from many sources. One type of image that you can insert is *clip art*. Clip art can include drawings, movies, sounds, or photographic images that are included with Microsoft Office or downloaded from the Web.

Activity 1.22 Inserting Clip Art

In this activity you will access Microsoft Office Online to insert a clip art image on the title slide.

1 Display **Slide 1**. On the Ribbon, click the **Insert tab**, and then in the **Illustrations group**, click **Clip Art** to display the **Clip Art** task pane.

2 In the **Clip Art** task pane, click in the **Search for** box and type **wedding cake** so that PowerPoint 2007 can search for images that contain the keywords *wedding cake*.

A message may display asking if you would like to include additional clip art images from Microsoft Office online. If this message displays, click Yes.

3 In the **Clip Art** task pane, click the **Search in arrow**, and if necessary, click to select the **Everywhere** check box. Click the **Search in** arrow again to collapse the search list.

When you click the Everywhere option, *All collections* displays in the Search in box. This action instructs PowerPoint to search for images stored on your system and on the Microsoft Office Online Web site.

4 Click the **Results should be arrow**, and then click as necessary to *deselect*—clear the selection by removing the check mark—the **Clip Art**, **Movies**, and **Sounds** check boxes so that only the **Photographs** check box is selected as shown in Figure 1.35.

With the Photographs check box selected, PowerPoint will search for images that were created with a digital camera or a scanner.

Type **wedding cake**
to search for images

Figure 1.35

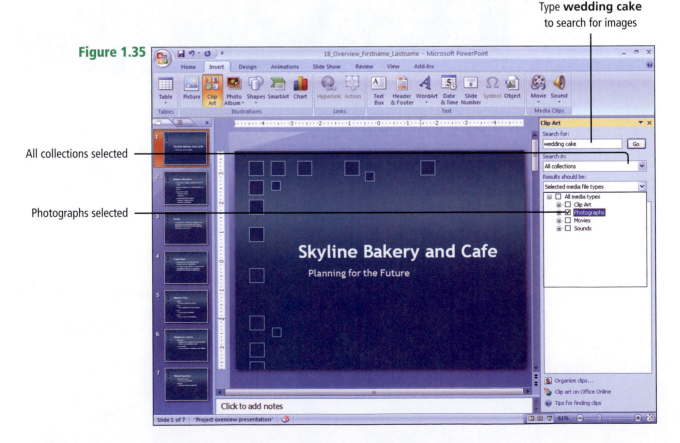

All collections selected

Photographs selected

5 In the **Clip Art** task pane, click **Go**. After a brief delay, several images display in the Clip Art task pane. Locate the image of the wedding cake shown in Figure 1.36.

Selected image

Figure 1.36

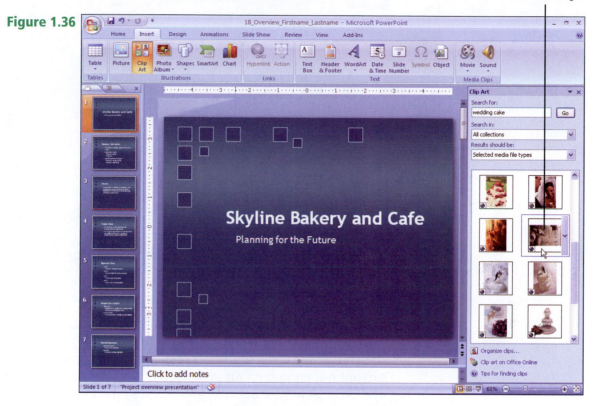

6 Click the wedding cake picture to insert it in the center of Slide 1, and then notice that the Ribbon has changed and the picture is surrounded by white square and circular handles, indicating that it is selected.

Because the picture is selected, **contextual tools** named *Picture Tools* display and add a **contextual tab**—*Format*—next to the standard tabs on the Ribbon as shown in Figure 1.37.

Contextual tools enable you to perform specific commands related to the selected object, and display one or more contextual tabs that contain related groups of commands that you will need when working with the type of object that is selected. Contextual tools display only when needed for a selected object; when you deselect the object,

Figure 1.37

Contextual tab

the contextual tools no longer display. In this case, the Format contextual tab contains four groups—Adjust, Picture Styles, Arrange, and Size. In a later activity, you will use the Picture Styles group to format the wedding cake picture.

7 **Close** ☒ the Clip Art task pane. **Save** 🖫 your changes.

Activity 1.23 Moving and Sizing Images

When an image is selected, it is surrounded by white ***sizing handles*** that are used to size the image. In the corners of the image, the handles are circular. When you point to a circular sizing handle, a diagonal pointer displays, indicating that you can resize the image by dragging up or down. In the center of each side of the selected image, the handles are square. When you point to a square handle, a left- and right-pointing arrow or an up- and down-pointing arrow displays. These arrows indicate the direction in which you can size the image. When you point to an image without positioning the pointer over a handle, a four-headed arrow displays, indicating that you can move the image.

1 If necessary, click to select the picture of the wedding cake so that the handles display.

2 Position the pointer anywhere over the image to display the Move pointer ⊕. Drag down and to the right until the lower right corner of the picture is aligned with the lower right corner of the slide as shown in Figure 1.38. Release the mouse button.

3 If necessary, select the picture, and then point to the upper left circular handle to display the Diagonal Resize pointer ⬉.

Figure 1.38

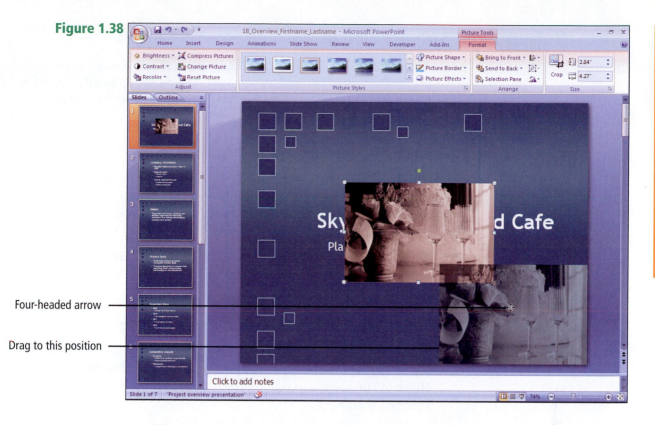

Four-headed arrow

Drag to this position

4 Drag down and to the right, noticing that as you do so, a semitransparent image displays the size of the picture. Continue to drag until the semitransparent image is approximately half the height and width of the original picture as shown in Figure 1.39. Release the mouse button to size the picture.

5 **Save** 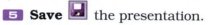 the presentation.

Figure 1.39

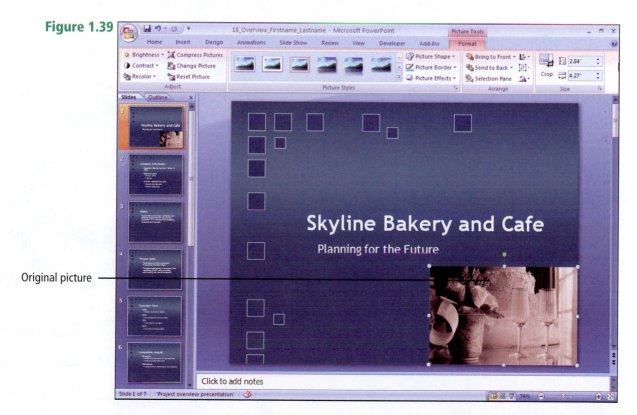

Original picture

Sizing a Picture

Using one of the corner sizing handles ensures that the original proportions of the image are maintained. When a top or side sizing handle is used, the picture is stretched either taller or wider, thus distorting the image.

Activity 1.24 Applying a Style to a Picture

Recall that when a picture is selected, the Picture Tools contextual tool and the Format contextual tab display on the Ribbon. You can use the Format tab to change the color and brightness of your picture; apply a shape, border, or effect; arrange multiple images; or size your picture.

1 If necessary, click the picture of the wedding cake to select it and notice that the Picture Tools are available.

2 On the **Format tab**, in the **Picture Styles group**, click the **More** button ⬇ to display the **Picture Styles gallery**.

3 In the displayed gallery, move your pointer over several of the picture styles to display the ScreenTip and to use Live Preview to see the effect of the style on your picture. Then, in the first row, click **Simple Frame, White**.

4 Click on a blank area of the slide so that the picture is not selected, and then compare your slide to Figure 1.40. Make any necessary adjustments to the size and position of the picture.

Figure 1.40

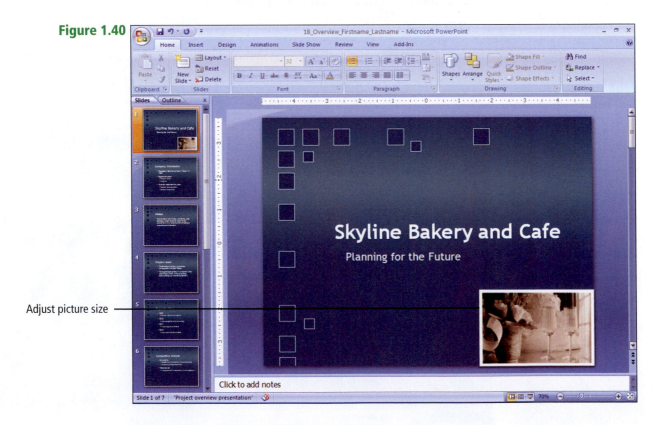

Adjust picture size

5 Click the **Insert tab**, and then, in the **Text group**, click the **Header & Footer** button to display the **Header and Footer** dialog box. Click the **Notes and Handouts tab**. Under **Include on page**, click to select the **Date and time** check box, and if necessary, click the **Update automatically** button so that the current date prints on the notes and handouts each time the presentation is printed. If necessary, *clear* the **Header** check box to omit this element from the header and footer. Click to select the **Page number** and **Footer** check boxes, noticing that when you do so, the insertion point displays in the Footer box. Using your own first and last names, type **1B_Overview_Firstname_Lastname** and then click **Apply to All**.

6 Check your *Chapter Assignment Sheet* or *Course Syllabus* or consult your instructor to determine if you are to submit your assignments on paper or electronically. To submit electronically, go to Step 8, and then follow the instructions provided by your instructor.

7 From the **Office** menu, point to the **Print arrow**, and then click **Print Preview** to make a final check of your presentation. In the **Page Setup group**, click the **Print What arrow**, and then click **Handouts, (4 slides per page)**. Your presentation will print on two pages. Click the **Print** button, and then click **OK** to print the handouts. Click **Close** ☒ to close Print Preview.

8 **Save** 🖫 the changes to your presentation, and then from the **Office** menu, click **Exit PowerPoint**.

Objective 8
Use the Microsoft Help System

As you work with PowerPoint 2007, you can get assistance by using the Help feature. You can ask questions and Help will provide you with information and step-by-step instructions for performing tasks.

Activity 1.25 Accessing PowerPoint Help

In this activity, you will use the Microsoft Help feature to learn more about this feature.

1 **Start** PowerPoint. In the upper right corner of your screen, click the **Microsoft Office PowerPoint Help** button. Alternatively, press F1.

You can browse the PowerPoint Help topics by clicking any of the listed items; or, near the top of the Help window, you can click in the search box and type a keyword to search for a specific item. If you have access to the Internet, PowerPoint will search Office Online for your help topic.

2 Near the upper left corner of the Help window, in the **Search** box, type **Printing Slides** as shown in Figure 1.41.

Search box

Figure 1.41

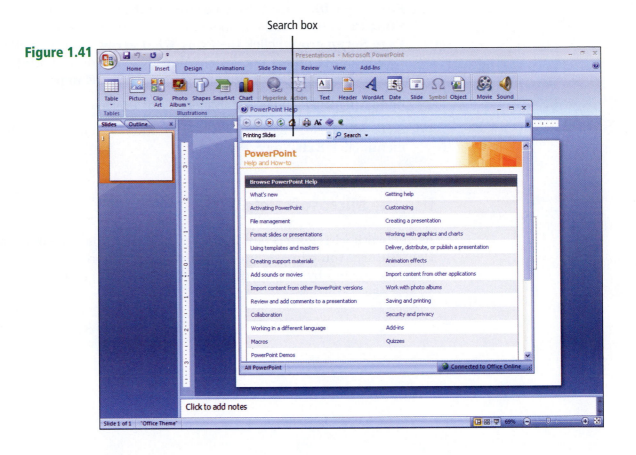

3 Press Enter or click **Search**. On the list of results, click **Print your slides** and then read the information that displays.

4 On the PowerPoint Help title bar, click the **Close** button. On the right side of the title bar, click the **Close** button to close PowerPoint.

End **You have completed Project 1B**

There's More You Can Do!

GO!
CD-ROM

From the student files that accompany this textbook, open the folder **02_theres_more_you_can_do**. Locate the Try IT! exercises for this chapter and follow the instructions to learn additional skills.

Try IT!—Set Slide Orientation and Size

In this Try IT! exercise, you will change the size and orientation of a slide.

Content-Based Assessments

Summary

In this chapter, you started PowerPoint and opened a PowerPoint presentation. You entered, edited, and formatted text in Normal view and worked with slides in Slide Sorter view; you added speaker notes; and you viewed the presentation as a slide show. The spelling checker tool was demonstrated, and you practiced how to change font style and size and add emphasis to text.

You created a new presentation, added content and clip art, and moved and deleted slides. You also added a footer to the notes and handouts pages and created a chapter folder to help organize your files. Each presentation was saved, previewed, printed, and closed. Finally, the Help program was introduced as a tool that can assist you in using PowerPoint.

Key Terms

Animation effects 8	**Header** 27	**Sizing handles** 42
Black slide 8	**Layout** 12	**Slide handouts** 27
Bulleted levels 14	**Live Preview** 21	**Slide Sorter view** 38
Clip art 39	**Mini toolbar** 15	**Synonym** 18
Contextual tabs 41	**Normal view** 11	**Task pane** 36
Contextual tools 41	**Notes pages** 27	**Template** 33
Deselect 40	**Placeholder** 13	**Text alignment** 23
Dragging 15	**Points** 20	**Theme** 25
Editing 11	**Presentation graphics software** 4	**Thesaurus** 18
Font 20		**Thumbnails** 6
Font styles 22	**Print Preview** 29	**Toggle buttons** 23
Footers 27	**ScreenTip** 24	**Transitions** 8
Formatting 20	**Shortcut menu** 16	
Gallery 12		

Content-Based Assessments

Matching

Match each term in the second column with its correct definition in the first column. Write the letter of the term on the blank line in front of the correct definition.

_____ **1.** A feature that introduces individual slide elements one element at a time.

_____ **2.** The PowerPoint view in which the window is divided into three panes—the Slide pane, the Slides/Outline pane, and the Notes pane.

_____ **3.** Outline levels represented by a symbol that are identified in the slides by the indentation and the size of the text.

_____ **4.** A feature that displays buttons that are commonly used with the selected object.

_____ **5.** A context-sensitive menu that displays commands and options relevant to the selected object.

_____ **6.** The action of holding down the left mouse button and moving the mouse pointer over text to select it.

_____ **7.** A set of characters (letters and numbers) with the same design and shape.

_____ **8.** A unit of measure to describe the size of a font.

_____ **9.** A container that reserves a portion of a slide for text, graphics, and other slide elements.

_____ **10.** A slide that is inserted at the end of every slide show to indicate that the presentation is over.

_____ **11.** The changing of the appearance of the text, layout, and design of a slide.

_____ **12.** A feature that displays formatting in your presentation so that you can decide whether or not you would like to apply the formatting.

_____ **13.** A feature that changes the horizontal placement of text within a placeholder.

_____ **14.** Printouts that contain the slide image in the top half of the page and notes that you have created in the Notes pane in the lower half of the page.

_____ **15.** A feature that displays your presentation as it will print, based on the options that you select.

A Animation

B Black slide

C Bulleted levels

D Dragging

E Font

F Formatting

G Live Preview

H Mini toolbar

I Normal view

J Notes pages

K Placeholder

L Point

M Print Preview

N Shortcut menu

O Text alignment

Fill in the Blank

Write the correct word in the space provided.

1. Microsoft Office PowerPoint 2007 is a presentation _____ program that you can use to effectively present information to your audience.

2. Miniature images of slides are known as _____.

3. A slide _____ controls the way in which a slide appears or disappears during an onscreen slide show.

4. The process of adding, deleting, or changing the contents of a slide is known as _____.

5. A _____ is a visual representation of a command's options.

6. The placement and arrangement of the text and graphic elements on a slide refer to its _____.

7. Tools that enable you to perform specific commands related to the selected object are _____ tools.

8. A file that contains the styles in a presentation, including the type and size of bullets and fonts, placeholder sizes and positions, background design and fill color schemes, and theme information, is known as a _____.

9. The _____ is a research tool that provides a list of synonyms for a selection.

10. Words with the same meaning are known as _____.

11. Font _____ add emphasis to text, and may include bold, italic, and underline.

12. A _____ button is one in which you can click the button once to turn it on and click it again to turn it off.

13. Text that prints at the top of a sheet of slide handouts or notes pages is known as a _____.

14. Text that displays at the bottom of every slide or that prints at the bottom of a sheet of slide handouts or notes is known as a _____.

15. The view in which all of the slides in your presentation display in miniature is _____ _____ view.

Content-Based Assessments

Skills Review

Project 1C — Hospitality

In this project, you will apply the skills you practiced from the Objectives in Project 1A.

Objectives: 1. *Open, View, and Save a Presentation;* **2.** *Edit a Presentation;* **3.** *Format a Presentation;* **4.** *Create Headers and Footers and Print a Presentation.*

In the following Skills Review, you will edit a presentation created by Shawna Andreasyan, the Human Resources Director, for new Skyline Bakery and Cafe employees. Your completed presentation will look similar to the one shown in Figure 1.42.

For Project 1C, you will need the following file:

p1C_Hospitality

You will save your presentation as
1C_Hospitality_Firstname_Lastname

Figure 1.42

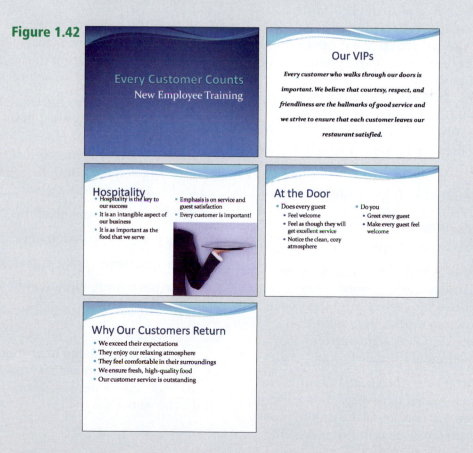

(Project 1C–Hospitality continues on the next page)

Content-Based Assessments

(Project 1C–Hospitality continued)

1. **Start** PowerPoint. Click the **Office** button, and then click **Open.** Navigate to the location where your student files are stored and open the file **p1C_Hospitality**. Click the **Office** button, and then click **Save As**. Navigate to your **PowerPoint Chapter 1** folder and using your own first and last name, save the file as **1C_Hospitality_Firstname_Lastname**.

2. Click the **Design tab**. In the **Themes group**, to the right of the last displayed theme, click the **More** button to display the **Themes gallery**. Recall that after the first theme—Office—the remaining themes display alphabetically. Under **Built-in**, locate and click the **Flow** theme to apply the theme to the entire presentation.

3. Display **Slide 2**, and then click in the paragraph. Click the **Home tab**, and then, in the **Paragraph group**, click the **Center** button to center align the paragraph within the placeholder. In the **Paragraph group**, click the **Line Spacing** button, and then click **2.0** to apply double-spacing to the paragraph. Then, click in the slide title, and click the **Center** button to center align the title.

4. On **Slide 2**, drag to select all of the text in the paragraph. Point to the Mini toolbar, and then click **Bold** and **Italic** to apply both font styles to the paragraph.

5. Display **Slide 4** and notice the red wavy underline under the last word of the last bullet. Point to *atmoshere*, and then click the right mouse button to display the shortcut menu. Click **atmosphere** to correct the spelling of the word.

6. On **Slide 4**, in the third bullet point, right-click the word *good* to display the shortcut menu. Near the bottom of the menu, point to **Synonyms**, and then in the synonyms

list, click **excellent** to use the Thesaurus to change *good* to *excellent*.

7. With **Slide 4** still displayed, on the **Home tab**, in the **Slides group**, click **Layout** to display the **Slide Layout gallery**. Click the **Two Content** layout.

8. Click in the placeholder on the right. Type **Do you** and then press Enter. Press Tab to increase the list level. Type **Greet every guest** and then press Enter. Type **Make every guest feel welcome**

9. In the placeholder at the left of **Slide 4**, drag to select the last three bulleted items. On the **Home tab**, in the **Paragraph group**, click the **Increase List Level** button to demote the three bulleted items one level below the first bulleted item.

10. With **Slide 4** still displayed, on the **Home tab**, in the **Slides group**, click the **New Slide arrow**, and then in the gallery, click **Title and Content** to create a new Slide 5.

11. On **Slide 5**, click in the title placeholder, type **Why Our Customers Return** and then click in the content placeholder. Type the following five bulleted items, pressing Enter at the end of each line to create a new bullet. Do not press Enter after the last item.

    We exceed their expectations

    They enjoy our relaxing atmosphere

    They feel comfortable in their surroundings

    We ensure fresh, high-quality food

    Our customer service is outstanding

12. With **Slide 5** displayed, click in the **Notes** pane and type **Remember that every single one of our customers is a VIP!** Make spelling corrections as necessary on the slide and in the notes.

(Project 1C–Hospitality continues on the next page)

Content-Based Assessments

Skills Review

(Project 1C–Hospitality continued)

13. Display **Slide 1** and drag to select the subtitle text—*New Employee Training*. On the Mini toolbar, click the **Font size button arrow**, and then change the font size to **44**.

14. Click the **Insert tab**, and then, in the **Text group**, click **Header & Footer** to display the **Header and Footer** dialog box.

15. Click the **Notes and Handouts tab**. Under **Include on page**, click to select the **Date and time** check box and, if necessary, click the **Update automatically** button so that the current date prints on the notes and handouts each time the presentation is printed. If necessary, clear the **Header** check box to omit this element from the header and footer. If necessary, click to select the **Page number** and **Footer** check boxes, noticing that when you do so, the insertion point displays in the Footer box. Using your own first and last names, in the Footer box type **1C_Hospitality_Firstname_Lastname** and then click **Apply to All**.

16. On the Ribbon, click the **Slide Show tab**, and then in the **Start Slide Show group**, click **From Beginning**. Press Spacebar or click the left mouse button to advance through the presentation and view the slide show.

17. Check your *Chapter Assignment Sheet* or *Course Syllabus* or consult your instructor to determine if you are to submit your assignments on paper or electronically. To submit electronically, go to Step 20, and then follow the instructions provided by your instructor.

18. From the **Office** menu, point to the **Print arrow**, and then click **Print Preview** to make a final check of your presentation. In the **Page Setup group**, click the **Print What arrow**, and then click **Handouts, (6 slides per page)**. Click the **Print** button, and then click **OK** to print the handouts.

19. In the **Page Setup group**, click the **Print What arrow**, and then click **Notes Pages**. Click the **Print** button, and in the **Print** dialog box, under **Print range**, click the **Slides** option button. In the **Slides** box, type **5** to instruct PowerPoint to print the notes pages for Slide 5. Click **OK**, and then close Print Preview.

20. **Save** changes to your presentation, and then from the **Office** menu, click **Exit PowerPoint**.

End **You have completed Project 1C**

PowerPoint

chapterone

Skills Review

Project 1D — Funding

In this project, you will apply the skills you practiced from the Objectives found in Project 1B.

Objectives: 5. *Create a New Presentation;* **6.** *Use Slide Sorter View;* **7.** *Add Pictures to a Presentation.*

In the following Skills Review, you will create the preliminary slides for a presentation that Lucinda dePaolo, Chief Financial Officer for Skyline Bakery and Cafe, will use to provide an overview of financial plans to a group of investors. Your completed presentation will look similar to the one shown in Figure 1.43.

For Project 1D, you will need the following files:

p1D_Background

p1D_Proposal_Template

p1D_Calculator

You will save your presentation as
1D_Funding_Firstname_Lastname

Figure 1.43

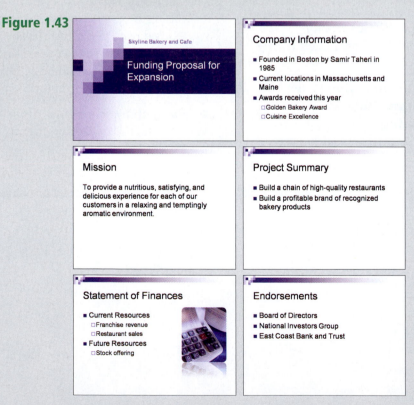

(Project 1D–Funding continues on the next page)

Skills Review

(Project 1D–Funding continued)

1. **Start** PowerPoint. From the **Office** menu, click **New** to display the **New Presentation** window. Under **Microsoft Office Online**, click **More Categories**, and then under **More categories**, click **Proposals**. Click the **Grant proposal** template, and then in the lower right corner of the **New Presentation** window, click **Download** to access the template from Microsoft Office Online. If a Microsoft Office window displays, click Continue. Alternatively, if you are unable to access the templates from Microsoft Office Online, the template for this project is available from your student data files. Click the Office button, and then click Open. Navigate to your student files and open the p1D_Proposal_Template presentation.

2. On **Slide 1**, drag to select the text *Organization Name*, and type **Skyline Bakery and Cafe** to replace it. Select the text that you just typed, and on the Mini toolbar, click the **Font Size button arrow**, and then click **24**. Drag to select the text in the title placeholder, and then type **Funding Proposal for Expansion**

3. Click the **Office** button, and then click **Save As**. In the **Save As** dialog box, click the **Save in** arrow, and then navigate to the location where you are storing your files for this chapter. In the **File name** box, delete any existing text, and then using your own first and last names type **1D_Funding_Firstname_Lastname** and then click **Save**.

4. Scroll through the presentation to view the content suggested for a funding proposal. Notice that in Slide 2, an introduction and mission statement are suggested. This content exists in another presentation and can be inserted without retyping the slides.

5. Display **Slide 1**. On the **Home tab**, in the **Slides group**, click the **New Slide arrow** to display the **Slide Layout gallery** and additional options for inserting slides. At the bottom of the gallery, click **Reuse Slides** to open the **Reuse Slides** task pane.

6. In the **Reuse Slides** task pane, click the **Browse** button, and then click **Browse File**. In the **Browse** dialog box, navigate to where your student files are stored and double-click **p1D_Background**. In the **Reuse Slides** task pane, point to either of the two slides that display and click the right-mouse button. From the shortcut menu, click **Insert All Slides** to insert both slides into the presentation. **Close** the **Reuse Slides** task pane.

7. On the status bar, locate the **View** buttons, and then click the **Slide Sorter** button to display the 15 slides in the presentation. Click to select **Slide 4**, and then press Delete to delete the slide. Click **Slide 5**, hold down ⇧ Shift and click **Slide 7** so that slides 5 through 7 are selected. Press Delete to delete the selected slides.

8. Click **Slide 6**, hold down ⇧ Shift and click **Slide 9** so that slides 6 through 9 are selected. With the four slides still selected, hold down Ctrl, and then click **Slide 11**. Press Delete to delete the selected slides. Six slides remain in the presentation.

9. Click **Slide 3** to select it. While pointing to **Slide 3**, press and hold down the left mouse button, and then drag the slide to the left until the displayed vertical bar is positioned to the left of **Slide 2**. Release the left mouse button to move the slide.

10. In the status bar, click the **Normal** button, and then **Save** your presentation. Display **Slide 4**, and then select the text in the

(Project 1D–Funding continues on the next page)

(Project 1D–Funding continued)

content placeholder. Replace the selected text with the following two bullets:

Build a chain of high-quality restaurants

Build a profitable brand of recognized bakery products

11. Display **Slide 5,** change the title to **Statement of Finances** and then select the text in the content placeholder. Replace the selected text with the following bullet points, increasing and decreasing the list level as indicated:

Current Resources

    Franchise revenue

    Restaurant sales

Future Resources

    Stock offering

12. Click the **Insert tab**, and then in the **Illustrations group**, click **Clip Art** to display the **Clip Art** task pane. In the **Clip Art** task pane, click in the **Search for** box, and then type **calculator**

13. In the **Clip Art** task pane, click the **Search in arrow**, and if necessary, click the **Everywhere** check box so that it is selected. Click the **Results should be arrow**, and then click as necessary to *clear* the **Clip Art**, **Movies**, and **Sounds** check boxes so that only **Photographs** is selected. Click **Go** to display the photographs of calculators. Click the picture of the white calculator with an adding machine tape on a blue background. Check Figure 1.43 at the beginning of this project if you are unsure of the picture that you should insert. **Close** the **Clip Art** task pane. (Note: If you cannot locate the picture, on the Insert tab, in the Illustrations group, click Picture. Navigate to your student files and then double-click p1D_Calculator.)

14. Position the pointer anywhere over the picture to display the ⊕ pointer. Drag to the right so that the picture is positioned approximately one-half inch from the right edge of the slide.

15. If necessary, click the picture of the calculator to select it and to activate the Picture Tools. On the Ribbon, click the **Format tab**, and then in the **Picture Styles group**, in the first row, click **Reflected Rounded Rectangle**.

16. Display **Slide 6**. Select the bulleted list text, and then replace it with the following bulleted items:

Board of Directors

National Investors Group

East Coast Bank and Trust

17. Click the **Insert tab**, and then in the **Text group**, click **Header & Footer** to display the **Header and Footer** dialog box.

18. Click the **Notes and Handouts tab**. Under **Include on page**, click to select the **Date and time** check box and, if necessary, click the **Update automatically** button so that the current date prints on the notes and handouts each time the presentation is printed. If necessary, clear the **Header** check box to omit this element from the header and footer. Click to select the **Page number** and **Footer** check boxes. Using your own first and last names, in the Footer box, type **1D_Funding_Firstname_Lastname** and then click **Apply to All**.

19. Check your *Chapter Assignment Sheet* or *Course Syllabus* or consult your instructor to determine if you are to submit your assignments on paper or electronically. To submit electronically, go to Step 21, and then follow the instructions provided by your instructor.

(Project 1D–Funding continues on the next page)

(Project 1D–Funding continued)

20. From the **Office** menu, point to **Print**, and then click **Print Preview** to make a final check of your presentation. In the **Page Setup group**, click the **Print What arrow**, and then click **Handouts, (6 slides per page)**. Click the **Print** button, and then

click **OK** to print the handouts. **Close** Print Preview.

21. **Save** changes to your presentation, and then from the **Office** menu, click **Exit PowerPoint**.

End **You have completed Project 1D**

Mastering PowerPoint

Project 1E—Recruitment

In this project, you will apply the skills you practiced from the Objectives found in Project 1A.

Objectives: 1. *Open, View, and Save a Presentation;* **2.** *Edit a Presentation;* **3.** *Format a Presentation;* **4.** *Create Headers and Footers and Print a Presentation.*

In the following Mastering PowerPoint project, you will edit a presentation created by Shawna Andreasyan regarding the new online recruiting program at Skyline Bakery and Cafe. Your completed presentation will look similar to Figure 1.44.

For Project 1E, you will need the following file:

p1E_Recruitment

You will save your presentation as
1E_Recruitment_Firstname_Lastname

Figure 1.44

(Project 1E–Recruitment continues on the next page)

Content-Based Assessments

PowerPoint
chapterone
Mastering PowerPoint

(Project 1E–Recruitment continued)

1. **Start** PowerPoint and **Open** the file **p1E_Recruitment**. Save the presentation as 1E_Recruitment_Firstname_Lastname

2. On **Slide 1**, change the **Font Size** for the title to **48** so that the entire title fits on one line. Add the subtitle **Online Recruiting Plan** and then apply **Italic** to the subtitle.

3. Add a **New Slide** to the presentation with the **Title and Content** layout. The slide title is **Need for Online Recruiting** In the content placeholder, type the following bullet points and correct any spelling errors that you make while typing:

Expansion into new geographic locations

Cost savings over traditional methods

New graduates search online for jobs

Reach a more diverse applicant pool

4. On **Slide 3**, **Center** the slide title, and then change the **Font** to **Arial Black**. Add the following speaker's notes, correcting spelling errors as necessary. **We currently use three major recruiting methods. This chart indicates the amount that will be spent on each method once online recruiting is established.**

5. Add a **New Slide** to the presentation with the **Title and Content** layout. The slide title is **Online Recruiting Advantages** In the content placeholder, type the following bullet points, and then correct any spelling errors that you make while typing. After you type the text, increase the list level of the fourth bullet point—*Automated database.*

Access to more qualified applicants

Streamlined application process

Improved manageability

Automated database

Easily maintained and updated

6. Display **Slide 3**, and then on the Ribbon, click the **Design tab**. Using the **More** button, display the **Themes gallery**. Under **Built-In**, apply the **Oriel** theme to **Slide 3** only. (Hint: Right-click the theme, and then click **Apply to Selected Slides.**)

7. Display **Slide 1** and view the slide show, pressing Spacebar to advance through the presentation. When the black slide displays, press Spacebar one more time return to the presentation.

8. Create a **Header and Footer** for the **Notes and Handouts**. Include only the **Date and time updated automatically**, the **Page number**, and a **Footer** with the filename **1E_Recruitment_Firstname_Lastname** using your own first and last names.

9. Check your *Chapter Assignment Sheet* or *Course Syllabus* or consult your instructor to determine if you are to submit your assignments on paper or electronically. To submit electronically, go to Step 11, and then follow the instructions provided by your instructor.

10. **Print Preview** your presentation, and then print **Handouts, (4 slides per page)** and the **Notes Pages** for **Slide 3**.

11. **Save** changes to your presentation, and then **Close** the presentation.

End **You have completed Project 1E**

Project 1F — Kitchen

In this project, you will apply the skills you practiced from Objectives in Project 1B.

Objectives: 5. *Create a New Presentation;* **6.** *Use Slide Sorter View;* **7.** *Add Pictures to a Presentation.*

In the following Mastering PowerPoint project, you will create a presentation that Peter Wing, Executive Chef for Skyline Bakery and Cafe, will use to describe the different types of chefs employed by the restaurant. Your completed presentation will look similar to Figure 1.45.

> ### For Project 1F, you will need the following files:
>
> p1F_Chefs
> p1F_Tools
> p1F_Nutrition_Template

You will save your presentation as
1F_Kitchen_Firstname_Lastname

Figure 1.45

(Project 1F– Kitchen continues on the next page)

Mastering PowerPoint

(Project 1F–Kitchen continued)

1. **Start** PowerPoint and begin a new presentation based on the **Nutrition** design template. You may search by using the keyword *Nutrition* or you may find the template in the **Design slides, Academic** category. If you do not have access to the online templates, open **p1F_Nutrition_Template** from your student files. **Save** the presentation as **1F_Kitchen_Firstname_Lastname**

2. The title for the first slide is **The Kitchen is Open!** and the subtitle is **Skyline Bakery and Cafe**

3. From your student files, add all of the slides in the **p1F_Chefs** presentation into the current presentation. Then, display the presentation in **Slide Sorter view** and rearrange the slides so that the *Kitchen Organization* slide is the second slide, and the *Director of Kitchen Operations* slide is the fourth slide.

4. Display **Slide 2** in **Normal** view and insert a clip art image by searching for **Photographs** in **All collections**, using the keyword **skillet** Insert the picture that contains a chef's hat, skillet, wooden spoon,

knife, and guest check. If you cannot find the picture, insert the picture found in your student files, p1F_Tools.

5. Drag the picture to the lower right corner of the slide, and then apply a **Picture Style—Bevel Rectangle**. (Hint: Picture Styles are found in the Format tab of the Picture Tools contextual tool.)

6. Create a **Header and Footer** for the **Notes and Handouts**. Include only the **Date and time updated automatically**, the **Page number**, and a **Footer** with the filename **1F_Kitchen_Firstname_Lastname** using your own first and last names.

7. Check your *Chapter Assignment Sheet* or *Course Syllabus* or consult your instructor to determine if you are to submit your assignments on paper or electronically. To submit electronically, go to Step 9, and then follow the instructions provided by your instructor.

8. **Print Preview** your presentation, and then print **Handouts, (4 slides per page)**.

9. **Save** changes to your presentation, and then **Close** the file.

End **You have completed Project 1F**

PowerPoint

chapterone

Mastering PowerPoint

Project 1G — Flyer

In this project, you will apply the skills you practiced from the Objectives found in Projects 1A and 1B.

Objectives: 2. *Edit a Presentation;* **3.** *Format a Presentation;* **4.** *Create Headers and Footers and Print a Presentation;* **5.** *Create a New Presentation;* **7.** *Add Pictures to a Presentation.*

In the following Mastering PowerPoint project, you will create a single slide to be used as a flyer for the annual employee baking contest. Your completed presentation will look similar to Figure 1.46.

For Project 1G, you will need the following files:

New blank PowerPoint presentation
p1G_Cookies

**You will save your presentation as
1G_Flyer_Firstname_Lastname**

Figure 1.46

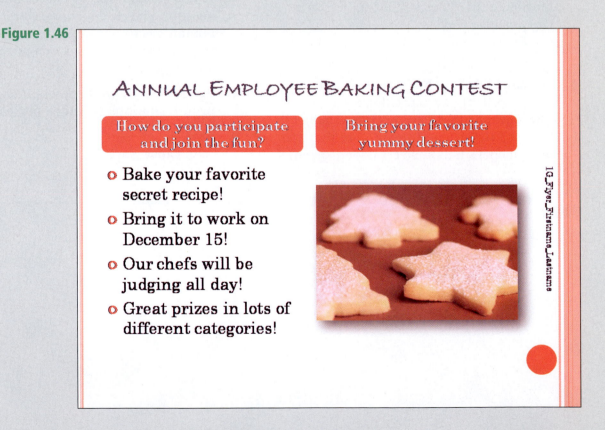

(Project 1G–Flyer continues on the next page)

Mastering PowerPoint

(Project 1G–Flyer continued)

1. **Start** PowerPoint and begin a new blank presentation. Change the **Layout** of the title slide to the **Comparison** layout. Change the **Design** of the presentation by applying the **Oriel** theme. **Save** your presentation as **1G_Flyer_Firstname_ Lastname**

2. The title of the slide is **Annual Employee Baking Contest** Change the **Font** to **Bradley Hand ITC** and the **Font Size** to **36**. Apply **Bold**, and then **Center** the title.

3. In the orange box on the left side of the slide, type **How do you participate and join the fun?** In the orange box on the right side of the slide, type **Bring your favorite yummy dessert! Center** the text in both boxes.

4. In the content placeholder on the left side of the slide, type the following bullet points:

   Bake your favorite secret recipe!

   Bring it to work on December 15!

   Our chefs will be judging all day!

   Great prizes in lots of different categories!

5. Click in the content placeholder on the right side of the slide and insert a clip art by using the keyword **cookies** Search for **Photographs** in **All collections**. Click the picture with the star-shaped cookies on the brown background. If you cannot find the picture, insert the picture found in your student files, **p1G_Cookies**.

6. Move the picture so that it is centered below the *Bring your favorite yummy dessert!* text. Then, apply **Picture Style— Drop Shadow Rectangle**.

7. Insert a **Footer** on the Slide (*not* the Notes and Handouts), that includes the file name **1G_Flyer_Firstname_Lastname** Because of the layout of this slide, the footer will display vertically on the right side of the slide.

8. Check your *Chapter Assignment Sheet* or *Course Syllabus* or consult your instructor to determine if you are to submit your assignments on paper or electronically. To submit electronically, go to Step 10, and then follow the instructions provided by your instructor.

9. **Print Preview** your presentation. There is only one slide in the presentation, so print **Slides**.

10. **Save** and **Close** your presentation.

End **You have completed Project 1G**

PowerPoint
chapter one

Mastering PowerPoint

Project 1H — Fresh

In this project, you will apply the skills you practiced from the Objectives found in Projects 1A and 1B.

Objectives: 2. *Edit a Presentation;* **3.** *Format a Presentation;* **4.** *Create Headers and Footers and Print a Presentation;* **5.** *Create a New Presentation;* **6.** *Use Slide Sorter View;* **7.** *Add Pictures to a Presentation.*

In the following Mastering PowerPoint project, you will create a presentation that describes some of the steps taken by Skyline Bakery and Cafe to ensure that their food is fresh. Your completed presentation will look similar to Figure 1.47.

For Project 1H, you will need the following files:

New blank PowerPoint presentation
p1H_Text
p1H_Apple_Template
p1H_Vegetables
p1H_Tomato

You will save your presentation as
1H_Fresh_Firstname_Lastname

Figure 1.47

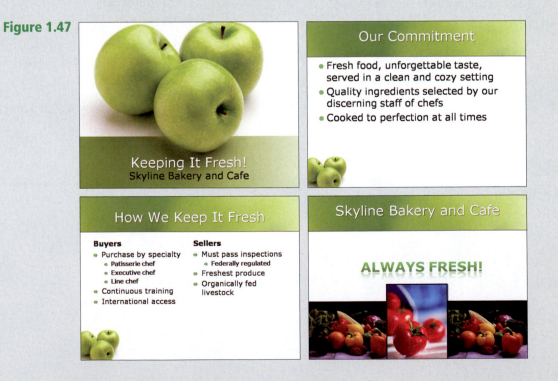

(Project 1H–Fresh continues on the next page)

Mastering PowerPoint

(Project 1H–Fresh continued)

1. **Start** PowerPoint and begin a new presentation by searching for a template with the keyword **Apple** Click the template with the three green apples. If the template is not available, from your student files, open **p1H_Apple_Template**.

2. The title of this presentation is **Keeping It Fresh!** and the subtitle is **Skyline Bakery and Cafe Save** the presentation as **1H_Fresh_Firstname_Lastname**

3. Add the two slides from the **p1H_Text** presentation. Display **Slide 3**, and then in the left bulleted list placeholder, increase the list level of the *Patisserie chef*, *Executive chef*, and *Line chef* bullet points. In the right bulleted list placeholder, increase the list level of the *Federally regulated* bullet point.

4. Add a **New Slide** with the **Title and Content** layout, and in the title placeholder, type **Our Commitment** In the bulleted list placeholder, type the following bullet points:

   Fresh food, unforgettable taste, served in a clean and cozy setting

   Quality ingredients picked by our discerning staff of chefs

   Cooked to perfection at all times

5. In **Slide Sorter** view, switch **Slides 2 and 4** so that **Slide 2** becomes the last slide and the **Our Commitment** slide becomes the second slide. Return the presentation to **Normal** view.

6. On **Slide 2**, in the second bullet point, use the shortcut menu to view **Synonyms** for the word *picked*. Change the word *picked* to **selected**.

7. Display **Slide 4**. Insert a clip art image by using the keyword **cabbage** Search for

Photographs in **All collections**. Click the picture with many different types and colors of vegetables. Move the picture down and to the left so that it covers the apples and is positioned in the lower left corner of the slide. If you cannot locate the picture, it is available in your student files. The filename is **p1H_Vegetables**.

8. Insert the vegetable picture again so that there are two copies of the same pictures on the slide. Move the picture down and to the right so that it is positioned in the lower right corner of the slide.

9. Insert another clip art image, this time by using the keywords **cherry tomato** Search for **Photographs** in **All collections**. Click the picture with tomatoes that look like they are spilling out of a bowl as shown in the figure at the beginning of this project. If you cannot locate the picture, it is available in your student files. The filename is **p1H_Tomato**. Drag the tomato picture straight down so that it overlaps the two vegetable pictures and its bottom edge aligns with the bottom edge of the slide. Apply **Picture Style—Simple Frame, Black**.

10. Create a **Header and Footer** for the **Notes and Handouts**. Include only the **Date and time updated automatically**, the **Page number**, and a **Footer** with the file name **1H_Fresh_Firstname_Lastname** and then view the slide show.

11. Check your *Chapter Assignment Sheet* or *Course Syllabus* or consult your instructor to determine if you are to submit your assignments on paper or electronically. To submit electronically, go to Step 13, and then follow the instructions provided by your instructor.

(Project 1H–Fresh continues on the next page)

Mastering PowerPoint

(Project 1H–Fresh continued)

12. Print Preview your presentation, and then print **Handouts, (4 slides per page)**. If the text or pictures do not display, on the Print Preview tab, in the Print group click Options, point to Color/Grayscale, and then click Color or Color (On Black and White Printer).

13. Save changes to your presentation. **Close** the presentation.

End **You have completed Project 1H**

Mastering PowerPoint

Project 1I — Holiday

In this project, you will apply the skills you practiced from Objectives found in Projects 1A and 1B.

Objectives: 1. *Open, View, and Save a Presentation;* **2.** *Edit a Presentation;* **3.** *Format a Presentation;* **4.** *Create Headers and Footers and Print a Presentation;* **5.** *Create a New Presentation;* **6.** *Use Slide Sorter View;* **7.** *Add Pictures to a Presentation;* **8.** *Use the Microsoft Help System.*

In the following Mastering PowerPoint project, you will create a presentation that details the holiday activities at Skyline Bakery and Cafe. Your completed presentation will look similar to Figure 1.48.

For Project 1I, you will need the following files:

New blank PowerPoint presentation
p1I_December
p1I_Green_Template
p1I_Coffee
p1I_Ornaments

You will save your presentation as
1I_Holiday_ Firstname_Lastname

Figure 1.48

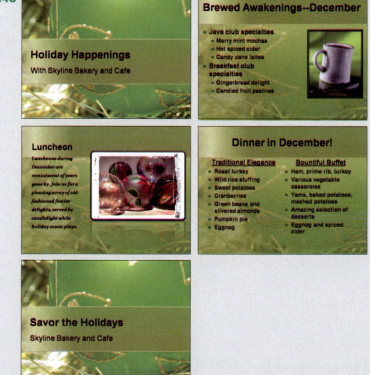

(Project 1I–Holiday continues on the next page)

Mastering PowerPoint

(Project 1I–Holiday continued)

1. **Start** PowerPoint and begin a new presentation by searching for the green and gold holiday template. If the template is not available, from your student files, open **p1I_Green_Template**. The title of the presentation is **Holiday Happenings** and the subtitle is **With Skyline Bakery and Cafe** Insert all of the slides from the presentation **p1I_December**. **Save** the presentation as **1I_Holiday_Firstname_Lastname**

2. On **Slide 2**, increase the list level for bullet points 2, 3, and 4 and for the last two bullet points. Change the **Layout** to **Two Content**, and then in the right placeholder insert a clip art photograph of a white coffee mug on a green background. If you cannot find the image, it is located with your student files—**p1I_Coffee**. Size the picture so that it is approximately as wide as the word *December* and as tall as the text in the left placeholder. Apply **Picture Style—Compound Frame, Black** and position the picture, using Figure 1.48 at the beginning of this project as your guide.

3. Display **Slide 3** and change the **Layout** to **Comparison**. In the *Click to add text* box on the left side of the slide, type **Traditional Elegance** and then in the box on the right side of the slide type **Bountiful Buffet Center** and **Underline** the text in both boxes, and then change the **Font Size** to **28**.

4. Insert a **New Slide** with the **Content with Caption** layout. In the *Click to add title* box, type **Luncheon** and then change the **Font Size** to **36**. In the text placeholder on the left side of the slide, type the following paragraph:

   Luncheons during December are reminiscent of years gone by. Join us for a pleasing array of old-fashioned festive delights, served by candlelight while holiday music plays.

5. Select the paragraph, and then change the **Font** to **Constantia** and the **Font Size** to **20**. Apply **Bold** and **Italic**, and then change the **Line Spacing** to **1.5**.

6. In the content placeholder on the right side of the slide, insert a clip art of five, brightly colored glass ornaments. Apply **Picture Style—Reflected Bevel, Black** and use Figure 1.48 at the beginning of this project as your guide for sizing and positioning the picture. If you cannot locate the picture, the file name in your student files is **p1I_Ornaments**.

7. Insert a **New Slide** with the **Title Slide** layout. In the title placeholder, type **Savor the Holidays** and in the subtitle placeholder type **Skyline Bakery and Cafe**

8. Move **Slide 4** so that it is between **Slides 2** and **3**. Add the **Date and time updated automatically**, the **Page number**, and the file name **1I_Holiday_Firstname_Lastname** to the **Notes and Handouts Footer.** Check the presentation for spelling errors, and then view the slide show from the beginning.

9. Check your *Chapter Assignment Sheet* or *Course Syllabus* or consult your instructor to determine if you are to submit your assignments on paper or electronically. To submit electronically, go to Step 11, and then follow the instructions provided by your instructor.

10. **Print Preview** your presentation, and then print **Handouts, (6 slides per page).**

11. **Save** changes to your presentation, and then **close** the file.

End **You have completed Project 1I**

GO!
CD-ROM

Business Running Case

Project 1J—Business Running Case

In this project, you will apply the skills you practiced in Projects 1A and 1B.

From the student files that accompany this textbook, open the folder **03_business_running_case.** Locate the Business Running Case project for this chapter. Follow the instructions and use the skills you have gained thus far to assist Jennifer Nelson in meeting the challenges of owning and running her business.

Outcomes-Based Assessments

Rubric

The following outcomes-based assessments are *open-ended assessments*. That is, there is no specific correct result; your result will depend on your approach to the information provided. Make *Professional Quality* your goal. Use the following scoring rubric to guide you in *how* to approach the problem, and then to evaluate *how well* your approach solves the problem.

The *criteria*—Software Mastery, Content, Format and Layout, and Process—represent the knowledge and skills you have gained that you can apply to solving the problem. The *levels of performance*—Professional Quality, Approaching Professional Quality, or Needs Quality Improvements—help you and your instructor evaluate your result.

	Your completed project is of Professional Quality if you:	Your completed project is Approaching Professional Quality if you:	Your completed project Needs Quality Improvements if you:
1-Software Mastery	Choose and apply the most appropriate skills, tools, and features and identify efficient methods to solve the problem.	Choose and apply some appropriate skills, tools, and features, but not in the most efficient manner.	Choose inappropriate skills, tools, or features, or are inefficient in solving the problem.
2-Content	Construct a solution that is clear and well organized, contains content that is accurate, appropriate to the audience and purpose, and is complete. Provide a solution that contains no errors of spelling, grammar, or style.	Construct a solution in which some components are unclear, poorly organized, inconsistent, or incomplete. Misjudge the needs of the audience. Have some errors in spelling, grammar, or style, but the errors do not detract from comprehension.	Construct a solution that is unclear, incomplete, or poorly organized, containing some inaccurate or inappropriate content; and contains many errors of spelling, grammar, or style. Do not solve the problem.
3-Format and Layout	Format and arrange all elements to communicate information and ideas, clarify function, illustrate relationships, and indicate relative importance.	Apply appropriate format and layout features to some elements, but not others. Overuse features, causing minor distraction.	Apply format and layout that does not communicate information or ideas clearly. Do not use format and layout features to clarify function, illustrate relationships, or indicate relative importance. Use available features excessively, causing distraction.
4-Process	Use an organized approach that integrates planning, development, self-assessment, revision, and reflection.	Demonstrate an organized approach in some areas, but not others; or, use an insufficient process of organization throughout.	Do not use an organized approach to solve the problem.

Outcomes-Based Assessments

Problem Solving

Project 1K — Catering

In this project, you will construct a solution by applying any combination of the Objectives found in Projects 1A and 1B.

> **For Project 1K, you will need the following file:**
>
> New blank PowerPoint presentation

You will save your presentation as
1K_Catering_Firstname_Lastname

Using the information provided, create a presentation that contains four to six slides that Nancy Goldman, Chief Baker, can use to describe the catering services offered by Skyline Bakery and Cafe. The presentation will be used at a business expo attended by representatives of many companies that frequently host business luncheons and dinners for their clients. The presentation should include a title slide, a slide that describes why customers would be interested in Skyline Bakery and Cafe's catering services, at least two slides with sample menus, and an ending slide that summarizes the presentation. The tone of the presentation should be positive and sales oriented so that the audience is encouraged to try Skyline's catering service.

The presentation should include a theme or template that is creative and is appropriate to the upbeat tone of the presentation. Use at least two different slide layouts to vary the way in which the presentation text is displayed. Search for clip art that visually represents the types of menu items described. Add the file name to the Notes and Handouts footer and check the presentation for spelling errors. Save the presentation as **1K_Catering_Firstname_Lastname** and submit it as directed.

 End **You have completed Project 1K** ——————

Outcomes-Based Assessments

PowerPoint
chapter one

Problem Solving

Project 1L — Picnic

In this project, you will construct a solution by applying any combination of the Objectives found in Projects 1A and 1B.

For Project 1L, you will need the following file:

New blank PowerPoint presentation

You will save your presentation as
1L_Picnic_Firstname_Lastname

In this project, you will create a one-slide flyer to be distributed to employees of Skyline Bakery and Cafe advertising the upcoming employee picnic. The picnic is held every summer at a large, regional park. The tone of the flyer is fun! Use two fonts that are informal and inviting and large enough to easily read if the flyer were posted on a bulletin board. Include in the flyer a slide title that will make the employees feel welcome and excited about attending. Choose a content layout that includes multiple placeholders for the information that you need to provide. The flyer should include information on location, date, time, and types of activities. Include a picture that is reminiscent of a picnic or large outdoor gathering. Refer to Project 1G for ideas on how to lay out the flyer.

Add the file name to the footer and check the presentation for spelling errors. Save the presentation as **1L_Picnic_Firstname_Lastname** and submit it as directed.

End **You have completed Project 1L**

Problem Solving

Project 1M — Customer Service

In this project, you will construct a solution by applying any combination of the Objectives found in Projects 1A and 1B.

> **For Project 1M, you will need the following files:**
>
> New blank PowerPoint presentation
> p1M_Mission_Statement

**You will save your presentation as
1M_Customer_Service_Firstname_Lastname**

In this project, you will create a six-slide customer service presentation to be used by Shawna Andreasyan, Director of Human Resources for Skyline Bakery and Cafe. All employees will be attending customer service training seminars and this presentation is a brief introduction to the overall topic of customer service.

Good customer service is grounded in the Skyline Bakery and Cafe's mission statement. The mission statement has been provided for you in presentation p1M_Mission_Statement and should be inserted early in the presentation. Think about the mission statement, and then in the next slide, use a title slide layout to make a brief statement that summarizes how the mission statement is tied to customer service. Then consider some of the following principles of good customer service. A company should make a commitment to customer service so that every employee believes in it and is rewarded by it. Employees should also understand that everyone is involved in good customer service. The company is not just about the product; people are critically important to the success of any business and good customer service ensures that success. Furthermore, employees who are rewarded for good customer service will likely continue to work with good practices, perhaps leading to increased sales.

Using the information in the previous paragraph and other information that you may gather by researching the topic of "restaurant customer service," create at least two additional slides that Shawna Andreasyan can use to describe the importance of good customer service and how it is rewarded at Skyline Bakery and Cafe. When creating the design template, search Microsoft Online for customer service or training templates; there are several available. The tone of this presentation is informative and serious. Keep this in mind when choosing a template, theme, fonts, and clip art. Add the date and file name to the Notes and Handouts footer and check the presentation for spelling errors. Save the presentation as **1M_Customer_Service_Firstname_Lastname** and submit it as directed.

End **You have completed Project 1M** ————————

Problem Solving

Project 1N — Menus

In this project, you will construct a solution by applying any combination of the Objectives found in Projects 1A and 1B.

> **For Project 1N, you will need the following file:**
>
> New blank PowerPoint presentation

You will save your presentation as 1N_Menus_Firstname_Lastname

In this exercise, you will create a presentation that contains special menus that are used for different holidays. Recognizing that holiday menus are frequently used in a number of presentations throughout the year, Peter Wang, Executive Chef, has decided to create sample menus in one presentation so that the menus are available when the marketing staff need to insert them into PowerPoint presentations.

Choose five holidays and create slides that include one holiday menu per slide. You may research holiday menus on the Internet, visit local restaurants to find out if they have special holiday menus, or you may use your own experience with family traditions in creating these menus. The slide title should identify the holiday and every slide should include a picture that portrays the holiday meal or represents the holiday in some way. Alternatively, consider using a Two Content layout in which the menu is in one column and a quote describing why the menu is special is in the other column. Keep your theme simple so that it does not interfere with the pictures that you have selected. Because these slides will likely be used in different presentations throughout the year, you may choose different fonts and font styles that characterize each holiday.

Add the date and file name to the Notes and Handouts footer and check the presentation for spelling errors. Save the presentation as **1N_Menus_Firstname_Lastname** and submit it as directed.

 You have completed Project 1N ————————————

Problem Solving

Project 1O — Opening

In this project, you will construct a solution by applying any combination of the Objectives found in Projects 1A and 1B.

For Project 1O, you will need the following file:

New blank PowerPoint presentation

**You will save your presentation as
1O_Opening_Firstname_Lastname**

In this project, you will create a presentation to be shown by Skyline Bakery and Cafe's Chief Executive Officer, Samir Taheri, at a Chamber of Commerce meeting. The presentation will explain the details of the company's grand opening of two new locations in Rhode Island taking place in June. The presentation should contain six to eight slides and the first two to three slides should include background information that may be taken from the following paragraph that describes the company and the new restaurant's location.

Skyline Bakery and Cafe is a chain of casual dining restaurants and bakeries based in Boston. Each restaurant has its own in-house bakery, which produces a wide variety of high-quality specialty breads, breakfast sweets, and desserts. Breads and sweets are sold by counter service along with coffee drinks, gourmet teas, fresh juices, and sodas. The full-service restaurant area features a menu of sandwiches, salads, soups, and light entrees. Fresh, high-quality ingredients and a professional and courteous staff are the hallmarks of every Skyline Bakery and Cafe.

The new restaurant is located in an outdoor lifestyle center where many residents gather in the evening to socialize. The restaurants are opening in June, so consider a summer theme as you develop ideas about the kinds of events that the owners may host during the grand opening. Include in the presentation four slides representing four different days of events—two at each of the new locations. The Comparison and Two Content slide layouts may be very effective for these four slides. Use fonts and clip art to enhance your presentation but do not clutter the presentation with excess images or many different types of fonts. Add the date and file name to the Notes and Handouts footer and check the presentation for spelling errors. Save the presentation as **1O_Opening_Firstname_Lastname** and submit it as directed.

End **You have completed Project 1O** ──────────

Outcomes-Based Assessments

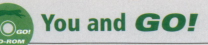
Project 1P — You and *GO!*

In this project, you will construct a solution by applying any combination of the Objectives found in Projects 1A and 1B.

From the student files that accompany this textbook, open the folder **04_you_and_go**. Locate the You and *GO!* project for this chapter and follow the instructions to create a presentation about a place to which you have traveled or would like to travel.

End **You have completed Project 1P** ————————————

GO! with Help

Project 1Q — *GO!* with Help

The PowerPoint Help system is extensive and can help you as you work. In this project, you will view information about getting help as you work in PowerPoint.

1 **Start** PowerPoint. At the right end of the Ribbon, click the **Microsoft Office PowerPoint Help** button to display the **PowerPoint Help** dialog box. In the **Search** box, type **keyboard shortcuts** and then press Enter.

2 In the displayed search results, click **Keyboard shortcuts for PowerPoint 2007**. Maximize the displayed window and read how you can use keyboard shortcuts in PowerPoint.

3 If you want, print a copy of the information by clicking the **Print** button at the top of the **Microsoft Office PowerPoint Help** window.

4 **Close** the Help window, and then **Close** PowerPoint.

End **You have completed Project 1Q** ————————————

Group Business Running Case

Project 1R — Group Business Running Case

In this project, you will apply the skills you practiced from the Objectives in Projects 1A and 1B.

Your instructor may assign this group case project to your class. If your instructor assigns this project, he or she will provide you with information and instructions to work as part of a group. The group will apply the skills gained thus far to help the Bell Orchid Hotel Group achieve its business goals.

End **You have completed Project 1R**

chaptertwo

Designing a PowerPoint Presentation

OBJECTIVES

At the end of this chapter you will be able to:

OUTCOMES

Mastering these objectives will enable you to:

1. Format Slide Elements
2. Insert and Format Pictures and Shapes
3. Apply Slide Transitions

PROJECT 2A
Format a Presentation

4. Reorganize Presentation Text and Clear Formats
5. Create and Format a SmartArt Graphic

PROJECT 2B
Enhance a Presentation with SmartArt Graphics

Montagna del Pattino

Montagna del Pattino was founded and built by the Blardone family in the 1950s. It has grown from one ski run and a small lodge to 50 trails, 6 lifts, a 300-room lodge, and a renowned ski and snowboard school. Luxurious condominiums on the property have ski in/ski out access. A resort store offers rental and sale of gear for enthusiasts who want the latest advances in ski and snowboard technology. A variety of quick service, casually elegant, and fine dining restaurants complete the scene for a perfect ski-enthusiast getaway.

Designing a PowerPoint Presentation

A PowerPoint presentation is a visual aid in which well-designed slides help the audience understand complex information, while keeping them focused on the message. Color is an important element that provides uniformity and visual interest. When used correctly, color enhances your slides and draws the audience's interest by creating focus. When designing the background and element colors for your presentation, use a consistent look throughout the presentation and be sure that the colors you use provide contrast so that the text is visible on the background.

Project 2A **Welcome**

In Activities 2.1 through 2.13, you will edit and format a presentation that Kirsten McCarty, Director of Marketing, has created for a travel fair that introduces potential resort visitors to the types of activities available at Montagna del Pattino. Your completed presentation will look similar to Figure 2.1.

For Project 2A, you will need the following files:

p2A_Snow
p2A_Snowboard
p2A_Welcome
p2A_Winter

You will save your presentation as
2A_Welcome_Firstname_Lastname

Figure 2.1
Project 2A—Welcome

Objective 1
Format Slide Elements

Recall that formatting is the process of changing the appearance of the text, layout, and design of a slide. You have practiced formatting text by changing the font and font size, and by applying bold and italic text styles. Other slide elements can be formatted, such as bulleted and numbered lists, and there are other methods that you can use to enhance text, including WordArt and the Format Painter.

Note — Comparing Your Screen with the Figures in This Textbook

Your screen will match the figures shown in this textbook if you set your screen resolution to 1024 × 768. At other resolutions, your screen will closely resemble, but not match, the figures shown. To view your screen's resolution, on the Windows desktop, right-click in a blank area, click Properties, and then click the Settings tab.

Activity 2.1 Selecting Placeholder Text and Using the Repeat Key

1 **Start** PowerPoint. From your student files, **Open** the file

p2A_Welcome. From the **Office** menu [icon], click **Save As**, and then click the **Create New Folder** button [icon]. Navigate to the location where you are saving your solution files, create a folder with the name **PowerPoint Chapter 2** and then click **OK**. In the **File name** box, type **2A_Welcome_Firstname_Lastname** and then click **Save** to save your file.

2 Display **Slide 2**. Click anywhere in the bulleted list on the left side of the slide and notice that the placeholder is surrounded by a dashed border, as shown in Figure 2.2.

The dashed border indicates that you can make editing changes to the placeholder text.

Activity 2.2 Changing a Bulleted List to a Numbered List

1 With **Slide 2** still displayed, click anywhere in the bulleted list on the left side of the slide, and then point to its dashed border to display the ⊕ pointer. Click the dashed border so that it displays as a solid line, indicating that all of the text is selected.

2 On the **Home tab**, in the **Paragraph group**, click the **Numbering** button 📋 ▾.

All of the bullets are converted to numbers. The color of the numbers is determined by the presentation theme.

Alert!

Did you display the Numbering gallery?

If you clicked the Numbering button arrow instead of the Numbering button, the Numbering gallery displays. Click the Numbering button arrow again to close the gallery, and then click the Numbering button to convert the bullets to numbers.

3 Select the bulleted list placeholder on the right side of the slide so that the border displays as a solid line. In the **Paragraph group**, click the **Numbering** button 📋 ▾.

4 **Save** 💾 the presentation.

Activity 2.3 Modifying the Bulleted List Style

The theme that is applied to your presentation includes default styles for the bulleted points in content placeholders. In this presentation, the default bullet is a blue circle. You can customize a bullet by changing its style, color, and size.

1 With **Slide 2** still displayed, click anywhere in the numbered list on the left side of the slide, and then point to its dashed border. Click the dashed border so that it displays as a solid line, indicating that all of the text is selected.

2 On the **Home tab**, in the **Paragraph group**, click the **Bullets button arrow** ⋮☰ ▾ to display the **Bullets gallery**, as shown in Figure 2.5. If your bullets gallery looks different, at the bottom of the Bullets and Numbering dialog box, click the Reset button.

The gallery displays several bullet characters that you can apply to the selection. Below the gallery, the Bullets and Numbering option, when clicked, displays the Bullets and Numbering dialog box.

Figure 2.5

Bullets button arrow

Bullets gallery

Click to display the Bullets and Numbering dialog box

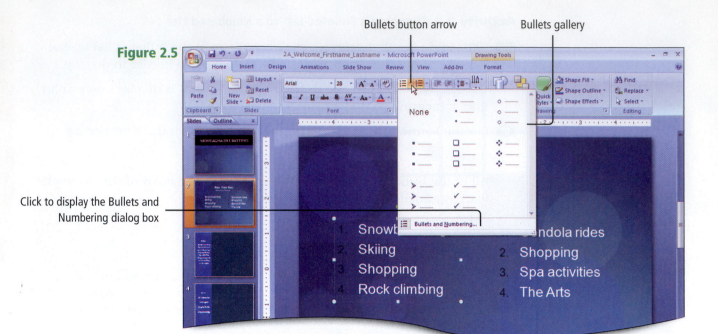

Did you replace the numbers with bullets?

If you replaced the numbers with bullets, then you clicked the Bullets *button* instead of the Bullets *arrow*. Click the Bullets arrow, and then continue with Step 3.

3 At the bottom of the **Bullets gallery**, click **Bullets and Numbering**. In the displayed **Bullets and Numbering** dialog box, point to each bullet style to display its ScreenTip. Then, in the second row, click **Star Bullets**. Below the gallery, click the **Color** button. Under **Theme Colors**, in the first row, click the first color—**Black, Background 1**. Click **OK** to apply the bullet style.

4 Click in the text in the numbered list placeholder on the right side of the slide. Point to the dashed border to display the ⊕ pointer, and then click the mouse button so that the placeholder border is solid, indicating that all of the text in the placeholder can be formatted at one time.

5 Press F4 to repeat the bullet formatting, and then compare your slide with Figure 2.6.

Figure 2.6

6 **Save** 💾 your changes.

More Knowledge

Using Other Symbols as Bullet Characters

Many bullets styles are available for you to insert in your presentation. In the Bullets and Numbering dialog box, click the Customize button to view additional bullet styles.

Activity 2.4 Applying WordArt Styles to Text

WordArt is a feature that applies combinations of decorative formatting to text, including shadows, reflections, and 3-D effects, as well as changing the line and *fill color* of text. A fill color is the inside color of text or of an object. You can choose from a gallery of WordArt styles to insert a new WordArt object or you can customize existing text by applying WordArt formatting.

1 Display **Slide 3**, and then drag to select the word *Relax*. On the **Format tab**, in the **WordArt Styles group**, click the **More** button

⏬ to display the **WordArt Styles gallery.**

The WordArt gallery is divided into two sections. If you choose a WordArt style in the *Applies to Selected Text* section, you must first select all of the text to which you want to apply the WordArt. If you choose a WordArt style in the *Applies to All Text in the Shape* section, the WordArt style is applied to all of the text in the placeholder.

2 Move your pointer over several of the WordArt styles and notice that Live Preview displays the formatting effects.

3 Under **Applies to Selected Text**, in the first row, click the second style—**Fill – None, Outline – Accent 2**.

The word *Relax* displays outlined in blue.

4 With the word *Relax* still selected, in the **Word Art Styles group**, click the **Text Fill button arrow**. Under **Theme Colors**, in the first row, click the first color—**Black, Background 1**, and then compare your slide with Figure 2.7.

Figure 2.7

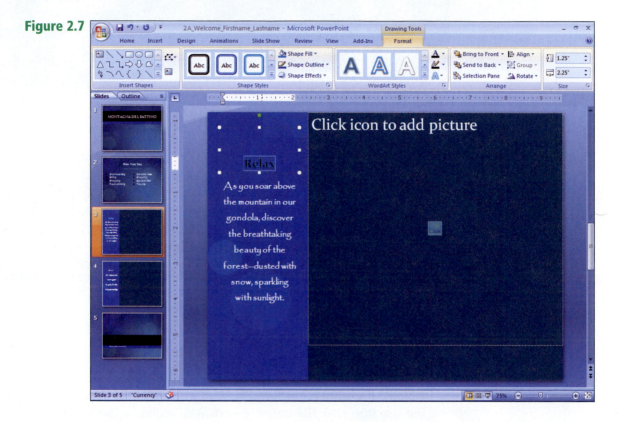

5 Display **Slide 5**. Click the **Insert tab**, and then in the **Text group**, click the **WordArt** button. In the gallery, click the first WordArt style in the first row—**Fill – Text 2, Outline – Background 2**.

In the center of your slide, a WordArt placeholder displays *Your Text Here*. When you type, your keystrokes will replace this text and fill the placeholder with wide letters. The placeholder will expand to accommodate the text. The WordArt is surrounded by sizing handles that are used to adjust its size by using the same technique that you learned when sizing clip art.

6 Type **Whatever Your Style!** to replace the WordArt placeholder text.

7 Look at the Slide pane and verify that the horizontal ruler displays above the slide and that the vertical ruler displays to the left of the slide. If the rulers do not display, on the Ribbon, click the View tab. In the Show/Hide group, click to select the Ruler check box.

8 Point to the WordArt border to display the ⊕ pointer. Using Figure 2.8 as a guide, drag down and to the left approximately 1 inch to move the WordArt.

Figure 2.8

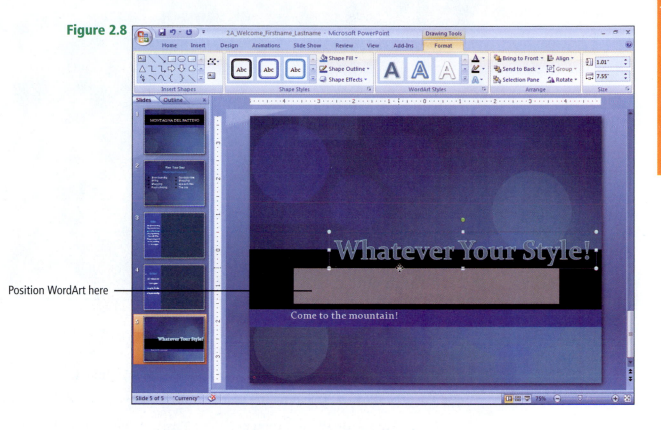

Position WordArt here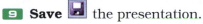

9 **Save** 💾 the presentation.

Activity 2.5 Using Format Painter

Format Painter copies *formatting* from one selection of text to another, thus ensuring formatting consistency in your presentation.

1 Display **Slide 3**, and then select the word *Relax*. On the **Home tab**, in the **Clipboard group**, double-click the **Format Painter** button 🖌, and then move your pointer anywhere into the Slide pane.

The pointer displays with a small paintbrush attached to it, indicating that Format Painter is active, as shown in Figure 2.9.

Figure 2.9

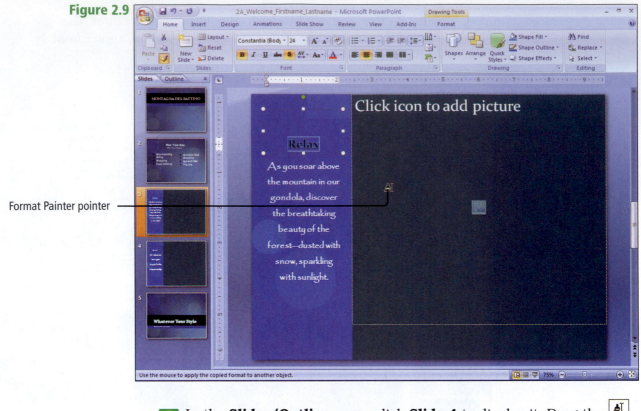

Format Painter pointer

2 In the **Slides/Outline** pane, click **Slide 4** to display it. Drag the [icon] pointer over the slide title—**Or Not!**

The WordArt formatting is applied to the title on Slide 4.

3 Display **Slide 2**. Drag the Format Painter pointer over the text **What's Your Preference?**, and then click the **Format Painter** button [icon] again to turn it off.

4 **Save** [icon] the presentation.

Alert!

Were you unable to use Format Painter more than one time?

When the Format Painter button is clicked one time instead of double-clicked, you can only use it to apply formatting to one selection. If you were only able to use Format Painter once, repeat Steps 1, 3, and 4.

Objective 2
Insert and Format Pictures and Shapes

PowerPoint 2007 provides a number of options for adding pictures and shapes to your presentation. You can draw lines, arrows, stars and banners, and a number of other basic shapes including ovals and rectangles. You can add text to a shape that you create and position it anywhere on a slide, and you can fill a shape with a picture. After you create a shape, you can add 3-D, glow, bevel effects, and shadows, or you can apply a predefined **Shape Style** that includes a combination of formatting effects.

Activity 2.6 Inserting a Picture Using a Content Layout

Many of the slide layouts in PowerPoint 2007 are designed to accommodate digital pictures that you have stored on your system or on a portable storage device.

1 Display **Slide 3**, which is formatted with the Content and Caption layout.

In the center of the large Content placeholder on the right side of the slide, the *Insert Picture* button displays.

2 In the center of the content placeholder, click the **Insert Picture from File** button  to open the **Insert Picture** dialog box. Navigate to the location in which your student files are stored, and then double-click **p2A_Winter**. Alternatively, click p2A_Winter, and then click Insert.

The picture fills the entire placeholder.

3 Display **Slide 4**. Using the technique that you practiced in **Step 2**, insert the picture **p2A_Snowboard**, and then compare your slide with Figure 2.10.

Figure 2.10

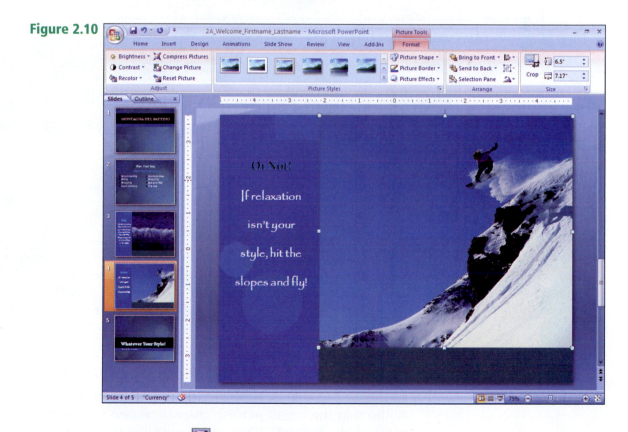

4 **Save** the presentation.

Workshop

Using Pictures Effectively in a Presentation

Large photographic images add impact to a presentation and help the audience visualize the message that you are trying to convey.

Activity 2.7 Changing the Size and Shape of a Picture

Recall that you can resize a picture by dragging the sizing handles. Alternatively, you can use the Picture contextual tools to specify a picture's height and width. You can also modify a picture by changing its shape.

1 Display **Slide 1**. Click the **Insert tab**, and then in the **Illustrations group**, click **Picture**. Navigate to the location where your student files are stored, and then double-click **p2A_Snow**.

The picture is inserted in the center of your slide and the Picture contextual tools tab displays on the Ribbon.

2 On the **Format tab**, in the **Size group**, notice that the height of the picture is 5.34 inches and the width of the picture is 6.68 inches, as shown in Figure 2.11.

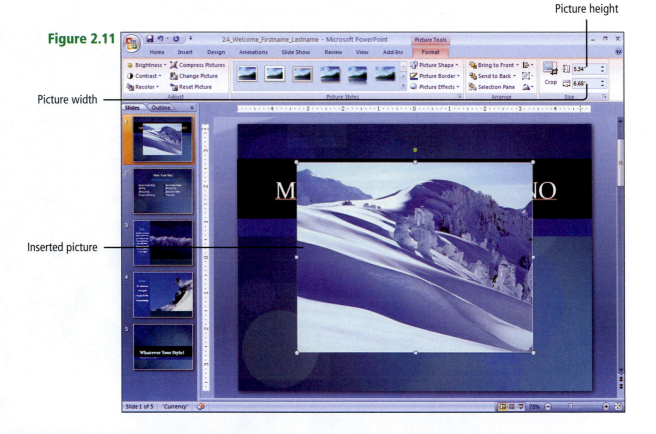

Figure 2.11

Picture height

Picture width

Inserted picture

3 On the **Format tab**, in the **Size group**, click in the **Shape Height box** so that 5.34 is selected. Type **3** and then press Enter. Notice that the height of the picture is resized to 3 inches and the width is also resized. When you change the height of a picture, the width is adjusted proportionately unless you type a new size in the Width box.

4 If necessary, select the picture. On the **Format tab**, in the **Picture Styles group**, click the **Picture Shape** button to display a gallery of shapes that you can apply to the picture. Under **Basic Shapes**, in the third row, click the third to last shape—**Cloud**.

5 Point to the picture to display the ⊕ pointer and then drag straight down so that the bottom edge of the cloud touches the bottom of the slide. Compare your slide with Figure 2.12.

Figure 2.12

6 **Save** 🖫 your presentation.

More Knowledge

Moving an Object by Using the Arrow Keys

You can use the directional arrow keys on your keyboard to move a picture, shape, or other object in small increments. Select the object so that its outside border displays as a solid line. Then, on your keyboard, press the directional arrow keys to precisely move the selected object.

Activity 2.8 Inserting and Positioning a Text Box

The slide layouts in PowerPoint 2007 are versatile and provide a variety of options for positioning text and objects on the slide. One way that you can customize a slide layout is by adding a ***text box***. A text box is an object that is used to position text anywhere on the slide. When you create a text box, the ***insertion point***—a blinking vertical line that indicates where text will be inserted—displays inside the text box, indicating that you can begin to type.

1 Display **Slide 4**. Click the **Insert tab**, and then in the **Text group**, click the **Text Box** button. Move the pointer into the slide to position the pointer below the picture as shown in Figure 2.13.

Figure 2.13

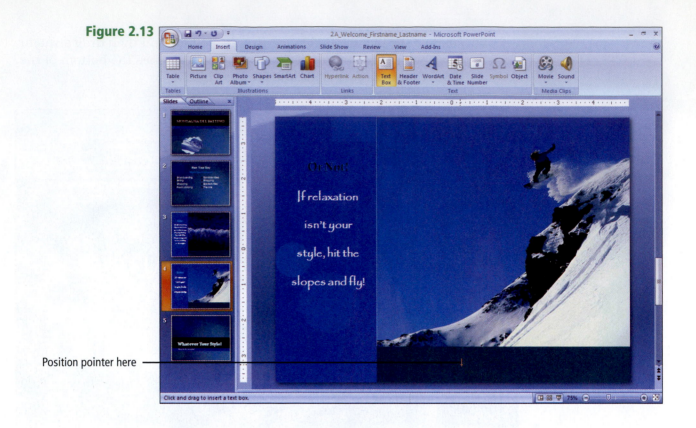

Position pointer here

2 Click to create a narrow rectangular text box. Type **Another View From Above** and notice that as you type, the width of the text box expands to accommodate the text.

Alert!

Does the text that you type in the text box display vertically, one character at a time?

If you move the pointer when you click to create the text box, PowerPoint sets the width of the text box and does not widen to accommodate the text. If this happened to you, your text may display vertically instead of horizontally or it may display on two lines. Point to the center right sizing handle and drag to the right so that the text box is approximately 3 inches wide. When you finish typing the text, adjust the width of the text box as necessary so that all of the text displays on one line.

3 Compare your slide with Figure 2.14 and if necessary, use the ⊹ pointer to adjust the size and position of the text box.

Do not be concerned if your text box does not match Figure 2.14 exactly. In a later Activity, you will practice using the Align tools to position slide elements precisely.

Position text box here

Figure 2.14

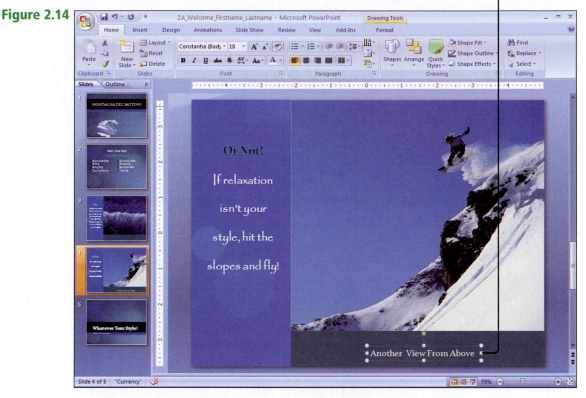

4 Display **Slide 3**. On the **Insert tab**, in the **Text group,** click the **Text Box** button. Click to create a text box in approximately the same position as the one that you created on Slide 4. Type **Spectacular Morning Vistas** and then click in a blank area of the slide.

5 Compare your slide with Figure 2.15, and if necessary, use the ⊕ pointer to adjust the position of the text box.

Figure 2.15

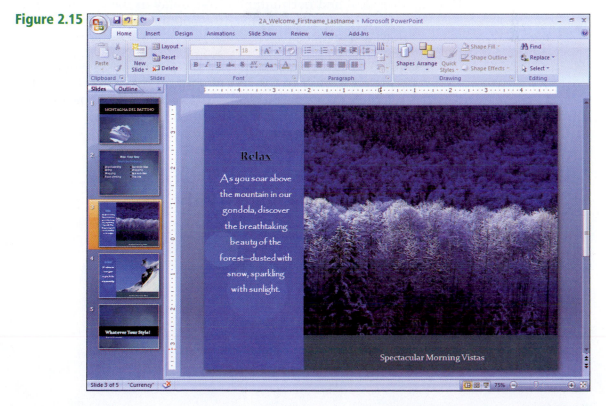

6 Save 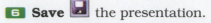 the presentation.

More Knowledge
Formatting a Text Box

You can format the text in a text box by using the same techniques that you use to format text in any other placeholder. For example, you can change fonts, font styles, and font sizes, and you can apply WordArt styles to the text in a text box.

Activity 2.9 Inserting, Sizing, and Positioning Shapes

Shapes can be used to help convey your message by illustrating an idea, a process, or a workflow. You can draw lines, arrows, stars and banners, and a number of other basic shapes including ovals and rectangles. Shapes can be sized and moved by using the same techniques that you used to size and move clip art images.

1 Display **Slide 1**, and then verify that the rulers display. If the rulers do not display, on the View tab, in the Show/Hide group, select the Ruler check box.

2 Click the **Insert tab**, and then in the **Illustrations group**, click the **Shapes button** to display the **Shapes gallery**. Under **Basic Shapes**, in the first row, click the seventh shape—**Diamond**.

3 Move the pointer into the slide until the ⊞ pointer—called the *crosshair pointer*—displays, indicating that you can draw a shape.

Notice that when you move the ⊞ pointer into the slide, *guides*— vertical and horizontal lines—display in the rulers to give you a visual indication of where the pointer is positioned so that you can draw a shape.

4 Move the ⊞ pointer so that the guides are positioned at approximately **1 inch to the left of zero** on the **horizontal ruler** and **1 inch above zero** on the **vertical ruler**, as shown in Figure 2.16.

Figure 2.16

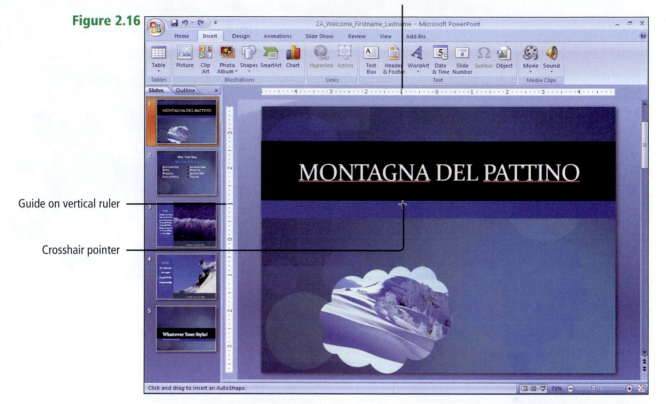

Guide on horizontal ruler

Guide on vertical ruler

Crosshair pointer

5 Hold down the left mouse button, and then drag down and to the right so that the guide displays at **1 inch to the right of zero** on the **horizontal ruler** and displays at **zero** on **the vertical ruler**. Release the mouse button to draw the diamond.

The Drawing Tools contextual tab displays on the Ribbon.

6 On the **Format tab**, in the **Size group**, look at the **Shape Height** and **Shape Width** boxes. If necessary, change the **Height** to **1** and the **Width** to **2** and then click on the diamond to change its size and to keep the diamond selected. Compare your slide with Figure 2.17. If necessary, move the diamond so that it is positioned correctly.

Figure 2.17

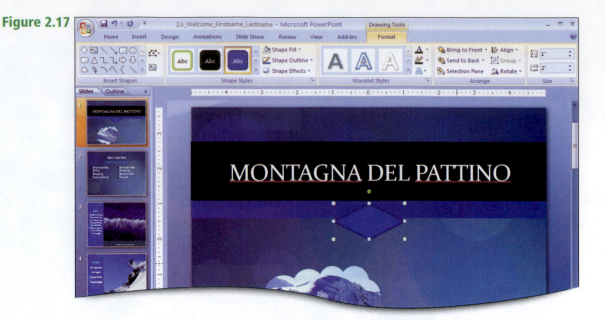

7 **Save** your presentation.

Another Way ─ **To Insert a Shape**

On the Home tab, in the Drawing group, click the Shapes button.

Activity 2.10 Adding Text to Shapes

Shapes can be used as containers for text. After you add text to a shape, you can change the font and font size, apply font styles, and change text alignment.

1 On **Slide 1**, if necessary, click the diamond so that it is selected.

Text can be typed in a shape when the shape is selected.

2 Type **Visit Today!** Notice that the text wraps to two lines and is centered.

3 Point to the left of the word *Today*, and then click so that the insertion point displays to the left of the word. Type **Us** and press Spacebar, and then click outside of the shape.

The text wraps to three lines and extends slightly outside of the diamond. The diamond shape is not large enough to accommodate the amount of text that you have typed.

4 Select the text *Visit Us Today!* On the **Home tab**, in the **Font group**, click the **Decrease Font Size** button ![A] to change the font size to **16**. Click outside of the shape.

The text displays on two lines and fits within the diamond shape.

5 Compare your slide with Figure 2.18. **Save** ![save] the presentation.

Figure 2.18

Text displays on two lines

Activity 2.11 Applying Shape and Picture Styles

Shapes and pictures can be formatted using a variety of effects, including 3-D, glow, bevel, and shadows. These effects soften the outer edges of a shape or image. Shapes can also be formatted by changing the inside fill color and the outside line color. Predefined combinations of these styles are available in the Shape Styles, Quick Styles, and Picture Styles galleries.

1 On **Slide 1**, click to select the diamond, and then click the **Format tab**. In the **Shape Styles group**, click the **Shape Fill** button, and then point to several of the theme colors and watch as Live Preview changes the inside color of the diamond.

2 Point to **Gradient** to display the **Gradient Fill** gallery. A *gradient fill* is a color combination in which one color fades into another. Under **Dark Variations**, in the second row, click the second variant—**From Center**.

The diamond is filled with a blue gradient in which the outer points of the diamond are light and the center of the diamond is a darker color.

3 In the **Shape Styles group**, click the **Shape Outline** button, and then point to **Weight**. Click **6 pt** and notice that a thick outline surrounds the diamond.

4 With the diamond still selected, in the **Shape Styles group**, click the **Shape Effects** button. Point to **Bevel**, and then under **Bevel**, in the first row, click the last bevel—**Cool Slant**.

The Cool Slant bevel applies a 3-dimensional effect to the diamond.

5 Select the snow picture in the shape of a cloud. Click the **Format tab**, and then in the **Picture Styles group**, click **Picture Effects**. Point to **Soft Edges**, and then click the second to last effect—**25 Point** to blur and soften the edges of the picture, giving it a more cloudlike effect.

6 Click on a blank part of the slide so that none of the objects are selected, and then compare your slide with Figure 2.19.

Figure 2.19

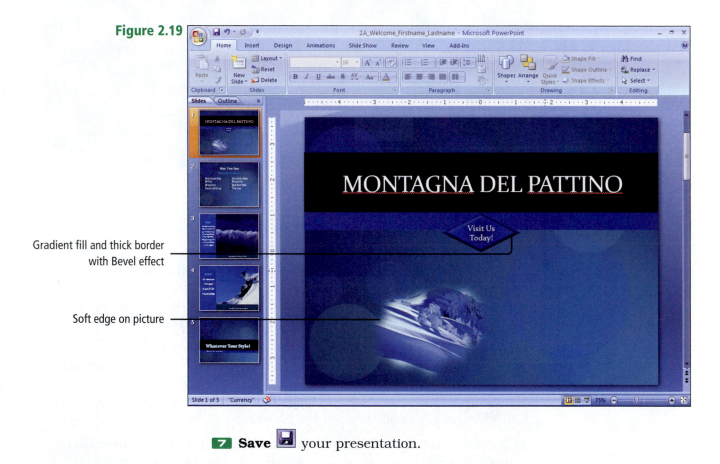

Gradient fill and thick border with Bevel effect

Soft edge on picture

7 **Save** your presentation.

More Knowledge

Applying a Quick Style or Shape Style to a Shape or Placeholder

You can quickly format an object such as a shape, text box, or placeholder by using one of the predefined Quick Styles or Shape Styles. Quick Styles and Shape Styles apply combinations of edges, shadows, line styles, gradients, and 3-D effects to the selected object. To apply a Quick Style, select the object, and then on the Home tab, click Quick Styles to display the gallery. To apply a Shape Style, select the object, and then on the Format Tab, in the Shape Styles group, click the More button to display the gallery.

Activity 2.12 Duplicating and Aligning Objects

You can duplicate an object by using a keyboard shortcut. You can align objects by dragging the object to another position on the slide or by using the Ribbon.

1 On **Slide 1**, click to select the picture. Press and hold down Ctrl, and then press D one time. Release Ctrl.

A duplicate of the picture overlaps the original picture and the duplicated image is selected.

2 Point to the duplicated image to display the ⊕ pointer. Drag the duplicated image to the right so that its left edge overlaps the right edge of the picture, using Figure 2.20 as a guide.

Figure 2.20

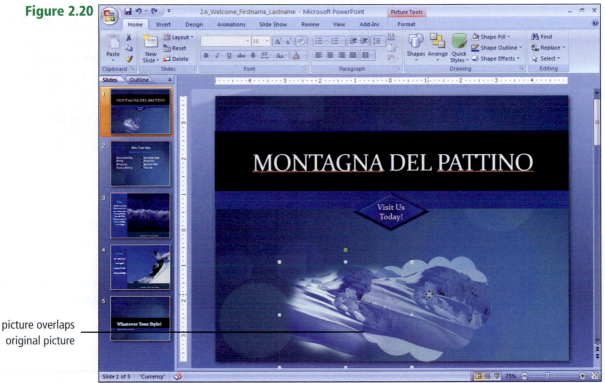

Duplicated picture overlaps original picture

3 Display **Slide 2**. Click the **Insert tab**, and then in the **Illustrations group**, click the **Shapes** button to display the **Shapes gallery**.

4 Under **Block Arrows**, in the first row, click the fourth arrow—**Down Arrow**. Position the ⊞ pointer at approximately **3 inches to the left of zero** on the **horizontal ruler** and at **1 inch below zero** on the **vertical ruler**, as shown in Figure 2.21.

Horizontal guide

Figure 2.21

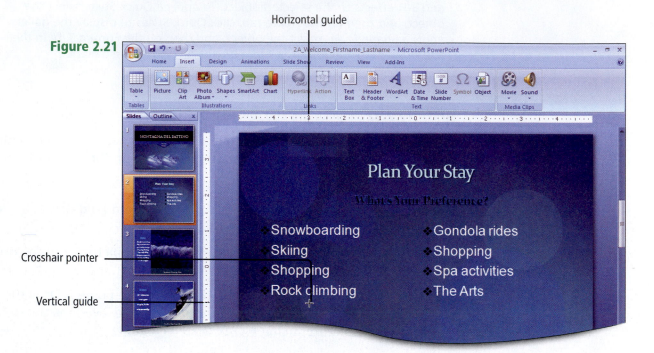

Crosshair pointer

Vertical guide

5 Drag approximately **1/2 inch to the right** and **1 inch down** to create the arrow and to display the Drawing Tools contextual tab. Check the size of the shape by looking at the **Format tab** in the **Size group**. If necessary, adjust the size of the arrow to a Height of 1 inch and a Width of 0.5 inch.

6 With the arrow selected, on the **Format tab**, in the **Shape Styles group**, click the **More** button ▼. In the last row, click the second effect—**Intense Effect – Accent 1.**

7 With the arrow still selected, hold down Ctrl, and then press D to duplicate the arrow. Drag the arrow to the right so that the arrow is positioned below the text on the right of the slide at approximately **2 inches to the right of zero** on the **horizontal ruler**.

8 With the arrow on the right selected, press ⇧Shift, and then click the arrow on the left so that both arrows are selected. Click the **Format tab**, and then in the **Arrange group**, click the **Align** button. Click **Align Selected Objects**.

The Align Selected Objects option enables you to align the objects that you select relative to each other. The Align to Slide option enables you to align objects with the edges of the slide determining placement.

9 On the **Format tab**, in the **Arrange group**, click the **Align** button ![Align icon], and then click **Align Top**.

With the two arrows selected, the lower arrow moves up so that its top edge is aligned with the top edge of the higher arrow. Thus, the tops of the two arrows are positioned at the same location on the vertical ruler. Compare your slide with Figure 2.22.

Figure 2.22

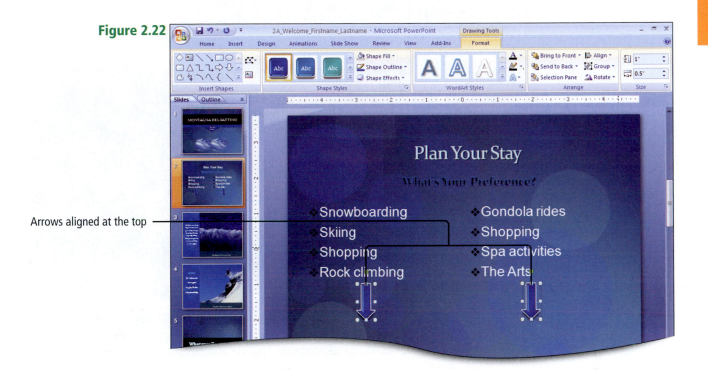

Arrows aligned at the top

10 Click the **Insert tab**, and then in the **Text group**, click **Text Box**. Position the pointer at approximately **4 inches to the left of zero** on the **horizontal ruler** and at **2.5 inches below zero** on the **vertical ruler.** Click to create a text box, type **High Energy** and then select the text that you typed. On the Mini toolbar, click the **Font Size button arrow** ![44] and then click **32**. Click the **Center** button ![Center icon]. If the text box does not expand to accommodate the text, use the center right sizing handle to widen the text box.

11 Click the **Format tab**, and then in the **Shape Styles group**, click the **More** button ![More icon]. In the last row, click the first style—**Intense Effect – Dark 1**.

12 Point to the outer edge of the text box to display the ![move pointer] pointer and then click to select the text box. Hold down (Ctrl), and then press (D) to duplicate the text box. Drag the duplicated textbox to the right so that it is positioned below the arrow on the right side of the slide. Select the text **High Energy**, and then type **Relaxation** to replace the text.

13 Use the ⇧Shift key to select the two text boxes—**High Energy** and **Relaxation**. On the **Format tab**, in the **Arrange group**, click the **Align** button. Click **Align Top** to align the top edges of the two text boxes, and then click anywhere on the slide so that none of the objects are selected.

14 Click the bulleted list placeholder on the left side of the slide. Press ⇧Shift and click the arrow on the left and the **High Energy** text box so that all three objects are selected, as shown in Figure 2.23.

Figure 2.23

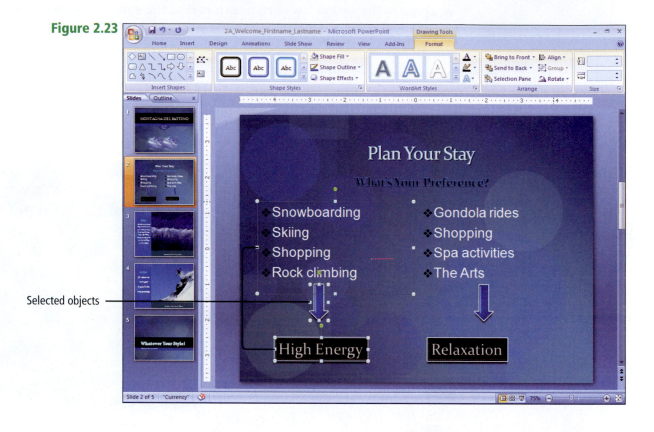

Selected objects

15 On the **Format tab**, in the **Arrange group**, click the **Align** button. Click **Align Selected Objects**. Click the **Align** button again, and then click **Align Center**.

The three objects are aligned at their center points.

16 Using the same procedure that you used in Steps 14 and 15, **Align Center** the placeholder, arrow, and text box on the right side of the slide.

17 **Save** 🖫 the presentation.

Objective 3
Apply Slide Transitions

Recall that a slide transition controls the way that a slide appears or disappears during an onscreen slide show. For example, when one slide leaves the screen, it may fade or dissolve into another slide. You can choose from a variety of transitions, and you can control the speed and method with which the slides advance during a presentation.

Activity 2.13 Applying Slide Transitions to a Presentation

In this activity, you will add slide transitions to all of the slides in the presentation.

1 If necessary, in the **Slides/Outline pane**, click the **Slides tab** so that the slide thumbnails display. Display **Slide 1**.

2 Click the **Animations tab**. In the **Transition to This Slide group**, click the **More** button to display the **Transitions gallery** as shown in Figure 2.24.

The slide transitions are categorized in six groups—No Transition, Fades and Dissolves, Wipes, Push and Cover, Stripes and Bars, and Random. You may need to scroll the gallery in order to view all of the transitions. The pictures illustrate the type of transition and the arrows indicate the direction in which the slide moves.

Figure 2.24

Transitions gallery

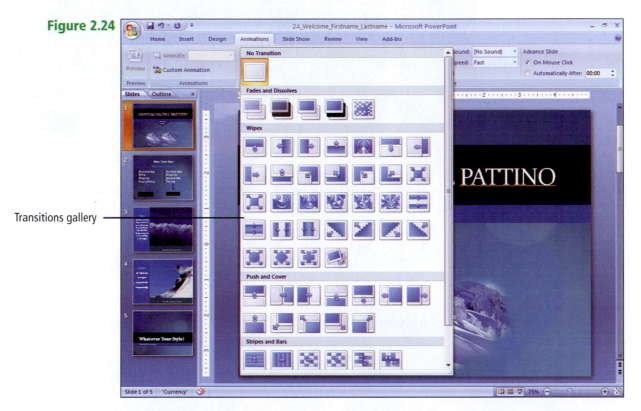

3 Point to several of the transitions to Live Preview the transition effects and to display the ScreenTip with the transition name. Under **Wipes**, locate and then click the **Box Out** transition.

4 In the **Transition to This Slide group**, click the **Transition Speed arrow**, and then click **Medium**.

5 In the **Transition to This Slide group** verify that under **Advance Slide**, **On Mouse Click** is selected. If it is not, click the On Mouse Click check box, as shown in Figure 2.25.

The On Mouse Click option enables you to control when the slide will advance to the next slide. During the slide show, you can click the mouse button or press Spacebar to advance the presentation.

Figure 2.25

On Mouse Click selected

Medium speed

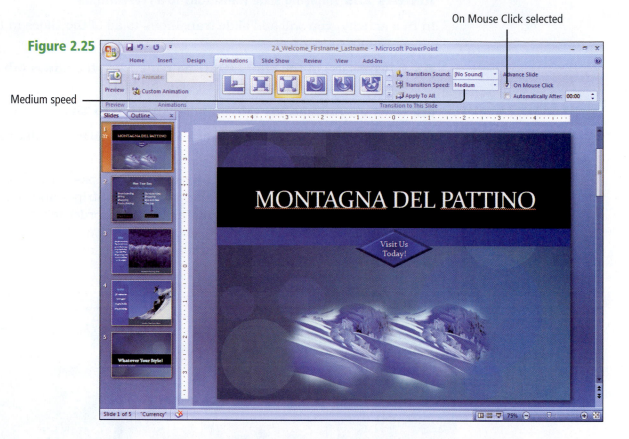

6 In the **Transition to This Slide group**, click the **Apply To All** button so that the medium speed Box Out transition is applied to all of the slides in the presentation. Notice that in the Slides/Outline pane, a star displays below each slide number, indicating that a transition has been applied.

Workshop

Applying Transitions

You can apply more than one type of transition in your presentation by displaying the slides one at a time, and then clicking the transition that you want to apply instead of clicking the Apply To All button. However, using too many different transitions in your presentation may distract the audience. Choose one basic transition to use on most of the slides in your presentation, and use one or two additional transitions if you feel that a particular slide would display effectively with a different transition.

7 Click the **Slide Show tab**. In the **Start Slide Show group**, click the **From Beginning** button, and then view your presentation, clicking the mouse button to advance through the slides. When the black slide displays, click the mouse button one more time to display the presentation in Normal view.

8 Create a **Header and Footer** for the **Notes and Handouts**. Include only the **Date and time updated automatically**, the **Page number**, and a **Footer** with the file name 2A_Welcome_Firstname_Lastname

9 Check your *Chapter Assignment Sheet* or *Course Syllabus* or consult your instructor to determine if you are to submit your assignments on paper or electronically. To submit electronically, go to Step 11, and then follow the instructions provided by your instructor.

10 **Print Preview** your presentation, and then print **Handouts, (6 slides per page)**.

11 **Save** changes to your presentation. **Close** the presentation.

End **You have completed Project 2A** ——————————

Project 2B **Itinerary**

In Activities 2.14 through 2.22, you will edit a presentation that Kirstin McCarty, Director of Marketing, has created that includes itineraries and contact information for resort guests. You will move and copy text, and you will create diagrams that will illustrate different types of itineraries. Your completed presentation will look similar to Figure 2.26.

For Project 2B, you will need the following files:

p2B_Itinerary
p2B_Reservations_Director
p2B_Ski_Lodge_Director
p2B_Spa_Director
p2B_Tour_Director

You will save your presentation as 2B_Itinerary_Firstname_Lastname

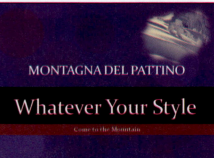

Figure 2.26
Project 2B—Itinerary

Objective 4
Reorganize Presentation Text and Clear Formats

When you select text or objects and then perform the Copy command or the Cut command, the selection is placed on the **Office Clipboard**—a temporary storage area maintained by your Microsoft Office program. From the Office Clipboard storage area, the object is available to **paste** into other locations, including other Office programs.

Activity 2.14 Moving and Copying Text

The **Cut** command removes selected text or graphics from your presentation and moves the selection to the Office Clipboard. From the Office Clipboard, the selection can be pasted to a new location. The **Copy** command duplicates a selection and places it on the Office Clipboard.

1 **Start** PowerPoint and from your student files, open **p2B_Itinerary**. **Save** the file in your **PowerPoint Chapter 2** folder as **2B_Itinerary_Firstname_Lastname**

2 Display **Slide 2**, and on the **Home tab**, in the **Slides group**, click the **New Slide arrow**. In the displayed gallery, click **Title and Content**. If you inserted a slide without displaying the gallery, on the Home tab, in the Slides group, click Layout, and then click Title and Content. In the title placeholder, type **High Energy Weekend?**

3 Display **Slide 4,** and then select all of the text in the bulleted list placeholder. On the **Home tab**, in the **Clipboard group**, click the

Copy button . Alternatively, hold down Ctrl and then press C.

4 Display **Slide 3**, and then click in the content placeholder. In the **Clipboard group**, click the **Paste** button to copy the selection to Slide 3. Alternatively, hold down Ctrl and then press V.

Below the pasted text an additional bullet may display and notice that a button displays, as shown in Figure 2.27. This is the Paste Options button that provides three options for formatting pasted text.

Figure 2.27

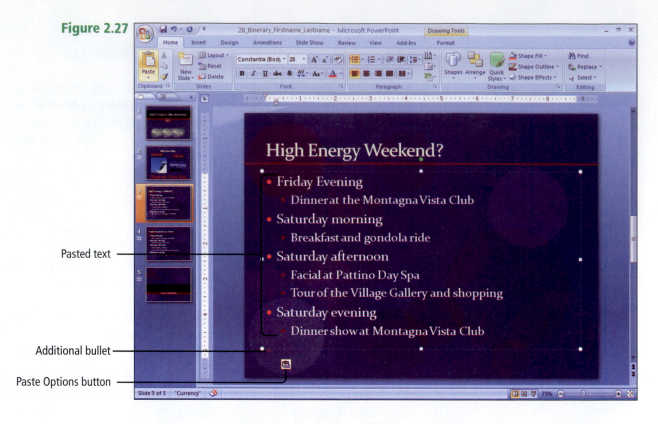

Pasted text

Additional bullet

Paste Options button

5 Pause your pointer over the Paste Options button so that a down arrow displays to its right, and then click the arrow to display the formatting options. Be sure that **Use Destination Theme** is selected so that the formatting of Slide 3 is applied to the pasted text.

Use Destination Theme applies the format of the slide to which you pasted the text to the selection, and *Keep Text Only* removes all formatting from the selection.

Note — Removing the Paste Options Button

You do not need to click the Paste Options button arrow every time you paste a selection. The default setting is *Use Destination Theme*. Thus, you need only click the arrow if you want to apply a different option. The Paste Options button will remain on the screen until you perform another action.

6 If necessary, use ⦗←Bksp⦘ or ⦗Delete⦘ to delete any extra bullets at the bottom of the pasted text. In the second bullet point, replace the text *Montagna Vista Club* with **Summit Clubhouse** In the fourth bullet point, replace *gondola ride* with **2-mile hike** Under *Saturday afternoon*, select both of the subordinate level bullet points, and then type **Skiing or snowboarding** to replace both of the selected bullet points. Select the last bullet point on the slide, and then replace it with **Party at Summit Clubhouse**

7 Click outside the content placeholder, and then compare your slide with Figure 2.28. Make spelling and layout corrections as necessary.

Figure 2.28

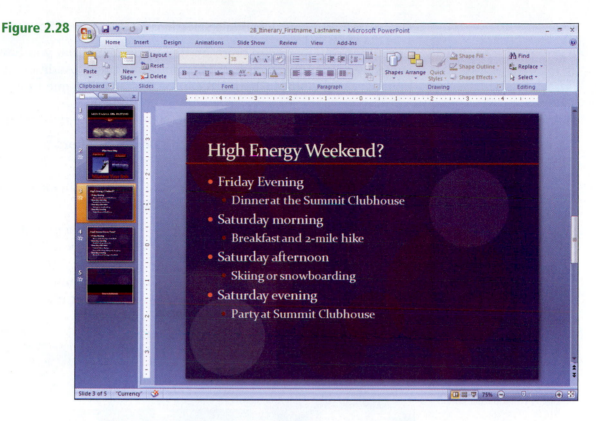

8 Display **Slide 2**. Click the WordArt text at the bottom of the slide—*Whatever Your Style*, and then click its dashed boundary box so that it displays as a solid line, indicating that all of the text is selected.

9 In the **Clipboard group**, click the **Cut** button 🔲. Alternatively, hold down Ctrl and then press X.

The text is removed from the slide and is stored on the Clipboard.

10 Display **Slide 5**. In the **Clipboard group**, click the **Paste** button to move the selection to the bottom of the last slide. Point to the edge of the pasted text to display the ⊕ pointer, and then drag up to position the text in the center of the black rectangle.

11 **Save** 🔲 the presentation.

More Knowledge

Using Drag-and-Drop Text Editing

Another method of moving text is the *drag-and-drop* technique, which uses the mouse to drag selected text from one location to another. To use drag-and-drop text editing, select the text you want to move, and then position the pointer over the selected text to display the 🔲 pointer. Drag the text to the new location. A vertical line attached to the pointer enables you to see exactly where the text will be pasted.

Activity 2.15 Copying Multiple Selections by Using the Office Clipboard

The Office Clipboard can store up to 24 selections that you have cut or copied, and each one can be pasted multiple times. Additionally, groups of items on the Office Clipboard can be pasted all at one time.

1 Display **Slide 1**. On the **Home tab**, in the lower right corner of the **Clipboard group**, click the **Dialog Box Launcher** ☐ to display the Clipboard task pane on the left side of the PowerPoint window.

2 In the **Clipboard** task pane, check to see if any items display. Compare your screen with Figure 2.29.

When the Office Clipboard is empty, *Clipboard empty* displays in the task pane. If items have been cut or copied, they will display on the Office Clipboard. In Figure 2.29, the WordArt text that was cut in the previous Activity displays. You may or may not have items displayed on the Office Clipboard, depending upon its last use.

Figure 2.29

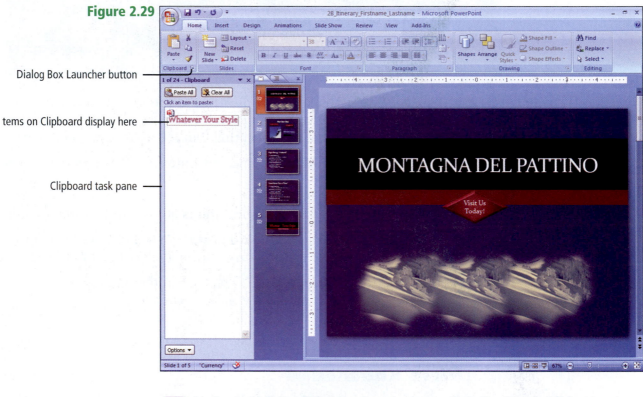

Dialog Box Launcher button

Items on Clipboard display here

Clipboard task pane

3 At the top of the **Clipboard** task pane, click the **Clear All** button to delete any items that are stored on the Office Clipboard.

4 Click in the slide title, and then click its dashed border so that it displays as a solid line. In the **Clipboard group**, click the **Copy** button ☐, and then notice that a boxed object displays in the Clipboard task pane.

The box appears to be empty, because the text is white, and the Clipboard task pane uses a white background. Even though the letters are not visible, they are still there.

5 At the bottom of the slide, three copies of the same picture display. Click any one of the three pictures to select it. In the **Clipboard**

group, click the **Copy** button, and then notice that the object displays in the Office Clipboard as the first item, and the previous item that you copied moves down.

You have collected two objects for copying.

6 Display **Slide 5**. In the **Clipboard** task pane, click **Paste All** to paste both objects to Slide 5.

The objects are pasted in the same location from which they were copied.

7 Drag the picture to the upper right corner of the slide.

8 Click the pasted text so that its dashed border displays. Point to the dashed border to display the pointer. Using Figure 2.30 as a guide, hold down Shift, and then drag the pasted text down approximately one inch.

Pressing Shift while dragging constrains the textbox from moving off center, allowing for precision placement.

Drag picture here

Figure 2.30

Drag text here

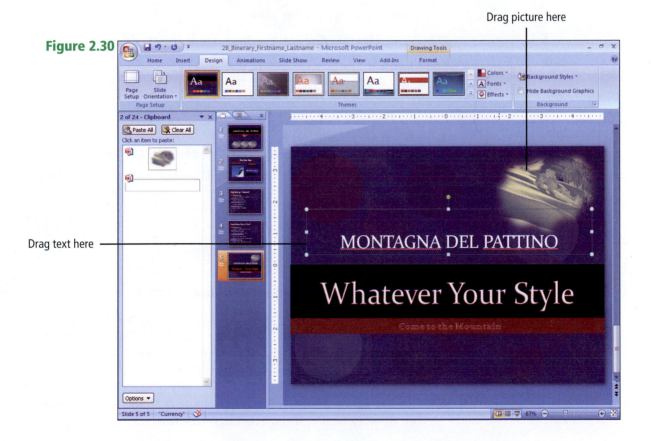

9 In the **Clipboard** task pane, click the **Clear All** button to delete the two selections from the Office Clipboard. **Close** the task pane.

10 **Save** the presentation.

More Knowledge

Pasting and Deleting Single Items from the Office Clipboard

When you point to an item on the Office Clipboard, a down arrow displays to its right. Click the arrow to display a menu with two options—Paste and Delete. You can paste and delete individual items from the Office Clipboard using this menu.

Activity 2.16 Undoing and Redoing Changes

PowerPoint remembers each change that you make so that you can undo them if you change your mind or perform an action by mistake. You can change your mind again and reverse an undo by using the Redo command.

1 Display **Slide 3**. In the fourth bullet point, select the words *2-mile*, and then type **Mountain Falls** to replace the selected words.

2 On the **Quick Access toolbar**, click the **Undo** button .

2-mile displays on the slide.

3 On the **Quick Access Toolbar**, click the **Redo** button .

Mountain Falls displays in the slide.

4 **Save** the presentation.

Alert! — **Did you repeat an action instead of redo an action?**

The Redo button is context-sensitive—it changes depending upon the action that you have performed. Before you click Undo, the Redo button displays as the Repeat button. Recall that the Repeat button repeats the last command or keystroke. In order to activate the Redo button, you must first Undo a command.

Activity 2.17 Clearing Formatting from a Selection

After applying multiple formats to a selection of text, you may decide that the selection is best displayed without the formats that you applied. You can clear formatting from a selection and return it to its default font and font size, and remove styles that have been applied.

1 Display **Slide 5** and notice that the text *Come to the Mountain* does not display well against the background.

2 Select *Come to the Mountain*, and then on the **Home tab**, in the **Font group**, click the **Clear All Formatting** button , and then click in a blank area of the slide.

The text is restored to its original formatting and contrasts with the background, making it easier to read.

3 **Save** the presentation.

Workshop

Creating Contrast on a Slide

Contrast is an important element of slide design because it helps in distinguishing text and objects from the slide background. Be sure that the font color that you choose contrasts with the background so that your audience can easily read the text. For example, if your background is dark, choose a light-colored font. If your background is light, choose a dark-colored font.

Objective 5
Create and Format a SmartArt Graphic

A **SmartArt graphic** is a designer-quality visual representation of information that you can create by choosing from among many different layouts to effectively communicate your message or ideas. SmartArt graphics can illustrate processes, hierarchies, cycles, lists, and relationships. You can include text and pictures in a SmartArt graphic, and you can apply colors, effects, and styles that coordinate with the presentation theme.

Activity 2.18 Creating a SmartArt Diagram by Using a Content Layout

When you create a SmartArt graphic, it is a good idea when choosing a layout to consider the message that you are trying to convey. Large amounts of text can make some types of SmartArt graphics difficult to read so keep that in mind when choosing a layout. The table in Figure 2.31 describes types of SmartArt layouts and suggested purposes.

Microsoft PowerPoint SmartArt Graphic Types	
Graphic Type	**Purpose of Graphic**
List	Show nonsequential information.
Process	Show steps in a process or timeline.
Cycle	Show a continual process.
Hierarchy	Show a decision tree or create an organization chart.
Relationship	Illustrate connections.
Matrix	Show how parts relate to a whole.
Pyramid	Show proportional relationships with the largest component on the top or bottom.

Figure 2.31

1 Display **Slide 4**, and then on the **Home tab**, in the **Slides group**, click the **New Slide** button to add a slide with the **Title and Content** layout. In the title placeholder, type **Contact Information** and then **Center** ☰ the title. Notice that in addition to adding text to this slide, you can insert a SmartArt graphic by clicking the Insert SmartArt Graphic button ▦ in the center of the slide, as shown in Figure 2.32.

Figure 2.32

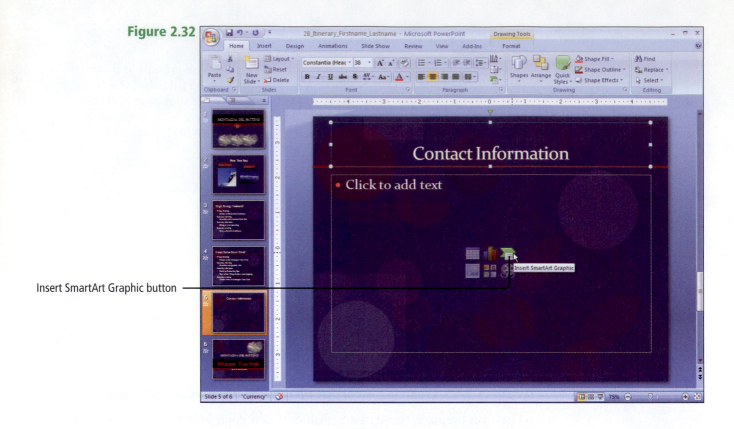

Insert SmartArt Graphic button

2 In the center of the slide, click the **Insert SmartArt Graphic**

button to open the **Choose a SmartArt Graphic** dialog box.

The dialog box is divided into three sections. The left section lists the diagram types. The center section displays the diagrams according to type. The third section displays the selected diagram, its name, and a description of its purpose and how text displays.

Another Way

To Insert a SmartArt Graphic

On the Insert tab, in the Illustrations group, click the SmartArt button.

3 Explore the types of diagrams available by clicking on several and reading their descriptions. Then, on the left side of the **Choose a SmartArt Graphic** dialog box, click **Hierarchy**. In the center section in the second row, click the last diagram—**Hierarchy List**—and then click **OK** to create a hierarchical diagram surrounded by a thick border, indicating the area that the diagram will cover on the slide. Notice that on the Ribbon, the SmartArt contextual tool displays two tabs—Design and Format, as shown in Figure 2.33.

The hierarchical diagram displays with two upper level shapes and two subordinate level shapes under each upper level shape. You will use the upper level shapes to enter the resort areas that customers frequently call, and the lower level shapes to enter the contact person's name and phone number. You can type text directly into the shapes or you can type text in the Text pane. The Text pane is displayed by clicking the Text pane tab on the left side of the SmartArt graphic border.

SmartArt
Design and Format tabs

Figure 2.33

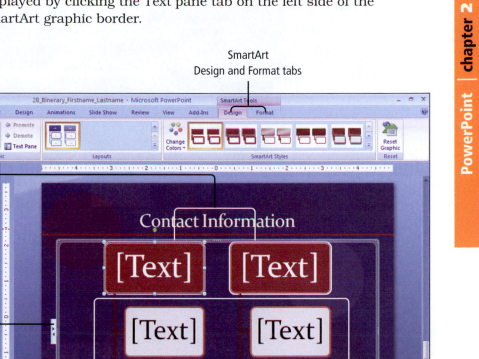

Upper level shapes

Text pane tab

Diagram border

Subordinate level shapes

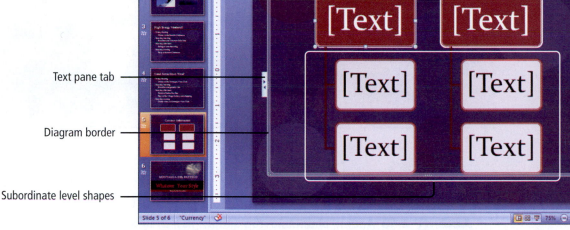

Note — Displaying and Closing the Text Pane

On the Ribbon, in the SmartArt Tools group, click the Design tab. In the Create Graphic group, click the Text pane button to toggle the Text pane on and off.

4 In the diagram, click in the dark red box on the left, and then type **Day Spa** Click in the box below it, and then type **Patricia Reeves** Click in the box below Patricia's name, and then type **555-0921**

The text is resized and when necessary, wraps to two lines in order to fit into each shape. When text is typed into additional shapes, the text in all shapes at the same level adjusts to the same size.

5 On the right side of the diagram, enter the following information in the boxes, and then click in a blank area of the slide. Compare your slide with Figure 2.34.

Ski Lodge

Victor Blardone

555-0563

Figure 2.34

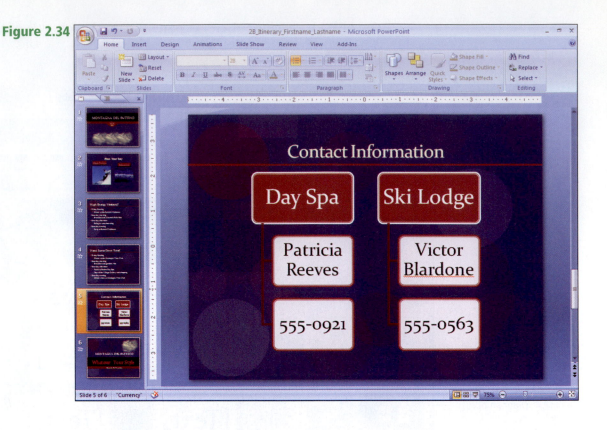

6 **Save** 📁 the presentation.

Activity 2.19 Adding and Removing Shapes in a Diagram

If a diagram does not have enough shapes to illustrate a concept or display the relationships, you can add more shapes.

1 Click in the shape that contains the text *Ski Lodge*. Click the **Design tab**. In the **Create Graphic group**, click the **Add Shape arrow**, and then click **Add Shape After** to insert an upper level shape to the right of the *Ski Lodge* shape. Type **Tours**

Alert! **Did you add a shape below the Ski Lodge shape?**

If you clicked the Add Shape button instead of the arrow, the new shape displays below the phone number shape. Click Undo to delete the shape, and then repeat Step 1, being sure to click the Add Shape arrow.

2 On the **Design tab**, in the **Create Graphic group**, click the **Add Shape** button.

When an upper level shape is selected and the Add Shape button is clicked, a lower level shape is added.

3 Type **Terry Anderson** and then click the **Add Shape** button. Type **555-0987** and then click the **Add Shape** button.

An additional shape is added below the phone number. You can promote the shape so that it is at the same level as the Day Spa, Ski lodge, and Tours shapes.

4 On the **Design tab**, in the **Create Graphic group**, click the **Promote** button to create a fourth, upper level shape. Type **Reservations** and notice that the text in all of the upper level shapes is resized. Add a shape, type **Anthony Johnson** and then add one more shape, and then type **555-0547**

5 On the **Design tab**, in the **Create Graphic group**, click the **Add Shape** button to create an extra shape below Anthony Johnson's phone number.

6 Press Delete to delete the shape, and then click on a blank area of the slide. Compare your slide with Figure 2.35.

Figure 2.35

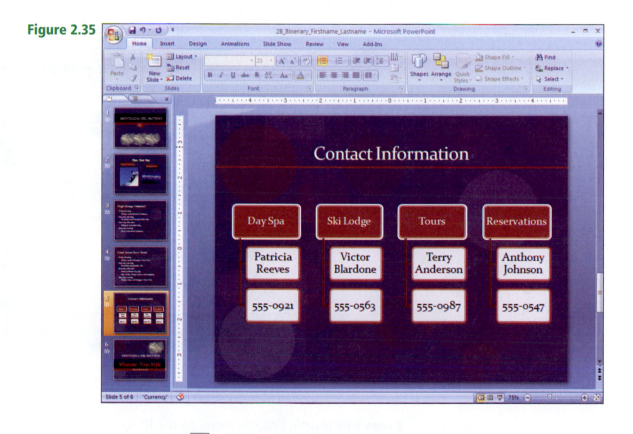

7 **Save** 🖫 the presentation.

More Knowledge

Deleting Shapes That Contain Text

To delete a shape that contains text, you must click its border. If you click the shape without clicking the border, you will delete text instead of the shape. When you delete an upper level shape that has subordinate shapes with text, the first subordinate shape is promoted to an upper level shape.

Activity 2.20 Changing the Diagram Type and Size

When you are creating a diagram, remember that it is important to choose the layout and type that provides the best visual representation of your information. In this Activity, you will change the diagram type to one that includes placeholders for pictures of each contact person.

1 Click anywhere in the diagram. Click the **Design tab**. In the **Layouts group**, click the **More** button ⏷, and then click **More Layouts** to display the **Choose a SmartArt Graphic** dialog box.

2 On the left side of the dialog box, click **List**, and then click **Horizontal Picture List**, as shown in Figure 2.36. Click **OK**.

The diagram is converted and contains shapes at the top of each group to insert pictures.

Figure 2.36

Horizontal Picture List

3 In the shape above the *Day Spa* information, click the **Insert Picture From File** button 🖼. Navigate to the location where your student files are stored, and then double-click **p2B_Spa_Director** to insert the picture of Patricia Reeves. Repeat this process in each of the three remaining shapes by inserting the files **p2B_Ski_Lodge_Director**, **p2B_Tour_Director**, and **p2B_Reservations_Director**.

Alert!

Did you move a shape when inserting a picture?

If you move the mouse when you click the Insert Picture from File button in one of the diagram shapes, the shape may move. If this happens, click the Undo button to reposition the shape. Then, click the Picture button, making sure that you hold the mouse steady.

4 Notice that the shapes of that contain the pictures are wider than they are long, and thus distort the pictures. You can adjust the size of all of the pictures at one time by sizing the SmartArt graphic.

5 The border surrounding a diagram contains sizing handles in the shape of three small circles in the corners and at the center of each side. You can use these sizing handles to size the diagram. Point to the center-right sizing handle to display the ↔ pointer, as shown in Figure 2.37.

Figure 2.37

Pointer positioned over sizing handle

6 Hold down the mouse button and drag to the left, noticing that as you do so the + pointer displays, as does a semitransparent rectangle that indicates the size of the SmartArt graphic. Continue to drag to the left until the pointer and semitransparent rectangle display between the Tours and Reservations shapes, as shown in Figure 2.38. Release the mouse button to size the diagram.

Figure 2.38

Crosshair pointer and transparent rectangle indicate new size of diagram

7 Point to the border surrounding the diagram to display the ⊕ pointer, and then drag to the right to center the diagram.

8 Compare your slide with Figure 2.39, and then **Save** 💾 your presentation.

Alert!

Did only a part of the diagram move?

Individual parts of a SmartArt diagram, such as text and picture shapes, can be moved. Be sure that when you move the diagram that you are pointing to the border that surrounds the SmartArt graphic and not an individual element. If you inadvertently moved a portion of the diagram instead of the entire diagram, click the Undo button, and then repeat step 7.

Figure 2.39

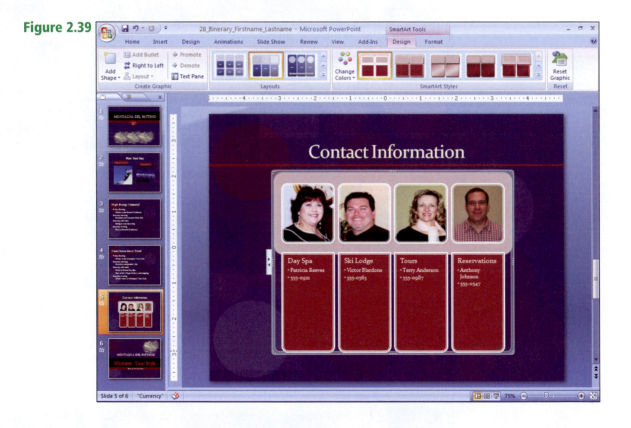

Activity 2.21 Creating a SmartArt Diagram from Bullet Points

You can convert an existing bulleted list into a SmartArt diagram. In this Activity, you will convert the bulleted lists on Slides 3 and 4 to list diagrams.

1 Display **Slide 3**. Right-click anywhere in the bulleted list placeholder to display the shortcut menu. Point to **Convert to SmartArt**, and at the bottom of the gallery, click **More SmartArt Graphics**.

2 In the **Choose a SmartArt Graphic** dialog box, click **List**, and then in the first row, point to each SmartArt graphic so that the ScreenTips display, and then click **Vertical Box List**. Click **OK**.

The entire bulleted list is converted to a diagram. It is not necessary to select all of the text in the bulleted list. By clicking in the list, PowerPoint converts all of the bullet points to the selected diagram.

3 Display **Slide 4**. Right-click anywhere in the bulleted list placeholder to display the shortcut menu. Point to **Convert to SmartArt**, and then at the bottom of the gallery, click **More SmartArt Graphics**. In the **Choose a SmartArt Graphic** dialog box, click **List**, and then use the ScreenTips to locate **Vertical Block List**. Click **Vertical Block List**, and then click **OK**.

4 **Save** the presentation.

Activity 2.22 Changing the Color and Style of a Diagram

SmartArt Styles are combinations of formatting effects that you can apply to diagrams. If you change the layout of a diagram, the SmartArt Style is applied to the new layout, as are any color changes that you have made.

1 Display **Slide 5** and click on the diagram. Click the **Design tab**. In the **SmartArt Styles group**, click the **Change Colors** button to display the color gallery.

The colors that display are coordinated with the presentation theme.

2 Under **Accent 1**, click the last style—**Transparent Gradient Range - Accent 1**—to change the color scheme of the diagram.

3 On the **Design tab**, in the **SmartArt Styles group**, click the **More** button to display the **SmartArt Styles gallery**. Point to several of the styles to Live Preview their effects on the diagram. Then, under **3-D**, in the first row, click the first style—**Polished**. Click in a blank area of the slide, and then compare your slide with Figure 2.40.

4 Display **Slide 3** and click on the diagram. Click the **Design tab**.

In the **SmartArt Styles group**, click the **More** button to display the **SmartArt Styles gallery**. Under **3-D**, in the first row, click the second style—**Inset**.

5 Display **Slide 4**. Using the same technique that you used in Step 4, under **Best Match for Document** apply the last style—**Intense Effect**.

Figure 2.40

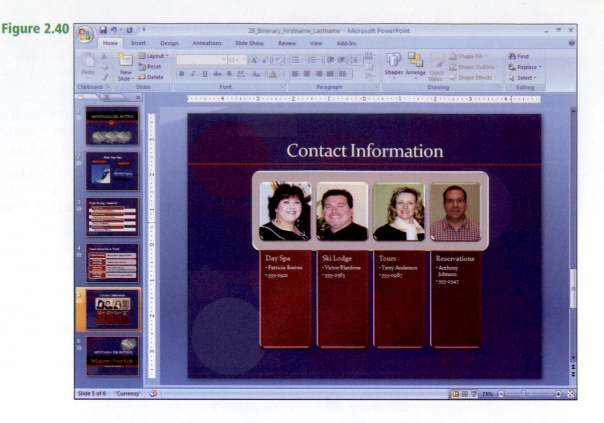

6 Click the **Slide Show tab**. In the **Start Slide Show group**, click **From Beginning**, and then view your presentation, clicking the mouse button to advance through the slides. When the black slide displays, click the mouse button one more time to display the presentation in Normal view.

7 Create a **Header and Footer** for the **Notes and Handouts**. Include only the **Date and time updated automatically**, the **Page number**, and a **Footer** with the file name **2B_Intinerary_Firstname_Lastname**

8 Check your *Chapter Assignment Sheet* or *Course Syllabus* or consult your instructor to determine if you are to submit your assignments on paper or electronically. To submit electronically, go to Step 10, and then follow the instructions provided by your instructor.

9 **Print Preview** your presentation, and then print **Handouts, (6 slides per page)**.

10 **Save** the changes to your presentation, and then **Close** the presentation.

End **You have completed Project 2B**

There's More You Can Do!

From My Computer, navigate to the student files that accompany this textbook. In the folder **02_theres_more_you_can_do_pg1_36**, locate and open the folder for this chapter. Open and print the instructions for this project, which are provided to you in Adobe PDF format.

Try IT! 1—Prepare a Presentation for Remote Delivery

In this Try IT! exercise, you will prepare a presentation for remote delivery by compressing images and packaging the presentation for CD.

Content-Based Assessments

Summary

In this chapter, you formatted a presentation by changing the bullet style and by applying WordArt styles to text. You copied formatting by using Format Painter and you also copied text and objects by using drag-and-drop and the Office Clipboard. You enhanced your presentations by inserting, sizing, and formatting shapes, pictures, and SmartArt diagrams. You gave your presentation a finished look by applying transitions to your slides, resulting in a professional-looking presentation.

Key Terms

Copy 109	**Gradient fill** 99	**Shape Style** 90
Crosshair pointer 96	**Guides** 96	**SmartArt graphic** 115
Cut 109	**Insertion point** 93	**SmartArt Styles** 123
Drag-and-drop 111	**Office Clipboard** 109	**Text box** 93
Fill color 87	**Paste** 109	**WordArt** 87
Format Painter 89	**Shapes** 96	

Content-Based Assessments

Matching

Match each term in the second column with its correct definition in the first column. Write the letter of the term on the blank line in front of the correct definition.

_____ **1.** A feature that applies combinations of decorative formatting to text, including shadows, reflections, and 3-D effects, and that changes the line and fill color of text.

_____ **2.** The inside color of text or an object.

_____ **3.** A feature that copies formatting from one selection of text to another, ensuring formatting consistency in your presentation.

_____ **4.** A combination of formatting effects that includes 3-D, glow, and bevel effects and shadows that can be applied to shapes.

_____ **5.** An object that is used to position text anywhere on the slide.

_____ **6.** The pointer that indicates that you can draw a shape.

_____ **7.** Vertical and horizontal lines that display in the rulers to give you a visual indication of the pointer position so that you can draw a shape.

_____ **8.** A blinking vertical line that indicates where text will be inserted.

_____ **9.** A color combination in which one color fades into another.

_____ **10.** The way a slide appears or disappears during an onscreen slide show.

_____ **11.** The action of placing text or objects that have been copied or moved from one location to another location.

_____ **12.** A temporary storage area maintained by your Microsoft Office program.

_____ **13.** The action of moving a selection by dragging it to a new location.

_____ **14.** A designer-quality visual representation of your information that you can create by choosing from among many different layouts to effectively communicate your message or ideas.

_____ **15.** Combinations of formatting effects that are applied to diagrams.

A Crosshair pointer

B Drag-and-drop

C Fill color

D Format Painter

E Gradient fill

F Guides

G Insertion point

H Office Clipboard

I Paste

J Shape Styles

K SmartArt graphic

L SmartArt Styles

M Text box

N Transition

O WordArt

Fill in the Blank

Write the correct word in the space provided.

1. When you click the dashed border of a placeholder, it displays as a _____ line.

2. To repeat the last command or text that you entered, press the _____ function key.

3. To copy formatting to multiple selections, _____-_____ Format Painter.

4. To horizontally or vertically position selected objects on a slide relative to each other, use the _____ tools.

5. When you apply slide transitions, you can control the _____ and the method with which the slides advance during the presentation.

6. The Clipboard can store up to _____ selections that you have cut or copied.

7. You can reverse an Undo by using the _____ command.

8. To show nonsequential information, use a _____ diagram.

9. To show steps in a process or timeline, use a _____ diagram.

10. To show a continual process, use a _____ diagram.

11. To show a decision tree or create an organization chart, use a _____ diagram.

12. To illustrate connections, use a _____ diagram.

13. To show how parts relate to a whole, use a _____ diagram.

14. To show proportional relationships with the largest component on the top or bottom, use a _____ diagram.

15. When you are creating a diagram, remember that it is important to choose the layout and type that provides the best _____ representation of your information.

PowerPoint
2 chaptertwo

Skills Review

Project 2C — Snowboarding

In this project, you will apply the skills you practiced from the Objectives in Project 2A.

Objectives: 1. *Format Slide Elements;* **2.** *Insert and Format Pictures and Shapes;* **3.** *Apply Slide Transitions.*

In the following Skills Review, you will edit a presentation created by Dane Richardson, the Director of Ski and Snowboarding Instruction, that describes the snowboarding events and services available at Montagna del Pattino. Your completed presentation will look similar to the one shown in Figure 2.41.

> ### For Project 2C, you will need the following files:
>
> p2C_Board
> p2C_Hillside
> p2C_Silhouette
> p2C_Snowboarding

You will save your presentation as
2C_Snowboarding_Firstname_Lastname

Figure 2.41

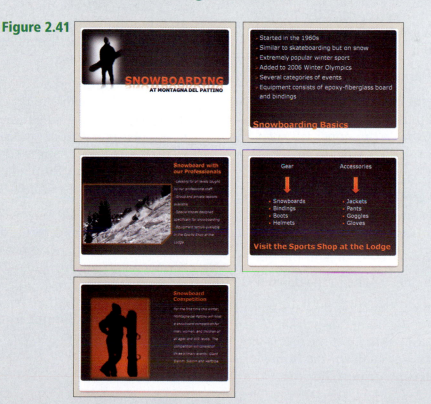

(Project 2C–Snowboarding continues on the next page)

(Project 2C–Snowboarding continued)

1. **Start** PowerPoint, and then from your student data files, open **p2C_Snowboarding**. Click the **Office** button, and then click **Save As**. Navigate to your *PowerPoint Chapter 2* folder and using your own first and last name, save the file as **2C_Snowboarding_Firstname_Lastname**

2. Display **Slide 1** and drag to select the title text. On the **Format tab**, in the **WordArt Styles group**, click the **More** button to display the **WordArt gallery**. Under **Applies to All Text in the Shape**, in the last row, click the last style—**Fill – Accent 1, Metal Bevel, Reflection**.

3. Click the **Insert tab**, and then in the **Illustrations group**, click **Picture**. Navigate to the location where your student files are stored, and then double-click **p2C_Silhouette** to insert the picture in the middle of the slide.

4. With the picture selected, click the **Format tab**. In the **Size group**, click in the **Height** box, and then type **4** Click on the picture to change its size, and then point to the picture to display the ⊕ pointer. Drag the picture up and to the left so that its upper left corner aligns with the upper left corner of the white rounded rectangle.

5. With the picture still selected, in the **Picture Styles group**, click **Picture Effects**. Point to **Soft Edges**, and then click **50 Point** to blur the edges of the image.

6. Display **Slide 2**, and then click in the bulleted list placeholder. Point to the dashed border so that the ⊕ pointer displays, and then click so that the border displays as a solid line, indicating that all of the text in the placeholder is selected. On the **Home tab**, in the **Paragraph group**, click the

Bullets button arrow to display the **Bullets gallery**, and then click **Arrow Bullets**.

7. Display **Slide 3**, and then select the bulleted list placeholder on the right side of the slide so that its solid border displays. Press F4 to repeat the bullet formatting that you applied in the previous step. If you have entered another action before pressing F4 and the bullet formatting does not repeat, click the Bullets button arrow, and then apply the Arrow Bullets style.

8. On **Slide 3**, in the placeholder on the left of the slide click the first button in the second row of buttons—**Insert Picture from File**. From your student files, double-click **p2C_Hillside**. In the **Picture Styles group**, click the **Picture Shape** button. Under **Basic Shapes**, in the third row, click the fourth shape —**Folded Corner**. In the **Picture Styles group**, click the **Picture Effects** button, point to **Glow**, and then under **Glow Variations**, in the third row, click the first effect—**Accent color 1, 11 pt glow**.

9. Click in the bulleted list placeholder on the right, and then click its border so that it displays as a solid line, indicating that all of the text is selected. On the **Home tab**, in the **Font group**, apply **Italic**, and then, in the **Paragraph group**, click the **Line Spacing** button. Click **2.0**. **Save** your presentation.

10. Display **Slide 4** and verify that the rulers display. If the rulers do not display, on the View tab, in the Show/Hide group, select the Ruler check box. Click the **Insert tab**, and then in the **Illustrations group**, click the **Shapes** button to display the **Shapes gallery**.

(Project 2C–Snowboarding continues on the next page)

Content-Based Assessments

Skills Review

(Project 2C–Snowboarding continued)

11. Under **Block Arrows**, in the first row, click the fourth arrow—**Down Arrow**. Position the crosshair pointer at approximately **2.5 inches to the left of zero** on the **horizontal ruler** and at **2 inches above zero** on the **vertical ruler**.

12. Drag approximately 0.5 inch to the right and 1 inch down to create the arrow. Check the size of the shape by looking at the **Format tab** in the **Size group**. If necessary, adjust the size of the arrow to a Height of **1** and a Width of **0.5**.

13. With the arrow selected, on the **Format tab**, in the **Shape Styles group**, click the **More** button. In the last row, click the second style—**Intense Effect – Accent 1**.

14. With the arrow still selected, hold down [Ctrl], and then press [D] to duplicate the arrow. Point to the arrow, and then drag to the right so that the arrow is positioned above the text on the right of the slide at approximately **2 inches to the right of zero** on the **horizontal ruler**.

15. With the arrow on the right selected, press [⇧ Shift], and then click the arrow on the left so that both arrows are selected. On the **Format tab**, in the **Arrange group**, click the **Align** button. Click **Align Selected Objects** to align the objects that you select relative to each other. On the **Format tab**, in the **Arrange group**, click the **Align** button, and then click **Align Top**.

16. Click the **Insert tab**, and then in the **Text group**, click **Text Box**. Position the pointer at approximately **3 inches to the left of zero** on the **horizontal ruler** and at **3 inches above zero** on the **vertical ruler**. Click to create a text box, and then type **Gear** Select the text that you typed, and then on the **Home tab**, in the **Font group**,

click the **Font Color arrow** and then click **White, Background 1**. Change the **Font Size** to **24**, and then click on a blank area of the slide.

17. Click the **Insert tab**, and then in the **Text group**, click **Text Box**. Position the pointer at approximately **1 inch to the right of zero** on the **horizontal ruler** and at **3 inches above zero** on the **vertical ruler**. Click to create a text box, and then type **Accessories** Select the text that you typed, and then on the **Home tab**, in the **Font group**, click the **Font Color button arrow** and then click **White, Background 1**. Change the **Font Size** to **24**.

18. Use the [⇧ Shift] key to select the two text boxes—*Gear* and *Accessories*. Click the **Format tab**, and then in the **Arrange group**, click the **Align** button. Click **Align Top** to align the top edges of the two text boxes, and then click anywhere on the slide so that none of the objects are selected. **Save** your presentation.

19. Click the bulleted list placeholder on the left side of the slide. Press [⇧ Shift], and then click the arrow on the left, and then press [⇧ Shift] and click the *Gear* text box so that all three objects are selected. On the **Format tab**, in the **Arrange group**, click the **Align** button. Click **Align Selected Objects**. Click the **Align** button again, and then click **Align Center**.

20. Using the same process that you used in Step 19, align center the placeholder, arrow, and text box on the right side of the slide. **Save** your presentation.

21. Display **Slide 5**. In the placeholder on the left side of the slide, click the **Insert Picture from File** button, and then navigate to your student files. Double-click

(Project 2C–Snowboarding continues on the next page)

(Project 2C–Snowboarding continued)

p2C_Board. On the **Format tab**, in the **Picture Styles group**, click the **Picture Effects** button, and then point to **Glow**. In the last row, click the first glow effect— **Accent color 1, 18 pt glow**.

22. On **Slide 5**, select the slide title. On the **Home tab**, in the **Clipboard group**, click the **Format Painter** button. Display **Slide 3**, and then drag the [icon] pointer over the title to apply the font, font size, and shadow effects from the title on **Slide 5** to the title on **Slide 3**.

23. Click the **Animations tab**. In the **Transition to This Slide group**, click the **More** button, and then under **Wipes**, in the first row, click the third transition— **Wipe Right**. In the **Transition to This Slide group**, click the **Apply To All** button. Click the **Slide Show tab**. In the **Start Slide Show group**, click **From Beginning** and then view your presentation, clicking the mouse button to advance from slide to slide.

24. Create a **Header and Footer** for the **Notes and Handouts**. Include only the **Date and time updated automatically**, the **Page number**, and a **Footer** with the file name 2C_Snowboarding_Firstname_Lastname

25. Check your *Chapter Assignment Sheet* or *Course Syllabus* or consult your instructor to determine if you are to submit your assignments on paper or electronically. To submit electronically, go to Step 27, and then follow the instructions provided by your instructor.

26. From the **Office** menu, point to the **Print arrow**, and then click **Print Preview** to make a final check of your presentation. In the **Page Setup group**, click the **Print What arrow**, and then click **Handouts, (6 slides per page)**. Click the **Print** button, and then click **OK** to print the handouts.

27. **Save** the changes to your presentation, and then close the file.

End **You have completed Project 2C**

Skills Review

Project 2D — Lessons

In this project, you will apply the skills you practiced from the Objectives in Project 2B.

Objectives: 4. *Reorganize Presentation Text and Clear Formats;* **5.** *Create and Format a SmartArt Graphic.*

In the following Skills Review, you will edit a presentation created by Dane Richardson, the Director of Ski and Snowboarding Instruction, that describes the ski and snowboarding lessons for children at Montagna del Pattino. Your completed presentation will look similar to the one shown in Figure 2.42.

For Project 2D, you will need the following files:

p2D_Cara
p2D_Dane
p2D_Lessons
p2D_Marty

**You will save your presentation as
2D_Lessons_Firstname_Lastname**

Figure 2.42

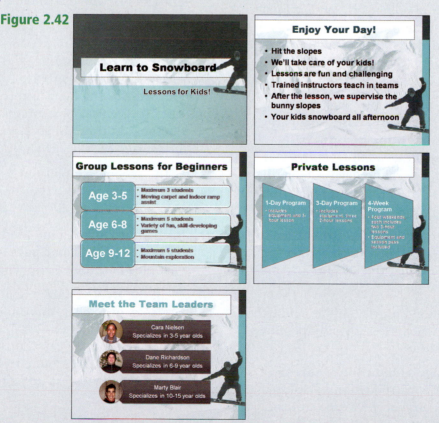

(Project 2D–Lessons continues on the next page)

Content-Based Assessments

PowerPoint
chapter two

Skills Review

(Project 2D–Lessons continued)

1. **Start** PowerPoint, and then from your student files, open **p2D_Lessons**. Click the **Office** button, and then click **Save As**. Navigate to your **PowerPoint Chapter 2** folder, and then using your own first and last name, save the file as **2D_Lessons_Firstname_Lastname**

2. Display **Slide 3**. On the **Home tab**, in the **Clipboard group**, click the **Dialog Box Launcher** to display the Clipboard task pane. In the **Clipboard** task pane, click the **Clear All** button. Drag to select the slide title—**Private Lessons**. In the **Clipboard group**, click the **Cut** button to move the title to the Office Clipboard.

3. Display **Slide 4**. Drag to select the title and on the **Home tab**, in the **Clipboard group**, click the **Cut** button to move the title to the Office Clipboard.

4. With **Slide 4** still displayed and the insertion point blinking in the title placeholder, in the **Clipboard** task pane, click **Private Lessons** to paste the item to the title placeholder.

5. Display **Slide 3**, and then click in the title placeholder. In the **Clipboard** task pane, click **Group Lesson for Beginners** to paste the item to the title placeholder. In the **Clipboard** task pane, click **Clear All**, and then **Close** the Clipboard task pane.

6. On **Slide 3**, right-click in the bulleted list placeholder to display the shortcut menu, and then point to **Convert to SmartArt**. In the first row, click the second graphic—**Vertical Block List**.

7. Click in the blank, fourth shape, and then press [Delete] to delete the extra shape. **Save** your presentation.

8. Click the **Design tab**. In the **SmartArt Styles group**, click the **Change Colors** button. Under **Primary Theme Colors**,

(Project 2D–Lessons continues on the next page)

click the third color set—**Dark 2 Fill**. In the **SmartArt Styles group**, click the **More** button. Under **3-D**, in the first row, click the third style—**Cartoon**.

9. Display **Slide 4**. Right-click in the bulleted list placeholder to display the shortcut menu. Point to **Convert to SmartArt**, and then click **More SmartArt Graphics**. Click **List**, and then in the fifth row, click **Trapezoid List**. Click **OK** to create a diagram with four shapes. Click in the blank, fourth shape, and then press [Delete] to delete the extra shape. In the **SmartArt tools Design tab**, click the **Change Colors** button. and then under **Primary Theme Colors**, click the third color—**Dark 2 Fill**.

10. Click the **Home tab**. In the **Slides group**, click the **New Slide** button to insert a slide with the **Title and Content** layout. Click in the title placeholder, and then type **Meet the Team Leaders**

11. In the content placeholder, click the **Insert SmartArt Graphic** button. In the fourth row, click the second graphic—**Vertical Picture Accent List**, and then click **OK**. Click in the first **Text** shape, type **Cara Nielsen** and then press [Enter]. Type **Specializes in 3–5 year olds**

12. In the second shape type **Dane Richardson** and then press [Enter]. Type **Specializes in 6-9 year olds**

13. In the third shape type **Marty Blair** and then press [Enter]. Type **Specializes in 10-15 year olds** and then **Save** your presentation.

14. Click the **Design tab**. In the **SmartArt Styles group**, click the **Change Colors** button. Scroll the color list, and then under **Accent 4**, click the second color set—**Colored Fill - Accent 4**. In the **SmartArt Styles group**, click the **More**

134 PowerPoint | Chapter 2: Designing a PowerPoint Presentation

Skills Review

(Project 2D–Lessons continued)

button. Under **Best Match for Document**, click the last style—**Intense Effect**.

15. To the left of Cara Nielsen's information, in the circle shape, click the **Insert Picture From File** button. Navigate to your student files, and then double-click **p2D_Cara** to insert the picture. Repeat this process for the remaining two circles, inserting the files **p2D_Dane**, and **p2D_Marty**.

16. Click the **Slide Show tab**. In the **Start Slide Show group**, click **From Beginning**, and then view your presentation, clicking the mouse button to advance from slide to slide. Create a **Header and Footer** for the **Notes and Handouts**. Include only the **Date and time updated automatically**, the **Page number**, and a **Footer** with the file name **2D_Lessons_Firstname_Lastname**

17. Check your *Chapter Assignment Sheet* or *Course Syllabus* or consult your instructor to determine if you are to submit your assignments on paper or electronically. To submit electronically, go to Step 19, and then follow the instructions provided by your instructor.

18. From the **Office** menu, point to the **Print arrow**, and then click **Print Preview** to make a final check of your presentation. In the **Page Setup group**, click the **Print What arrow**, and then click **Handouts, (6 slides per page)**. Click the **Print** button, and then click **OK** to print the handouts. **Close** Print Preview.

19. **Save** changes to your presentation, and then from the **Office** menu, click **Exit PowerPoint**.

End **You have completed Project 2D** _____

PowerPoint

2 **chapter two**

Mastering PowerPoint

Project 2E — Condos

In this project, you will apply the skills you practiced from the Objectives in Project 2A.

Objectives: 1. *Format Slide Elements;* **2.** *Insert and Format Pictures and Shapes;* **3.** *Apply Slide Transitions.*

In the following Mastering PowerPoint project, you will create a presentation that Kirsten McCarty, Director of Marketing will use to showcase the new timeshare condos at Montagna del Pattino. Your completed presentation will look similar to Figure 2.43.

For Project 2E, you will need the following files:

New blank PowerPoint presentation
p2E_Condominiums
p2E_Timeshare

You will save your presentation as
2E_Condos_Firstname_Lastname

Figure 2.43

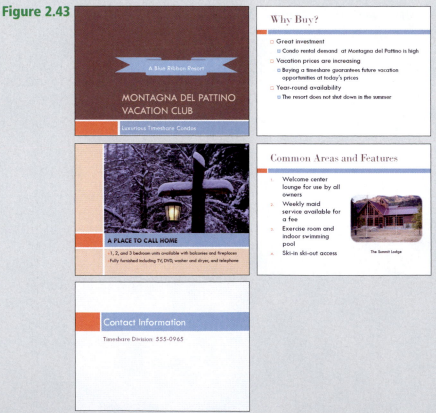

(Project 2E–Condos continues on the next page)

Content-Based Assessments

Mastering PowerPoint

(Project 2E–Condos continued)

1. **Start** PowerPoint, and then begin a new blank presentation. On the **Design tab**, display the **Themes gallery**, and then under **Built-In**, apply the **Median** theme. The title of the presentation is **Montagna del Pattino Vacation Club** and the subtitle is **Luxurious Timeshare Condos Save** the presentation as **2E_Condos_Firstname_Lastname**

2. On the **Insert tab**, display the **Shapes gallery**. Under **Stars and Banners**, in the second row, click the second shape—**Down Ribbon**. Position the crosshair pointer at **1 inch above zero on the vertical ruler** and aligned with the **M** in *Montagna*. Drag down approximately 1 inch and to the right so that the ribbon shape extends to the **o** in *Pattino*. In the **Format tab**, verify the **Size** of the shape and if necessary, change the **Height** to **1** and the **Width** to **6**

3. In the shape, type **A Blue Ribbon Resort** and then apply a **Shadow Shape Effect,** using **Inner** style—**Inside Center**. Select the text, and then change the **Font Size** to **24**.

4. Add a new slide to the presentation with the **Title and Content** layout. The slide title is **Why Buy?** Type the following bullet points, increasing and decreasing the list levels as indicated. Correct any spelling errors that you make while typing.

   Great investment

       More affordable than buying a vacation home

   Vacation prices are increasing

       Buying a timeshare guarantees future vacation opportunities at today's prices

   Year-round availability

       The resort does not shut down during summer

(Project 2E–Condos continues on the next page)

5. Add a **New Slide** to the presentation with the **Picture with Caption** layout. The slide title is **A Place to Call Home** Select the title text. On the **Format tab**, display the **WordArt Styles gallery**, and then apply the **Fill – White**, **Warm Matte Bevel** style—the first style under **Applies to All Text in the Shape**. In the text placeholder, type the following two bullet points, increase the **Font Size** to **20**, and then apply the **Star Bullets** bullet style.

   1-, 2-, and 3-bedroom units available with balconies and fireplaces

   Fully furnished including TV, DVD, washer and dryer, and telephone

6. From your student files, insert the picture **p2E_Condominiums** in the picture placeholder.

7. Add a **New Slide** to the presentation with the **Two Content** layout. The slide title is **Common Areas and Features** Type the following bullet points in the placeholder on the left, and then correct any spelling errors that you make while typing.

   Welcome center lounge for use by all owners

   Weekly cleaning service available for a fee

   Exercise room and indoor swimming pool

   Ski-in and ski-out access

8. Apply **Numbering** to the list. On the right side of the slide, from your student files, insert the picture **p2E_Timeshare**. On the **Format tab**, display the **Picture Shape** gallery, and then under **Rectangles**, apply the second shape—**Rounded Rectangle**. Apply a **5 Point**, **Soft Edges Picture Effect**.

9. Insert a **Text Box** approximately 0.5 inch below the picture, and then type **The Summit Lodge** Use ⬆Shift to select the picture and the text box. Using the **Drawing Tools Format tab** (Note: Be sure to use

Mastering PowerPoint

(Project 2E–Condos continued)

the *Drawing Tools*, not the Picture Tools), **Align Center** the picture and the text box.

10. Add a **New Slide** to the presentation with the **Section Header** layout. The title of the slide is **Contact Information** and the subtitle is **Timeshare Division: 555-0965**

11. Display **Slide 2** and change the title **Font** to **Bodoni MT**. Use **Format Painter** to copy the formatting to the slide title on **Slide 4**. Apply the **Wipe Down Transition**, and then change the **Transition Speed** to **Medium** for all of the slides in the presentation. View the slide show from the beginning.

12. Create a **Header and Footer** for the **Notes and Handouts**. Include only the **Date and time updated automatically**, the **Page**

number, and a **Footer** with the file name **2E_Condos_Firstname_Lastname** using your own first and last name.

13. Check your *Chapter Assignment Sheet* or *Course Syllabus* or consult your instructor to determine if you are to submit your assignments on paper or electronically. To submit electronically, go to Step 15, and then follow the instructions provided by your instructor.

14. **Print Preview** your presentation, and then print **Handouts, (6 slides per page)**.

15. **Save** changes to your presentation, and then **Close** the presentation.

End **You have completed Project 2E**

Mastering PowerPoint

Project 2F — Job Listings

In this project, you will apply the skills you practiced from the Objectives in Project 2B.

Objectives: 4. *Reorganize Presentation Text and Clear Formats;* **5.** *Create and Format a SmartArt Graphic.*

In the following Mastering PowerPoint Assessment, you will create a presentation that Leah Huynh, Director of Human Resources will use to describe some of the seasonal employment opportunities available at Montagna del Pattino. Your completed presentation will look similar to Figure 2.44.

> **For Project 2F, you will need the following files:**
>
> New blank PowerPoint presentation
> p2F_Employment
> p2F_Snowflake_Template

You will save your presentation as
2F_Job_Listings_Firstname_Lastname

Figure 2.44

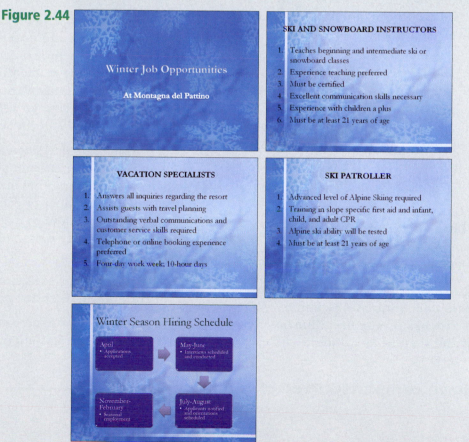

(Project 2F–Job Listings continues on the next page)

(Project 2F—Job Listings continued)

1. **Start** PowerPoint, and then open **p2F_Snowflake_Template** from your student files. **Save** the file as **2F_Job_Listings_Firstname_Lastname**

2. The title for the first slide is **Winter Job Opportunities** The subtitle is **At Montagna del Pattino**

3. Several slides for this presentation are contained in a file that lists summer and winter seasonal employment opportunities. From the file **p2F_Employment**, reuse **Slides 2—Ski and Snowboard Instructors**; **3—Vacation Specialists**; and **4—Ski Patroller**. (Hint: In the New Slide gallery, click Reuse Slides).

4. Display **Slide 2**, and then select and **Copy** the last bullet point—*Must be at least 21 years of age*. **Paste** the selection to **Slide 4** so that it is the fifth bullet point. On **Slide 4**, **Cut** the second to last bullet point—*Four-day work week; 10-hour days*, and then paste it to **Slide 3** so that it is the fifth bullet point.

5. Display **Slide 2**, and then select the bullet list placeholder so that its border displays as a solid line. Apply **Numbering** to the list and then use F4 to repeat the numbering for the bulleted lists on **Slides 3 and 4**.

6. Display **Slide 4**, and then add a new slide with the **Title and Content** layout. The title of the new slide is **Winter Season Hiring Schedule**

7. In the content placeholder, insert the second **Process** type **SmartArt Graphic —Accent Process**. In the first blue box, type **April** and then in its attached white box, type **Applications accepted** In the second blue box, type **May-June** and then in its attached white box, type **Interviews scheduled and conducted** In the third blue box, type **July-August** and then in its attached white box, type **Applicants notified and orientations scheduled**

8. Click in the third blue box, and then in the **SmartArt Tools** click the **Design tab**. Add a shape at the same level, and then in the blue box, type **November-February** In its attached white box, type **Seasonal employment** Notice that this diagram does not use the slide space efficiently and the font size of the text is small and difficult to read. Change the **Layout** of the **SmartArt** to a **Process** layout—**Basic Bending Process** and its color to the second **Accent 2** scheme—**Colored Fill - Accent 2**. Apply **3-D Style Cartoon**.

9. Create a **Header and Footer** for the **Notes and Handouts**. Include only the **Date and time updated automatically**, the **Page number**, and a **Footer** with the file name **2F_Job_Listings_Firstname_Lastname** using your own first and last name.

10. Check your *Chapter Assignment Sheet* or *Course Syllabus* or consult your instructor to determine if you are to submit your assignments on paper or electronically. To submit electronically, go to Step 12, and then follow the instructions provided by your instructor.

11. **Print Preview** your presentation, and then print **Handouts, (6 slides per page)**.

12. **Save** changes to your presentation, and then **Close** the presentation.

End **You have completed Project 2F**

PowerPoint

2 chapter two

Mastering PowerPoint

Project 2G — Packages

In this project, you will apply the skills you practiced from the Objectives in Projects 2A and 2B.

Objectives: 1. *Format Slide Elements;* **2.** *Insert and Format Pictures and Shapes;* **3.** *Apply Slide Transitions;* **5.** *Create and Format a SmartArt Graphic.*

In the following Mastering PowerPoint project, you will edit a presentation that Kirsten McCarty, Director of Marketing, will be showing at a travel fair to highlight the vacation packages offered at Montagna del Pattino. Your completed presentation will look similar to Figure 2.45.

For Project 2G, you will need the following files:

p2G_Fireworks
p2G_Mountain
p2G_Packages
p2G_Ski_Lift
p2G_Sunset

You will save your presentation as 2G_Packages_Firstname_Lastname

Figure 2.45

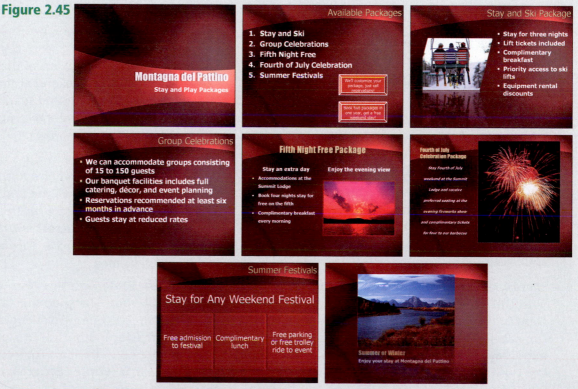

(Project 2G–Packages continues on the next page)

(Project 2G–Packages continued)

1. **Start** PowerPoint, and then from your student files, open **p2G_Packages**. **Save** your presentation as **2G_Packages_Firstname_Lastname**

2. Display **Slide 2**, and then change the bulleted list to **Numbering**. Insert a **Basic Shape Bevel** at **1 inch to the right of zero on the horizontal ruler** and at **0.5 inch below zero on the vertical ruler**. Size the bevel so that its **Height** is **1.3** inches and its **Width** is **3** inches. In the bevel, type **We'll customize your package; just call for reservations! Center** the text.

3. Select the shape so that its outer border is solid, and then duplicate the shape by using [Ctrl] + [D]. Drag the new shape down so that it almost touches the bottom of the slide. Replace the text with **Book two packages in one year; get a free weekend stay!**

4. Select both shapes, and then **Arrange** the shapes, using **Align Left** so that the left edge of the two shapes align. Apply a **Shape Style** found in the third row, **Light 1 Outline, Colored Fill – Accent 1** to both shapes.

5. Display **Slide 3**. In the placeholder on the left side of the slide, use the **Insert Picture from File** button in the placeholder to insert from your student files **p2G_Ski_Lift**. Change the **Picture Shape** under **Basic Shapes** to **Parallelogram**, and then apply the first **Reflection** effect—**Tight Reflection, touching.**

6. Display **Slide 4**, and then add a **New Slide** with the **Comparison** layout. Type and **Center** the title **Fifth Night Free Package** In the caption box on the left, type **Stay an extra day** and then in the caption box on the right, type **Enjoy the evening view**

(Project 2G–Packages continues on the next page)

Center both captions, and then in the content placeholder on the left, type the following bullet points:

Accommodations at the Summit Lodge

Book four nights, stay for free on the fifth

Complimentary breakfast every morning

7. Select the placeholder so that its outer edge displays as a solid line, and then change the **Line Spacing** to **1.5** and the **Font Size** to **20**. With the placeholder border displayed as a solid line, the change is applied to all of the text.

8. In the placeholder on the right side of the slide, use the **Insert Picture from File** button in the placeholder to insert from your student files **p2G_Sunset**. Apply the second **Glow Picture Effect** in the second row—**Accent color 2, 8 pt. glow**. **Save** the presentation.

9. Add a **New Slide** to the presentation with the **Content with Caption** layout. The slide title is **Fourth of July Celebration Package Center** the title and increase the **Font Size** to **24**. Remove the **Bold** formatting. In the text placeholder on the left of the slide, type **Stay Fourth of July weekend at the Summit Lodge and receive preferred seating at the evening fireworks show and complimentary tickets for four to our barbecue**

10. Change the **Font Size** of the text that you typed to **16**, and then change the **Line Spacing** to **2.5**. **Center** the text and apply **Italic**. In the placeholder on the right side of the slide, use the **Insert Picture from File** button to insert **p2G_Fireworks** from your student files.

11. Add a **New Slide** with the **Title and Content** layout. The slide title is **Summer Festivals** In the content placeholder, use the **SmartArt Graphic** button to insert a **List** graphic found in the fifth row—**Table List**. Apply the **3-D Powder SmartArt Style** to

(Project 2G–Packages continued)

the graphic. In the long rectangular box at the top of the SmartArt graphic, type **Stay For Any Weekend Festival** and then select the text and display the **WordArt Styles** gallery. In the first row of WordArt styles, apply **Fill – White, Outline – Accent 1** to the selection. In the three remaining boxes, type the following points, one in each box from left to right.

Free admission to festival

Complimentary lunch

Free parking or free trolley ride to event

12. Display **Slide 8**. Click the **Insert Picture from File** button in the placeholder to insert from your student files **p2G_Mountain**. Apply the second **Reflection** effect in the first row—**Half Reflection, touching**.

13. Display **Slide 2**, and then select the title. Change the **Font** to **Tahoma**. Use the **Format Painter** to apply the formatting to the titles on **Slides 3**, **4**, and **7**. (Hint: Double-click Format Painter so that you can apply the formatting multiple times).

14. In the **Transitions** gallery, under **Wipes**, apply the **Uncover Left-Up** transition, and then change the **Transition Speed** to **Medium** for all of the slides. View the **Slide Show** from the beginning.

15. Create a **Header and Footer** for the **Notes and Handouts**. Include only the **Date and time updated automatically**, the **Page number**, and a **Footer** with the file name **2G_Packages_Firstname_Lastname** using your own first and last name.

16. Check your *Chapter Assignment Sheet* or *Course Syllabus* or consult your instructor to determine if you are to submit your assignments on paper or electronically. To submit electronically, go to Step 18, and then follow the instructions provided by your instructor.

17. **Print Preview** your presentation and then print **Handouts, (4 slides per page)**.

18. **Save** your presentation, and then **Close** the file.

End **You have completed Project 2G**

Content-Based Assessments

Mastering PowerPoint

Project 2H—Family

In this project, you will apply the skills you practiced from the Objectives in Projects 2A and 2B.

Objectives: 2. *Insert and Format Pictures and Shapes;* **3.** *Apply Slide Transitions;* **4.** *Reorganize Presentation Text and Clear Formats;* **5.** *Create and Format a SmartArt Graphic.*

In the following Mastering PowerPoint project, you will create a presentation based on the activities that the Gillis family enjoyed while spending a day at Montagna del Pattino. Your completed presentation will look similar to Figure 2.46.

For Project 2H, you will need the following files:

New blank PowerPoint presentation
p2H_Baby
p2H_Group
p2H_Memories
p2H_Snowflake
p2H_Winner

You will save your presentation as 2H_Family_Firstname_Lastname

Figure 2.46

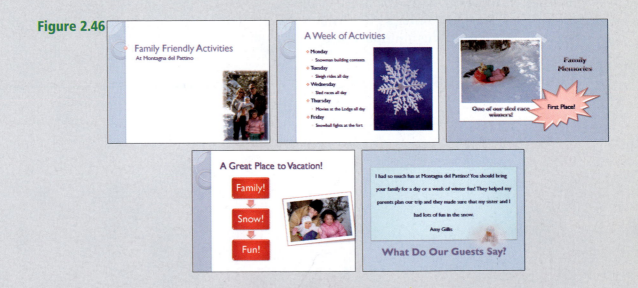

(Project 2H–Family continues on the next page)

Content-Based Assessments

(Project 2H–Family continued)

1. **Start** PowerPoint, and then begin a new blank presentation. On the **Design tab**, display the **Themes** gallery, and then under **Built-In**, apply the **Solstice** theme. Change the **Theme Colors** to the fifth theme under **Built-In—Civic**. **Save** the file as **2H_Family_Firstname_Lastname**

2. The title of this presentation is **Family Friendly Activities** and the subtitle is **At Montagna del Pattino** From your student files, insert the **p2H_Group** picture. Adjust the picture **Height** to **4.5** and the **Width** to **3**. Drag the picture to the lower right corner of the slide. Change the picture shape to **Bevel**, and then apply a **Soft Edges Picture Effect** of **10 Point**.

3. Add a **New Slide** with the **Two Content** layout, and then in the title placeholder, type **A Week of Activities** In the content placeholder on the left, type the following bullet points, increasing and decreasing the list level as necessary:

   Monday

   Snowman building contests

   Tuesday

   Sleigh rides all day

   Wednesday

   Sled races

   Thursday

   Movies at the lodge

   Friday

   Snowball fights at the fort

4. Click the **Insert Picture from File** button in the placeholder on the right to insert from your student files **p2H_Snowflake**.

5. Add a **New Slide** with the **Picture with Caption** layout. In the title placeholder, type **Family Memories** and then apply **WordArt Style Gradient Fill – Black, Outline – White, Outer Shadow**. Increase the **Font Size** to **32** and **Center** the title. In the Picture placeholder, from your student files insert **p2H_Winner**. In the caption box below the picture, type **One of our sled race winners!** In the slide title, select the word *Family*, and then use **Format Painter** to apply the WordArt style to the caption. **Center** the caption and change the **Line Spacing** to **1.0**.

6. On the **Insert tab**, display the **Shapes** gallery. Under **Stars and Banners**, in the first row, click the second shape— **Explosion 2**. Draw a shape that extends from **zero on the horizontal** and **vertical rulers** to **4 1/2 to the right of zero on the horizontal ruler** and **3 below zero on the vertical ruler**. Type **First Place!** in the shape, and then change the **Font Size** to **28**. Display the **Shape Styles gallery**, and then in the fourth row apply **Subtle Effect – Accent 1**. Apply the **Bevel Shape Effect Soft Round**—the second effect in the second row.

7. Add a **New Slide** with the **Two Content** layout, and then in the title placeholder, type **A Great Place to Vacation!** In the content placeholder on the left, insert the **Vertical Process SmartArt** graphic. In the first box, type **Family!** In the second box, type **Snow!** In the last box, type **Fun!** Apply **SmartArt Style 3-D Polished** to the graphic.

8. In the placeholder on the right of the slide, from your student files, insert the picture **p2H_Memories**. Apply **Picture Style Rotated, White**, and then apply the **Glow Picture Effect—Accent color 1, 5 pt glow**.

(Project 2H–Family continues on the next page)

(Project 2H–Family continued)

9. Add a **New Slide** with the **Comparison** layout, and then in the title placeholder at the bottom of the slide, type **What Do Our Guests Say?** Click in the white placeholder at the top left of the slide, and then press ⇧Shift and click the white placeholder at the top right to select both placeholders. **Delete** both placeholders.

10. Click in the placeholder on the left, and then type **I had so much fun at Montagna del Pattino! You should bring your family for a day or a week of winter fun! They helped my parents plan our trip and they made sure that my sister and I had lots of fun in the snow.** Press Enter, and then type **Amy Gillis**

11. In the placeholder on the right, use the **Insert Picture from File** button to insert from your student files **p2H_Baby**. Change the shape of the picture to the **32-Point Star**, and then apply the **Soft Edges 50 Point Picture Effect** so that the baby almost appears to be crawling on the slide. Drag the picture to the right so that the points of the stars and its border box aligns with the right edge of the slide.

12. With the picture selected, press ⇧Shift, and then click the slide title to select both the picture and the title. On the **Drawing Tools Format tab**, in the **Arrange group**, click **Align**, and then click **Align Bottom** to align the bottom edges of the two objects. The baby displays slightly above the word *Say*.

13. Select the text in the bulleted list placeholder, and then on the **Home tab**, click the **Bullets** button to toggle the bullets off. **Center** all of the text in the placeholder.

Point to the placeholder's right-center sizing handle and drag to the right to **4.5 inches to the right of zero on the horizontal ruler** to resize the placeholder. Apply the **Shape Style** found in the fourth row—**Subtle Effect – Accent 3**, and then change the **Line Spacing** of the text to **2.0.**

14. Display **Slide 2**, and then click in the first bullet point—**Monday**. Change the Bullet style to **Star Bullets**. Use F4 or Format Painter to apply the same bullet style to each bullet point that includes a day of the week. In the fourth bullet point, **Copy** the words *all day* to the end of the sixth and eighth bullet points after the words *races*, and *lodge*.

15. Apply the **Box In** transition and change the **Transition Speed** to **Medium**. Click **Apply To All**, and then view the slide show from the beginning.

16. Create a **Header and Footer** for the **Notes and Handouts**. Include only the **Date and time updated automatically**, the **Page number**, and a **Footer** with the file name **2H_Family_Firstname_Lastname**

17. Check your *Chapter Assignment Sheet* or *Course Syllabus* or consult your instructor to determine if you are to submit your assignments on paper or electronically. To submit electronically, go to Step 19, and then follow the instructions provided by your instructor.

18. **Print Preview** your presentation, and then print **Handouts, (6 slides per page).**

19. **Save** changes to your presentation, and then **Close** the file.

End **You have completed Project 2H**

Mastering PowerPoint

Project 2I — Summer

In this project, you will apply the skills you practiced from all the Objectives in Projects 2A and 2B.

Objectives: 1. *Format Slide Elements;* **2.** *Insert and Format Pictures and Shapes;* **3.** *Apply Slide Transitions;* **4.** *Reorganize Presentation Text and Clear Formats;* **5.** *Create and Format a SmartArt Graphic.*

In the following Mastering PowerPoint Assessment, you will edit a presentation that Kirsten McCarty, Director of Marketing, will be showing at a travel fair describing the summer activities at Montagna del Pattino. Your completed presentation will look similar to Figure 2.47.

For Project 2I, you will need the following files:

p2I_Art
p2I_Balloons
p2I_Fireworks
p2I_Summer

You will save your presentation as
2I_Summer_Firstname_Lastname

Figure 2.47

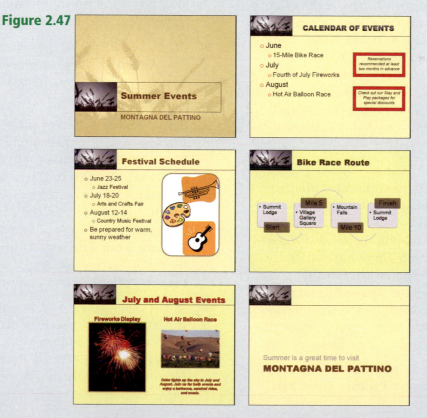

(Project 2I–Summer continues on the next page)

PowerPoint
chapter two

Mastering PowerPoint

(Project 2I–Summer continued)

1. **Start** PowerPoint, and then from your student files open the file **p2I_Summer**. **Save** the presentation as **2I_Summer_Firstname_Lastname**

2. On **Slide 2**, apply a **WordArt Style—Gradient Fill – Accent 6, Inner Shadow** found in the fourth row—to the title, and then decrease the **Font Size** to **32**. Select the bulleted list placeholder so that its border displays as a solid line, and then display the **Bullets and Numbering** dialog box. Change the bullet style to the third style in the first row of the Bullets gallery—**Hollow Round Bullets**. Change the bullet **Color** to the first color under **Standard Colors—Dark Red**.

3. On **Slide 2**, display the **Shapes** gallery. Under **Basic Shapes**, insert the fifth shape in the second row—**Frame**. Position the pointer at **1.5 inches to the right of zero on the horizontal ruler** and at **1.5 inches above zero on the vertical ruler**. Draw the shape with a **Height** of **1.5** and a **Width** of **3.25**, using the **Format Tab** to adjust the size as necessary. In the frame, type **Reservations recommended at least two months in advance** Apply **Italic** and **Center** the text.

4. Duplicate the frame shape by using Ctrl + D, and then drag the duplicated shape down so that it is approximately 0.5 inch below the first shape. Align the left edges of the shapes, and then in the second shape, replace the text with **Check out our Stay and Play packages for special discounts** On the **Format tab**, click the **Shape Fill arrow**, and then under **Standard Colors**, click the first color—**Dark Red**. Use F4 to repeat the fill color formatting to the other frame shape.

5. Display **Slide 3**. In the placeholder on the right, use the **Insert Picture from File**

button to insert from your student files, **p2I_Art**. Change the **Picture Shape** to a **Rounded Rectangle**. Apply the fourth **Glow Effect** in the first row—**Accent color 4, 5 pt glow**.

6. Display **Slide 4**. Select the title, and then in the **Font group**, click the **Clear All Formatting** button to remove the WordArt formatting from the selection.

7. On **Slide 4**, right-click in the content placeholder text, and then point to **Convert to SmartArt**. Click **More SmartArt Graphics** to display the **Choose a SmartArt Graphics** dialog box. Click **Process**, and then in the first row, double-click the last graphic—**Alternating Flow** to convert the text to a diagram. Click in the **Mile 10** shape, and then in the **Create Graphic group**, click **Add Shape**. In the gray box, type **Finish** and then in the brown box, type **Summit Lodge**

8. Change the color of the SmartArt to the first **Accent 1** color—**Colored Outline - Accent 1**, and then apply **3-D Style Powder**.

9. Display **Slide 5**. Select the *Fireworks Display* text, and then apply the second **Word Art Style** in the first row. Change the **Text Fill** color to **Dark Red**. Use the **Format Painter** to apply the same formatting to the *Hot Air Balloon Race* text. In the placeholder on the left, use the **Insert Picture from File** button to insert the picture **p2I_Fireworks**. Apply the **Glow Picture Effect Accent color 2, 8 pt glow**.

10. In the placeholder on the right, use the **Insert Picture from File** button to insert the picture **p2I_Balloons**. Apply the **Soft Edges Picture Effect 5 Point**. Size the picture to a **Height** of **2.5** and a **Width** of

(Project 2I–Summer continues on the next page)

Mastering PowerPoint

(Project 2I–Summer continued)

3.75 and then drag the picture up so that its top edge is positioned at **1 inch above zero on the vertical ruler**. It should *not* align with the fireworks picture.

11. Insert a 4-inch-wide **Text Box** positioned at **zero on the horizontal ruler** and at **2 inches below zero on the vertical ruler**. Type **Color lights up the sky in July and August. Join us for both events and enjoy a barbecue, carnival rides, and music.** Apply **WordArt Style Fill – None, Outline – Accent 2**, and then change the **Text Fill** to **Dark Red**. Apply **Italic**, and then change the **Font Size** to **16**. **Center** the text.

12. Use ⌖ Shift to select the text box that you created in Step 11, the balloon picture, and the *Hot Air Balloon Race* text box. **Align Center** the three objects. (Hint: Use the Drawing Tools Format tab).

13. In the first row of the **Wipes** transitions, apply the **Wedge Transition** to all of the slides in the presentation, and then view the slide show.

14. Create a **Header and Footer** for the **Notes and Handouts**. Include only the **Date and time updated automatically**, the **Page number**, and a **Footer** with the file name **2I_Summer_Firstname_Lastname** using your own first and last name.

15. Check your *Chapter Assignment Sheet* or *Course Syllabus* or consult your instructor to determine if you are to submit your assignments on paper or electronically. To submit electronically, go to Step 17, and then follow the instructions provided by your instructor.

16. **Print Preview** your presentation, and then print **Handouts, (6 slides per page)**.

17. **Save** changes to your presentation, and then **Close** the presentation.

End **You have completed Project 2I**

Content-Based Assessments

 PowerPoint
chapter two

 Business Running Case

Project 2J — Business Running Case

In this project, you will apply the skills you practiced in Projects 2A and 2B.

From My Computer, navigate to the student files that accompany this textbook. In the folder **03_business_running_case_pg37_86**, locate and open the folder for this chapter. Open and print the instructions for this project, which are provided to you in Adobe PDF format. Follow the instructions and use the skills you have gained thus far to assist Jennifer Nelson in meeting the challenges of owning and running her business.

End **You have completed Project 2J** ———————————

Outcomes-Based Assessments

Rubric

The following outcomes-based assessments are *open-ended assessments*. That is, there is no specific correct result; your result will depend on your approach to the information provided. Make *Professional Quality* your goal. Use the following scoring rubric to guide you in *how* to approach the problem and then to evaluate *how well* your approach solves the problem.

The *criteria*—Software Mastery, Content, Format and Layout, and Process—represent the knowledge and skills you have gained that you can apply to solving the problem. The *levels of performance*—Professional Quality, Approaching Professional Quality, or Needs Quality Improvements—help you and your instructor evaluate your result.

	Your completed project is of Professional Quality if you:	Your completed project is Approaching Professional Quality if you:	Your completed project Needs Quality Improvements if you:
1-Software Mastery	Choose and apply the most appropriate skills, tools, and features and identify efficient methods to solve the problem.	Choose and apply some appropriate skills, tools, and features, but not in the most efficient manner.	Choose inappropriate skills, tools, or features, or are inefficient in solving the problem.
2-Content	Construct a solution that is clear and well organized, contains content that is accurate, appropriate to the audience and purpose, and is complete. Provide a solution that contains no errors of spelling, grammar, or style.	Construct a solution in which some components are unclear, poorly organized, inconsistent, or incomplete. Misjudge the needs of the audience. Have some errors in spelling, grammar, or style, but the errors do not detract from comprehension.	Construct a solution that is unclear, incomplete, or poorly organized, containing some inaccurate or inappropriate content; and contains many errors of spelling, grammar, or style. Do not solve the problem.
3-Format and Layout	Format and arrange all elements to communicate information and ideas, clarify function, illustrate relationships, and indicate relative importance.	Apply appropriate format and layout features to some elements, but not others. Overuse features, causing minor distraction.	Apply format and layout that does not communicate information or ideas clearly. Do not use format and layout features to clarify function, illustrate relationships, or indicate relative importance. Use available features excessively, causing distraction.
4-Process	Use an organized approach that integrates planning, development, self-assessment, revision, and reflection.	Demonstrate an organized approach in some areas, but not others; or, use an insufficient process of organization throughout.	Do not use an organized approach to solve the problem.

Outcomes-Based Assessments

Problem Solving

Project 2K—Adult Lessons

In this project, you will construct a solution by applying any combination of the skills you practiced from the Objectives in Projects 2A and 2B.

> **For Project 2K, you will need the following file:**
>
> New blank PowerPoint presentation

**You will save your presentation as
2K_Adult_Lessons_Firstname_Lastname**

Using the information provided, create a presentation that contains four to six slides that Dane Richardson, Director of Ski and Snowboard Instruction, can use to describe the adult ski and snowboard lessons offered at Montagna del Pattino. The presentation will be used as a part of a larger presentation on resort activities to be shown to an audience of varying skiing abilities at a regional ski and snowboard convention.

The resort offers Adult Group Lessons that are comprised of individuals with similar skill levels. Two-hour group lessons include equipment. Private lessons, which are one-on-one instruction geared toward an individual's skill level and preferences, are also available. The resort offers 8-week programs which are group lessons for those who prefer more in-depth, ongoing instruction. The resort also offers several specialty lessons. The Ladies Only group lessons are geared specifically toward women and participants are encouraged to bring a friend. The Backcountry Adventure is a chance for advanced skiers to explore lesser-known areas of the resort. Finally, the Racing Camps are for recreational skiers seeking to fine-tune their skills, and feature gate running and on-hill training.

Use the techniques that you learned in this chapter to insert and format graphics to visually enhance your presentation. The tone of the presentation should be positive and encouraging so that the audience—regardless of skill level—will be interested in visiting the resort and attending the Ski and Snowboard School. Add the file name to the Notes and Handouts footer and check the presentation for spelling errors. Save the presentation as **2K_Adult_Lessons_Firstname_Lastname** and submit it as directed.

Note: You can find many appropriate images available to Office users. To access these images, click the Insert tab, and then from the Illustrations group, click the Clip Art button. In the Clip Art task pane, type a key word—such as *ski*—in the *Search for* box. You can specify the image type (clip art or photographs) and where to search. The largest variety of photographs can be found by including Web Collections in the *Search in* box. You can also use images from earlier projects in this chapter, or images from your personal collection.

End **You have completed Project 2K**

Problem Solving

Project 2L — Festivals

In this project, you will construct a solution by applying any combination of the skills you practiced from the Objectives in Projects 2A and 2B.

For Project 2L, you will need the following file:

New blank PowerPoint presentation

You will save your presentation as
2L_Festivals_Firstname_Lastname

In this project, you will create a presentation that Justin Mitrani, Hotel Manager, is creating as part of a collection of presentations, given to guests on CDs, that describes the seasonal festivals and events held at Montagna del Pattino. The events that are sponsored at the resort include a Celtic Festival, a Chili Cook-Off, and a Country Music Festival. The tone of the presentation should be fun and interesting so that guests will be encouraged to return to the resort during the events. Research these types of events on the Internet to develop content and use a SmartArt graphic to highlight the dates of the festivals. Include pictures and shapes that are relevant to the events and format the pictures, using the techniques that you learned in this chapter. (See the note at the end of Project 2K for hints about locating images.) Add the file name to the Notes and Handouts footer and check the presentation for spelling errors. Save the presentation as **2L_Festivals_Firstname_Lastname** and submit it as directed.

End **You have completed Project 2L** ——————————

Problem Solving

Project 2M — Orientation

In this project, you will construct a solution by applying any combination of the skills you practiced from the Objectives in Projects 2A and 2B.

For Project 2M, you will need the following file:

New blank PowerPoint presentation

**You will save your presentation as
2M_Orientation_Firstname_Lastname**

In this exercise, you will create an orientation presentation consisting of four to six slides to be used by Justin Mitrani, Hotel Director for Montagna del Pattino. This presentation will be used to introduce new employees to the resort and to the importance of customer service. Begin the presentation with slides that include information about the resort. You can summarize from the following information, and you can expand upon this information by researching mountain ski resorts.

Montagna del Pattino was founded and built by the Blardone family in the 1950s. It has grown from one ski run and a small lodge to 50 trails, 6 lifts, a 300-room lodge, and a renowned ski and snowboard school. Luxurious condominiums on the property have ski in/ski out access. A resort store offers rental and sale of gear for enthusiasts who want the latest advances in ski and snowboard technology. A variety of quick service, casually elegant, and fine dining restaurants complete the scene for a perfect ski-enthusiast getaway.

Include at least two slides that describe why customer service and hospitality are important at the resort. Guests who return year after year are impressed by the friendly attitude and helpfulness of the staff and the cleanliness of the facilities. Stress the importance of greeting guests and making them feel at home, thus exemplifying the family-friendly atmosphere that is a hallmark of the resort. Use a process SmartArt graphic to illustrate how hospitality and customer service lead to satisfied guests.

The tone of this presentation is informative and should include examples of how customer service is provided on a daily basis. Keep this in mind when choosing a theme, diagrams, bullet styles, and pictures. (See the note at the end of Project 2K for hints about locating images.) Add the date and file name to the Notes and Handouts footer and check the presentation for spelling errors. Save the presentation as **2M_Orientation_Firstname_Lastname** and submit it as directed.

End **You have completed Project 2M**

Problem Solving

Project 2N — Restaurants

In this project, you will construct a solution by applying any combination of the skills you practiced from the Objectives in Projects 2A and 2B.

For Project 2N, you will need the following file:

New blank PowerPoint presentation

You will save your presentation as
2N_Restaurants_Firstname_Lastname

In this exercise, you will create a presentation that contains information about the restaurants that are onsite at Montagna del Pattino resort. This presentation is being used by Justin Mitrani, Hotel Director, at a Chamber of Commerce meeting. Mr. Mitrani's purpose is to inform Chamber members of the restaurant and catering services available at the resort in an effort to expand catering, conference, and business meeting operations. Create a presentation about the restaurant services, using the following information.

The resort offers a variety of quick service, casually elegant, and fine dining restaurants. The Summit Clubhouse and the Montagna Vista Club are fine dining restaurants known for their superb buffets and desserts. The Mediterranean buffet includes Whole Chicken, slow-roasted and quartered, Rice Pilaf with Pine Nuts and Raisins, Classic Greek Salad with Vinaigrette, Hummus, and Baklava. The Italian buffet includes Lasagna, Italian Vegetable Sauté, Classic Caesar salad, Garlic Bread and Bread Sticks, and Cheesecake. Other buffets include the All American Barbecue, the Cajun Cookout, and the Heartland buffet. The Summit Clubhouse can accommodate large groups of up to 150 guests and the Montagna Vista Club is best suited for more intimate gatherings of no more than 65 guests. The restaurants offer full bar service, event-planning services, and coordination with hotel operations to accommodate conference guests who plan to stay overnight. The Summit Clubhouse includes three conference rooms off of the main banquet room that can be used for smaller group meetings. The resort recently hired a full-time conference and catering director who will act as a liaison with business representatives to coordinate event planning.

Using the preceding information, create a presentation with a minimum of six slides that describes the resort restaurants, menus, banquet and conference facilities, and services. Create a SmartArt graphic that demonstrates the catering and event-planning process. The process may include an initial meeting with the catering director, a meeting to choose

(Project 2N–Restaurants continues on the next page)

Problem Solving

(Project 2N–Restaurants continued)

the date and location, and other meetings to choose menus and finalize reservations. Illustrate your presentation with pictures that will entice the intended audience to use the Montagna del Pattino resort for their catering and business meeting needs. (See the note at the end of Project 2K for hints about locating images.) Add the date and file name to the Notes and Handouts footer and check the presentation for spelling errors. Save the presentation as **2N_Restaurants_Firstname_Lastname** and submit it as directed.

End **You have completed Project 2N**

Problem Solving

Project 2O — Triathlon

In this project, you will construct a solution by applying any combination of the skills you practiced from the Objectives in Projects 2A and 2B.

For Project 2O, you will need the following file:

New blank PowerPoint presentation

You will save your presentation as
2O_Triathlon_Firstname_Lastname

In this exercise, you will create a presentation to be shown by Montagna del Pattino's President, Albert Blardone, at a company meeting that details the Annual Triathlon sponsored by the resort. The presentation will explain the details of the triathlon including the events, the routes, major sponsors, prizes, and medical and security measures. The triathlon takes place in July and is attended by international competitors who excel in three sporting events—swimming, cycling, and running. The triathlon is open to men and women of all ages. Men and women compete concurrently but in separate categories. In addition to gender, the athletes are further categorized according to the following age brackets: 18 to 24; 25 to 35; 36 to 45; and over 45.

Conduct research on triathlon events and begin the presentation with at least two slides that describe traditional triathlon competitions. The next two slides should include the categories in which competitors are separated and a diagram that illustrates the race route. The 1600-meter swimming event takes place in Lake Hennessy, which adjoins Montagna del Pattino. The 50-mile cycling event begins at the lake and finishes at the Brownsville Town Square. The 26-mile marathon finishes at Montagna del Pattino Summit Lodge. Refer to Project 2I_Summer, Slide 4 to see an example of how this information can be included in a SmartArt graphic.

As you conduct your research, explore the types of sponsors involved in triathlon events and the prizes awarded to winners. Include this information on two slides and conclude the presentation with one slide that discusses the mobile medical facilities that will be available to competitors and bystanders as heat exhaustion can affect both athletes and fans. The event draws a large number of spectators, with rooms at the Summit Lodge typically reserved two months in advance. Use the techniques that you learned in this chapter to illustrate the presentation. (See the note at the end of Project 2K for hints about locating images.) Add the date and file name to the Notes and Handouts footer and check the presentation for spelling errors. Save the presentation as **2O_Triathlon_Firstname_ Lastname** and submit it as directed.

End **You have completed Project 2O** —————

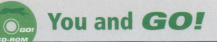 You and *GO!*

Project 2P — You and *GO!*

In this project, you will construct a solution by applying any combination of the skills you practiced from the Objectives in Projects 2A and 2B.

From My Computer, navigate to the student files that accompany this textbook. In the folder **04_you_and_go_pg87_102**, locate and open the folder for this chapter. Open and print the instructions for this project, which are provided to you in Adobe PDF format. Follow the instructions to create a presentation about a career in which you are interested.

End **You have completed Project 2P** —————————

GO! with Help

Project 2Q — *GO!* with Help

The PowerPoint Help system is extensive and can help you as you work. In this project, you will view information about creating a photo album in PowerPoint.

1. **Start** PowerPoint. On the right side of the Ribbon, click the **Microsoft Office PowerPoint Help** button to open the PowerPoint Help window. In the **Search** box, type **Create a Photo Album** and then press Enter.

2. In the displayed search results, click **Create a photo album**. Maximize the displayed window, and then read about photo albums and how you can create them in PowerPoint.

3. If you want, print a copy of the information by clicking the printer button at the top of Microsoft Office PowerPoint Help window.

4. Close the **Help** window, and then **Close** PowerPoint.

End **You have completed Project 2Q** —————————

PowerPoint
2 chapter two

Group Business Running Case

Project 2R — Group Business Running Case

In this project, you will apply the skills you practiced from the Objectives in Projects 2A and 2B.

Your instructor may assign this group case project to your class. If your instructor assigns this project, he or she will provide you with information and instructions to work as part of a group. The group will apply the skills gained thus far to help the Bell Orchid Hotel Group achieve its business goals.

End **You have completed Project 2R** —————————————

3 chapterthree

Enhancing a Presentation with Animation, Tables, and Charts

OBJECTIVES

At the end of this chapter you will be able to:

OUTCOMES

Mastering these objectives will enable you to:

1. Customize Slide Backgrounds and Themes
2. Animate a Slide Show

PROJECT 3A
Customize a Presentation

---

3. Create and Modify Tables
4. Create and Modify Charts

PROJECT 3B
Present Data with Tables and Charts

Select National Properties

Select National Properties is a diversified real estate company that develops, builds, manages, and acquires a wide variety of properties nationwide. Among the company's portfolio of properties are shopping malls, mixed-use town center developments, high-rise office buildings, office parks, industrial buildings and warehouses, multifamily housing developments, educational facilities, and hospitals. Residential developments are mainly located in and around the company's hometown, Chicago; commercial and public buildings in the portfolio are located nationwide. The company is well respected for its focus on quality and commitment to the environment and economic development of the areas where it operates.

Enhancing a Presentation with Animation, Tables, and Charts

Recall that the presentation theme applies a consistent look to a presentation. You can customize a presentation by modifying the theme and by applying animation to slide elements, and you can enhance your presentations by creating tables and charts that help your audience understand numeric data and trends just as pictures and diagrams help illustrate a concept. The data that you present should determine whether a table or a chart would most appropriately display your information. The charts most commonly used in PowerPoint presentations are bar, column, line, and pie. Styles applied to your tables and charts unify these slide elements by complementing your presentation theme.

Project 3A New Homes

In Activities 3.1 through 3.8, you will edit and format a presentation that Shaun Walker, President of Select National Properties, has created for a City Council meeting that describes a proposed residential development. Your completed presentation will look similar to Figure 3.1.

For Project 3A, you will need the following files:

p3A_Bedroom

p3A_Community

p3A_Family_Room

p3A_New_Homes

You will save your presentation as
3A_New_Homes_Firstname_Lastname

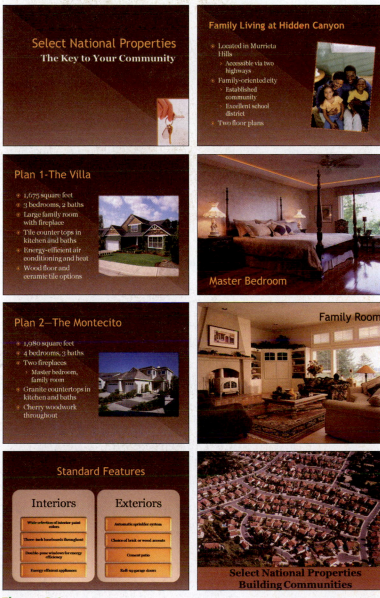

Figure 3.1
Project 3A—New Homes

Objective 1
Customize Slide Backgrounds and Themes

You have practiced customizing presentations by applying themes with unified design elements, backgrounds, and colors that provide a consistent look in your presentation. You can further customize a slide by changing the background color, applying a background style, or by inserting a picture on the slide background.

Activity 3.1 Applying a Background Style

Recall that the presentation theme is a coordinated, predefined set of colors, fonts, lines, and fill effects. In this activity, you will open a presentation in which the Verve theme is applied, and then you will change the theme colors for the entire presentation and the background style for the first slide.

> ### Note — Comparing Your Screen with the Figures in This Textbook
>
> Your screen will match the figures shown in this textbook if you set your screen resolution to 1024 x 768. At other resolutions, your screen will closely resemble, but not match, the figures shown. To view your screen's resolution, on the Windows desktop, right-click in a blank area, click Properties, and then click the Settings tab.

1 **Start** PowerPoint. From your student files, **Open** the file

p3A_New_Homes. From the **Office** menu [icon], click **Save As**, and then click the **Create New Folder** button [icon]. Navigate to the location where you are saving your solution files, create a folder with the name **PowerPoint Chapter 3** and then click **OK**. In the **File name** box, type **3A_New_Homes_Firstname_Lastname** and then click **Save** to save your file.

2 Click the **Design tab**, and then in the **Themes group**, click the **Colors** button. Click **Trek** to change the theme color for the entire presentation.

3 With **Slide 1** displayed, on the **Design tab**, in the **Background group**, click the **Background Styles** button to display the Background Styles gallery, as shown in Figure 3.2.

A *background style* is a slide background fill variation that combines theme colors in different intensities.

Background Styles gallery

Figure 3.2

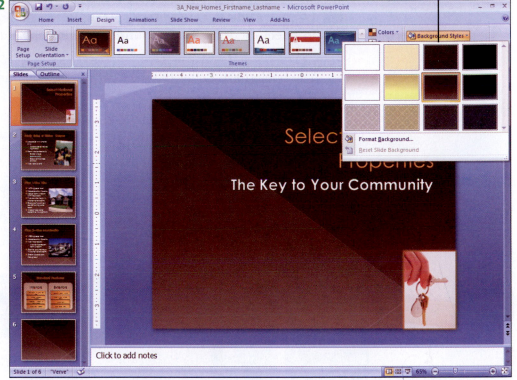

4 Point to each of the background styles to use Live Preview to view the style on **Slide 1**. Then, in the first row, *right-click* **Style 2** to display the shortcut menu. Click **Apply to Selected Slides**.

The background style is applied to Slide 1.

5 **Save** your presentation.

More Knowledge

Applying Background Styles to All Slides in a Presentation

You do not need to display the shortcut menu to apply a background style to all of the slides in a presentation. Click the background style that you wish to apply and the style will be applied to all of the slides in the presentation.

Activity 3.2 Hiding Background Graphics

Slide themes and backgrounds often contain graphic elements that display on slides with various layouts. In the Verve theme applied to this presentation, the background includes a triangle and a line that intersect near the lower right corner of the slide. Sometimes the background graphics interfere with the slide content. When this happens, you can hide the background graphics.

1 Display **Slide 6** and notice that on this slide, you can clearly see the triangle and line on the slide background.

You cannot delete these objects because they are a part of the slide background.

2 Display **Slide 5**. On the **Design tab**, in the **Background group**, click to select the **Hide Background Graphics** check box, and then compare your slide with Figure 3.3.

The background objects no longer display behind the SmartArt diagram.

Hide Background Graphics check box is checked

Figure 3.3

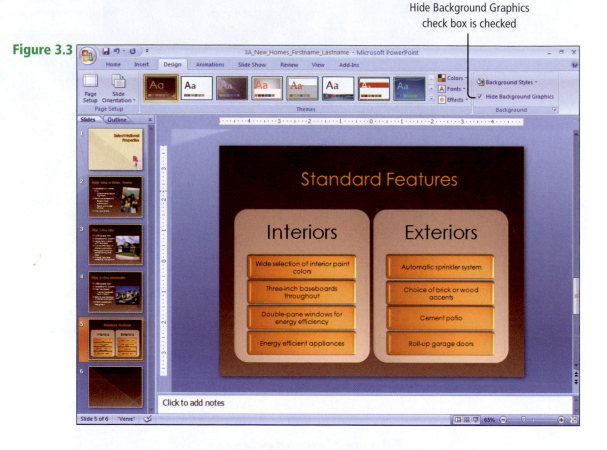

3 Display **Slide 1**. On the **Design tab**, in the **Background group**, select the **Hide Background Graphics** check box to toggle the graphics off.

4 Click the **Hide Background Graphics** check box again to toggle the graphics on.

5 **Save** the presentation.

Activity 3.3 Formatting a Slide Background with a Picture

You can insert a picture on a slide background so the image fills the entire slide.

1 Display **Slide 3**, and then click the **Home tab**. In the **Slides group**, click the **New Slide arrow**, and then click the **Title Only** layout.

2 Click the **Design tab**. In the **Background group**, click the **Hide Background Graphics** check box, and then click the **Background Styles** button. Below the displayed gallery, click **Format Background**.

The Format Background dialog box displays, providing options for customizing slide backgrounds.

3 If necessary, on the left side of the dialog box, click Fill. On the right side of the dialog box, under **Fill**, click the **Picture or texture fill** option button as shown in Figure 3.4, and then notice that on the slide background, a textured fill displays.

Your background may differ

Figure 3.4

Fill selected

Picture or texture fill option button selected

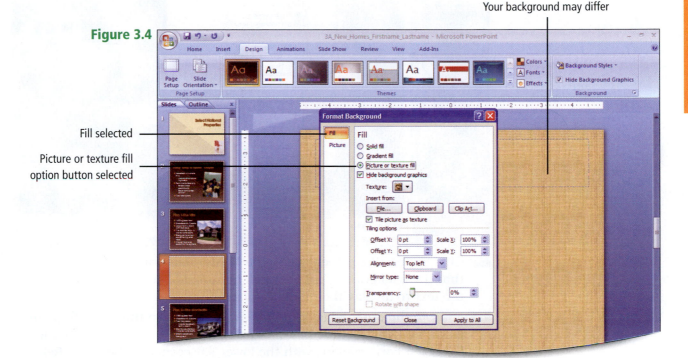

4 Under **Insert from**, click the **File** button to display the **Insert Picture** dialog box. Navigate to the location where your student files are located, and then click **p3A_Bedroom**. Click **Insert**.

Notice that the picture displays on the background of Slide 4.

5 In the **Format Background** dialog box, under **Stretch options**, verify that the **Left**, **Right**, **Top**, and **Bottom Offsets** are set to **0%** and make changes as necessary. Compare your dialog box with Figure 3.5.

The Stretch options enable you to control the way in which the picture displays on the slide background by cropping portions of the picture and then stretching it to fit on the background. Setting the Offsets to 0% ensures that the slide background is formatted with the original picture in its entirety.

6 Click **Close** and notice that the picture has been applied to the slide background.

When a picture is applied to the slide background using the Format Background option, the picture is not treated as an object. Thus, you cannot move it or size it.

Figure 3.5

Picture displays on slide background

Set all Offsets to 0%

7 Click in the title placeholder, type **Master Bedroom** and then notice that the background picture does not provide sufficient contrast with the text to display the title effectively.

8 Point to the outer edge of the title placeholder so that the ⊕ pointer displays. Drag the title placeholder down and to the left so that its lower left corner aligns with the lower left corner of the slide. Release the mouse button, and then compare your slide with Figure 3.6.

The brown background of the floor provides good contrast for the title text.

Figure 3.6

Workshop

Overlaying Text on a Picture

When you insert a picture on a slide background, it is a good idea to choose a picture that has a solid area in which you can overlay a text box or title. For example, in the picture that you inserted on Slide 4, the lower left corner has a brown area that provides good contrast for light-colored text. When the picture that you choose does not contain a solid area, you can create one by filling the text box with color.

9 Display **Slide 5**, and then insert a **New Slide** with the **Title Only** layout.

10 On the **Design tab**, in the **Background group**, click the **Hide Background Graphics** check box, and then click the **Background Styles** button. Click **Format Background**. Under **Fill**, click the **Picture or texture fill** option button. Under **Insert from**, click **File**. Navigate to your student files, click **p3A_Family_Room**, and then click **Insert**. Under **Stretch options**, change as necessary the **Left**, **Right**, **Top**, and **Bottom Offsets** to **0%**. **Close** the **Format Background** dialog box to format the slide background with the picture.

11 In the title placeholder, type **Family Room** Select the text, and then on the Mini toolbar, click the **Font Color button arrow** to display the **Theme Colors gallery**. In the first row, click the first color, **Black**, **Background 1**. On the Mini toolbar, click the **Align Text Right** button .

12 Point to the outer edge of the placeholder to display the pointer, and then drag the placeholder up and to the right so that its upper right corner aligns with the upper right corner of the slide. Compare your slide with Figure 3.7.

Figure 3.7

13 Display **Slide 8**. Using the process that you practiced in **Step 10**, insert the picture **p3A_Community** on the background of **Slide 8**.

Notice that the background does not provide sufficient contrast for the slide title to be easily read. You can apply a Shape Style to the title placeholder so that the text is visible.

14 Click in the title placeholder, and then click the **Format tab**. In the **Shape Styles group**, click the **More** button ⬇. In the second row of the **Shape Styles gallery**, click the third style—**Colored Fill – Accent 2**.

15 Point to the outer edge of the placeholder to display the ⊕ pointer, and then drag the placeholder down so that its bottom edge aligns with the bottom of the slide. Click outside of the placeholder, and then compare your slide with Figure 3.8.

Figure 3.8

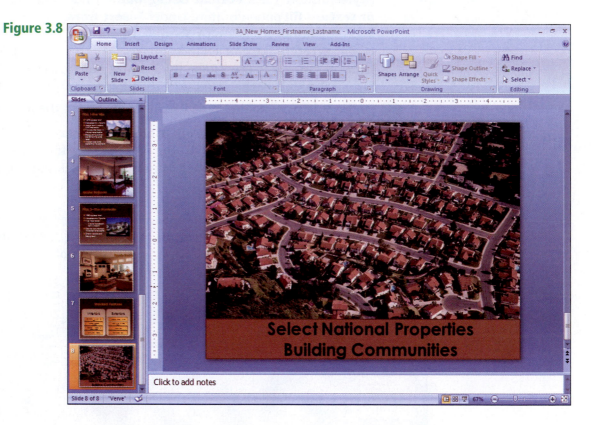

16 **Save** 💾 your presentation.

Activity 3.4 Applying a Background Fill Color and Resetting a Slide Background

1 Display **Slide 1**, and then click the **Design tab**. In the **Background group**, click the **Background Styles** button, and then click **Format Background**. In the **Format Background** dialog box, if necessary, click the Solid Fill option button, and then click the **Color** button 🎨▾. Under **Theme Colors**, in the last row, click the second color—**Black**, **Text 1**, **Lighter 5%**. Click **Close**.

The solid fill color is applied to the slide background.

2 On the **Design tab**, in the **Background group**, click the **Background Styles** button. Below the gallery, click **Reset Slide Background**.

After making many changes to a slide background, you may decide that the original theme formatting best displays the text and graphics on a slide. The Reset Slide Background feature restores the original theme formatting to a slide.

3 **Save** 🖫 the presentation.

Activity 3.5 Modifying Font Themes

Every presentation theme includes a ***font theme*** that determines the font applied to two types of slide text—headings and body. The ***headings font*** is applied to slide titles and the ***body font*** is applied to all other text. Sometimes the heading and body fonts are the same, but are different sizes. In other font themes, the heading and body fonts are different. When you apply a new font theme to the presentation, the text on every slide is updated with the new heading and body fonts.

1 If necessary, display **Slide 1**. Click anywhere in the title placeholder. Click the **Home tab**, and then in the **Font group**, click the **Font button arrow** Calibri (Headings) ▾. Notice that at the top of the Font list, under **Theme Fonts**, *Century Gothic (Headings)* and *Century Gothic (Body)* display as shown in Figure 3.9.

Figure 3.9

Theme fonts

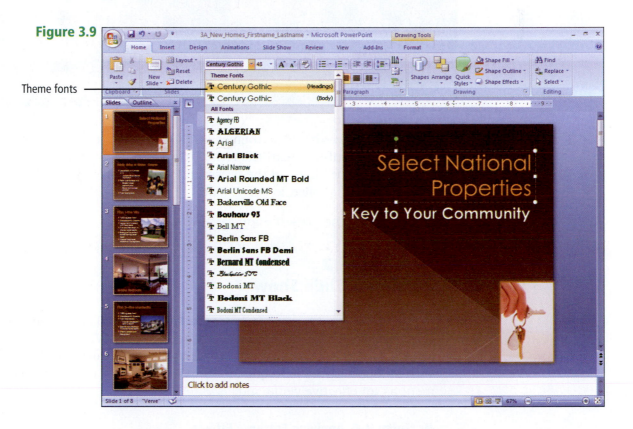

2 Click anywhere on the slide to close the Font list.

3 Click the **Design tab**, and then in the **Themes group**, click the **Fonts** button.

The list displays the name of each font theme and the pair of fonts in the theme. The first and larger font in each pair is the Headings font and the second and smaller font in each pair is the Body font.

4 Scroll the **Theme Fonts** list and notice that the last theme—*Verve*—is selected as shown in Figure 3.10.

Current font theme

Figure 3.10

5 Point to several of the themes and watch as Live Preview changes the title and subtitle text. Click the **Urban** theme, and then scroll through the slides in the presentation, noticing that the font changes have been applied to every slide.

6 **Save**  the presentation.

Objective 2
Animate a Slide Show

Animation effects are used to introduce individual slide elements so that the slide can progress one element at a time. When used correctly, animation effects focus the audience's attention, providing the speaker with an opportunity to emphasize important points using the slide element as an effective visual aid.

Activity 3.6 Applying Entrance Effects

Entrance effects are animations that bring a slide element onto the screen.

1 Display **Slide 1**. Click the **Animations tab**, and then in the

Transition to This Slide group, click the **More** button ▼. Under **Wipes**, click the transition that contains four arrows pointing inward toward a center box—**Box In**. Click the **Transition Speed arrow**, and then click **Medium**. Click the **Apply To All** button.

2 Display **Slide 2**, and then click the bulleted list placeholder. In the **Animations group**, click the **Custom Animation** button. At the top of the displayed **Custom Animation** task pane, click the **Add Effect** button, and then point to **Entrance**. Compare your screen with Figure 3.11.

A list of the most recently used animation effects displays. At the bottom of the list, the *More Effects* option displays.

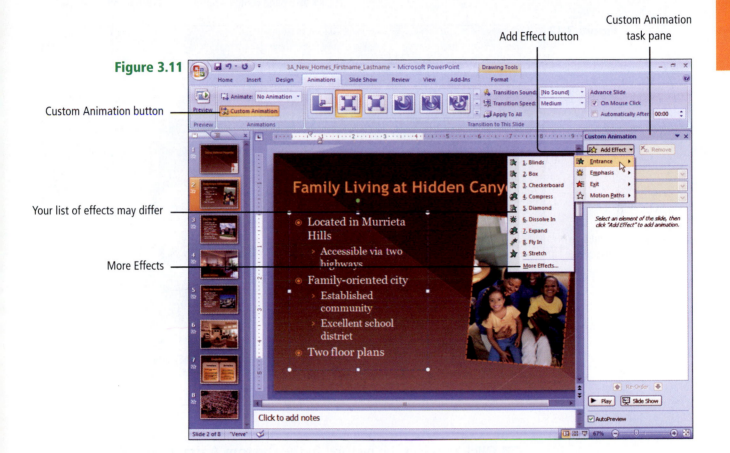

Custom Animation task pane

Add Effect button

Figure 3.11

Custom Animation button

Your list of effects may differ

More Effects

3 Click **More Effects** to display the **Add Entrance Effect** dialog box. Scroll through the list to view the *Basic*, *Subtle*, *Moderate*, and *Exciting* entrance effects.

4 At the bottom of the **Add Entrance Effect** dialog box, if necessary, click to select the **Preview Effect** check box. Click several of the effects in each of the four categories to view the animation.

5 Under **Basic**, click **Blinds**, and then click **OK**. Compare your screen with Figure 3.12.

Notice that the numbers *1, 2,* and *3* display to the left of the bulleted list placeholder, indicating the order in which the bullet points will display. For example, the first bullet point and its subordinate bullet are both numbered *1*. Thus, both will display at the same time.

In the task pane, the **custom animation list** indicates that an animation effect has been applied to the selected item. The custom animation list displays the animation sequences for a slide. The mouse image next to item 1 in the custom animation list indicates that the animation will display the bulleted list placeholder text when the left mouse button is clicked or when the $\boxed{\text{Spacebar}}$ is pressed. Below item 1, a button with two downward-pointing arrows displays. This is the *Click to expand contents* button, which when clicked, displays the animation for bullet points 1, 2, and 3.

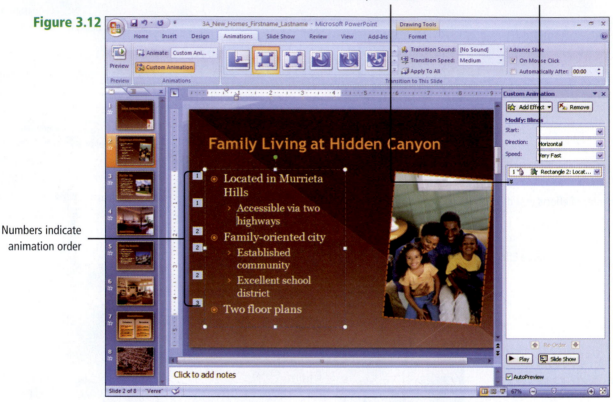

Click to expand contents button   Custom animation list

Figure 3.12

Numbers indicate
animation order

6 Click to select the picture. In the **Custom Animation** task pane, click the **Add Effect** button, point to **Entrance**, and then click **More Effects**. In the displayed **Add Entrance Effect** dialog box, under **Basic**, click **Dissolve In**, and then click **OK**.

The task pane displays item number 4 in the custom animation list, and the number 4 also displays on the slide next to the picture. These numbers only display when the Custom Animation task pane is open.

7 At the bottom of the task pane, click the **Play** button.

For the active slide only, the slide transition and each animation display. Additionally, the task pane indicates the number of seconds that elapse with each animation. This is a good way to test the animations you have applied to a single slide, without switching to Slide Show view.

8 **Save** 💾 the presentation.

More Knowledge

Removing Animation Effects

You can remove animation that you have applied to a slide element by clicking the element in the Custom Animation task pane, and then clicking the Remove button. If you have applied an animation effect to a slide element, and then change your mind and decide to apply a different one, be sure to remove the animation that you do not wish to use. Otherwise, when you view your slide show, all of the animation effects will display one after another.

Activity 3.7 Setting Effect and Timing Options

After animation is applied, you can set *effect options*. Using effect options, you can change the direction of the effect and play a sound when an animation takes place. Effect options also enable you to control the levels of text that display. For example, you can animate text by first-level paragraphs, so that first-level bullet points and their subordinate text display all at once. Or, you can animate text by second-, third-, fourth-, or fifth-level paragraphs so that each bullet on the slide, regardless of level, displays individually. Finally, you can use the effect options to control how text displays when the next animation sequence occurs. For example, after you have discussed a bullet point, you can click the mouse button to display the next point and dim the previous point, thus keeping the audience focused on the new bullet point.

1 With **Slide 2** displayed, click in the bulleted list placeholder. If necessary, display the Custom Animation task pane by clicking the Custom Animation button, in the Animations group.

2 In the **custom animation list**, notice that item 1 is selected and a downward-pointing arrow displays to the right of the item. In the **custom animation list**, click the **item 1 arrow**, and then point to **Effect Options**, as shown in Figure 3.13.

Figure 3.13

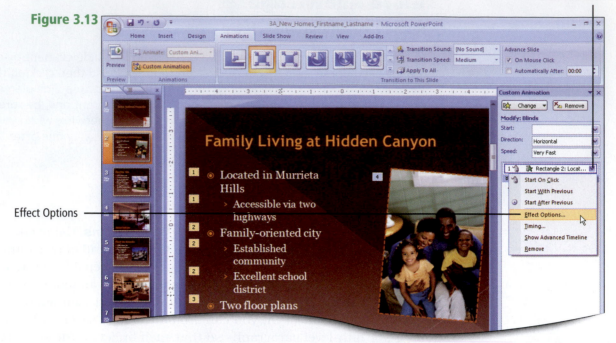

Item 1 arrow

Effect Options

[3] Click **Effect Options** to display the **Blinds** dialog box.

When you click the Effect Options command, the dialog box that displays is named according to the applied animation.

[4] In the **Blinds dialog box**, if necessary, click the **Effect tab**. Under **Enhancements**, click the **After animation arrow**.

Use the After Animation options to choose how the text will display after it is animated and you click the mouse button. The default—*Don't Dim*—keeps the text onscreen without any changes. You can dim the text by choosing a color that blends with the slide background, or you can hide the text so that it does not display at all.

[5] In the row of colors, click the **fifth color**, as shown in Figure 3.14, and then click **OK** to apply the effect option.

Figure 3.14

After animation arrow

Click this color

---

6 Click to select the picture. Near the top of the **Custom Animation** task pane, under **Modify: Dissolve In**, click the **Start arrow** to display three options—On Click, With Previous, and After Previous.

The *On Click* option begins the animation sequence for the selected slide element when the mouse button is clicked or the ⌴Spacebar⌴ is pressed. The *With Previous* option begins the animation sequence at the same time as the item preceding it in the custom animation list. The *After Previous* option begins the animation sequence for the selected slide element immediately after the completion of the previous animation or transition.

7 Click **After Previous**. In the **Custom Animation** task pane, under **Modify: Dissolve In**, click the **Speed arrow**, and then click **Fast**. Compare your task pane with Figure 3.15.

Figure 3.15

Change Start option

Change Speed

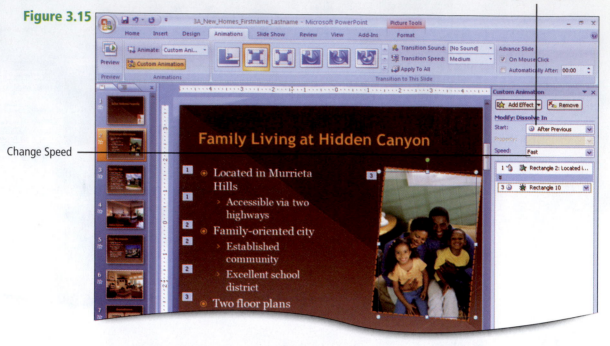

8 In the **Custom Animation** task pane, click **Play** to view the animation applied to the slide.

9 Display **Slide 4**, and then click in the title placeholder. In the **Custom Animation** task pane, click **Add Effect**, and then point to **Entrance**. Click **More Effects**. Under **Basic**, click **Fly In**, and then click **OK**.

10 In the **Custom Animation task pane**, click the **Start arrow**, and then click **After Previous** so that the title displays immediately after the slide transition. If necessary, click the **Direction arrow**, and then click **From Bottom**. In the **Custom Animation** task pane, click **Play** to view the animation applied to the slide.

11 Display **Slide 6**, and then click in the title placeholder. In the **Custom Animation** task pane, click **Add Effect**, and then point to **Entrance**.

Recall that the Animation Effects list displays the most recently applied animations.

12 In the **Animation Effects list**, click **Fly In**. Click the **Start arrow**, and then click **After Previous**. Click the **Direction arrow**, and then click **From Top**. In the **Custom Animation** task pane, click **Play** to view the animation applied to the slide.

13 **Close** ☒ the **Custom Animation** task pane, and then **Save** 🖫 the presentation.

Workshop

Applying Animation Effectively

It is not necessary to animate every item on every slide in your presentation. Too much animation can distract your audience by focusing their attention on what the presentation is going to do instead of the message that you are trying to convey. Remember, the purpose of animation is to draw attention to important text and graphics!

Activity 3.8 Applying Animation to a SmartArt Graphic

The most efficient method of animating a SmartArt graphic is to use one of the choices in the Animate list. Your animation choice can be modified using the Custom Animation task pane.

1 Display **Slide 7**, and then click anywhere in the *Interiors/Exteriors* SmartArt graphic to select it.

2 On the **Animations tab**, in the **Animations group**, click the **Animate arrow** to display the Animate list, as shown in Figure 3.16.

Animate arrow

Figure 3.16

Animate list

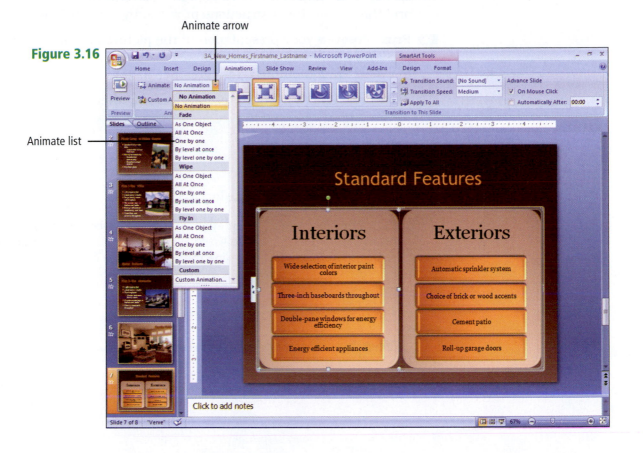

3 Point to several of the **Animate** options and notice as Live Preview displays the animation effects.

4 Under **Wipe**, click **By level at once**.

The *By level at once* option animates all shapes at the same level at the same time. In this case, the light-colored Interiors and Exteriors boxes will display at the same time, and then all of the gold boxes will display.

5 Click the **Slide Show tab**. In the **Start Slide Show group**, click **From Current Slide** to view the animation on Slide 7. Press [Spacebar] to advance through the SmartArt graphic animation effects. After the animations for Slide 7 are complete, press [Esc] to end the slide show and return to the presentation.

6 In the **Start Slide Show group**, click **From Beginning**, and then view your presentation, clicking the mouse button to advance through the slides. Notice the animation that is applied to each slide, and then when the black slide displays, click the mouse button one more time to display the presentation in Normal view.

7 Insert a **Header and Footer** for the **Notes and Handouts**. Include the **Date and time updated automatically**, the **Page number**, and a **Footer** with the file name **3A_New_Homes_Firstname_Lastname**

8 Check your *Chapter Assignment Sheet* or *Course Syllabus* or consult your instructor to determine if you are to submit your assignments on paper or electronically. To submit electronically, go to Step 10, and then follow the instructions provided by your instructor.

9 **Print Preview** your presentation. If the pictures on the background of Slides 4, 6, and 8 do not display, Print Preview your presentation in Color. Print **Handouts, (4 slides per page)**.

10 **Save** the changes to your presentation, and then **Close** the presentation.

More Knowledge
Showing Selected Slides During a Slide Show

When you are delivering a presentation, you can right-click to display the shortcut menu, and then point to Go to Slide to view a list of the slides in the presentation. Then, click the slide that you want to display.

 You have completed Project 3A

Project 3B **Developments**

In Activities 3.9 through 3.14, you will add a table and two charts to a presentation that Shaun Walker, President of Select National Properties, is creating to apprise investors of the status of several new residential developments. Your completed presentation will look similar to Figure 3.17.

For Project 3B, you will need the following file:

p3B_Developments

You will save your presentation as
3B_Developments_Firstname_Lastname

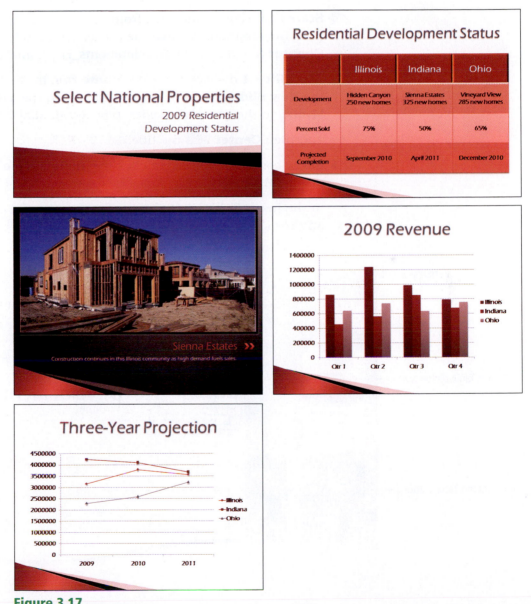

Figure 3.17
Project 3B—Developments

Objective 3
Create and Modify Tables

A *table* is a format for information that organizes and presents text and data in columns and rows. The intersection of a column and row is a *cell* and is the location in which you type text in a table.

Activity 3.9 Creating a Table

There are several ways to insert a table. You can create a table in Microsoft Office Word or Excel, and then paste and edit it in PowerPoint. You can also draw a table using the Draw Table pointer—a feature that is useful when the rows and columns contain cells of different sizes. You can insert a slide with a Content Layout and then click the Insert Table button, or you can click the Insert tab and then click Table. In this Activity, you will use a Content Layout to create a table.

1 **Start** PowerPoint, and then from your student files, open **p3B_Developments**. **Save** the presentation in your **PowerPoint Chapter 3** folder as **3B_Developments_Firstname_Lastname**

2 With **Slide 1** displayed, on the **Home tab**, in the **Slides group**, click the **New Slide** button to insert a slide with the **Title and Content** layout. In the title placeholder, type **Residential Development Status** and then **Center** the title.

3 In the content placeholder, click the **Insert Table** button to display the Insert Table dialog box, as shown in Figure 3.18.

In the Insert Table dialog box, you can enter the number of columns and rows that you want the table to contain.

Figure 3.18

Insert Table dialog box

Insert Table button

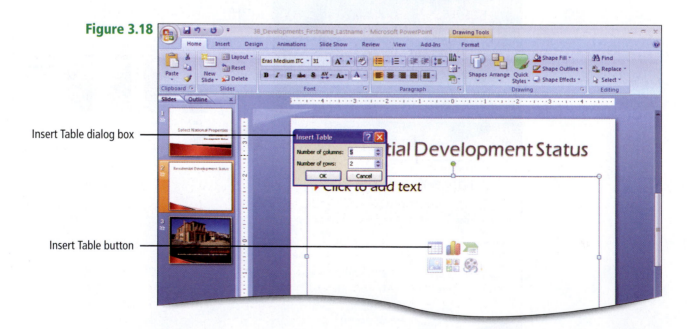

4 In the **Insert Table** dialog box, in the **Number of columns box** type **3** and then press `Tab`. In the **Number of rows** box type **2** and then compare your dialog box with Figure 3.19.

Figure 3.19

3 columns
2 rows

5 Click **OK** to create a table with three columns and two rows. Notice that the insertion point is blinking in the upper left cell of the table.

The table extends from the left side of the content placeholder to the right side and the three columns are equal in width. By default, a style is applied to the table.

6 With the insertion positioned in the first cell of the table, type **Illinois** and then press `Tab`.

Pressing `Tab` moves the insertion point to the next cell in the same row. If the insertion point is positioned in the last cell of a row, pressing `Tab` moves the insertion point to the first cell of the next row.

Alert!

Did you press `Enter` instead of `Tab`?

In a table, pressing `Enter` creates another line in the same cell, similar to the way you add a new bullet point in a content placeholder. If you press `Enter` by mistake, you can remove the extra line by pressing `←Bksp`.

7 With the insertion point positioned in the second cell of the first row, type **Indiana** and then press `Tab`. Type **Ohio** and then press `Tab` to move the insertion point to the first cell in the second row, and then compare your table with Figure 3.20.

Figure 3.20

Type this text

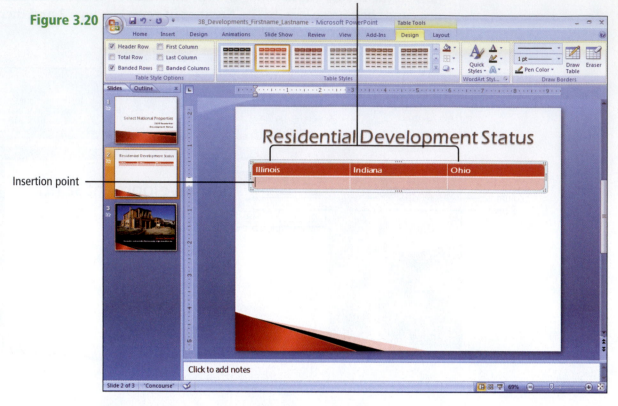

Insertion point

8 With the insertion positioned in the first cell of the second row, type **Hidden Canyon** and then press ⏎ to create a second line in the cell. Type **250 new homes** and then press ⭾. Type **Sienna Estates** and then press ⏎ to create a second line in the cell. Type **325 new homes** and then press ⭾. Type **Vineyard View** and then press ⏎. Type **285 new homes** and then press ⭾ to insert a new blank row.

When the insertion point is positioned in the last cell of a table, pressing ⭾ inserts a new blank row at the bottom of the table.

9 In the first cell of the third row, type **September 2010** and then press ⭾. Type **April 2011** and then press ⭾ Type **December 2010** and then compare your table with Figure 3.21.

Figure 3.21

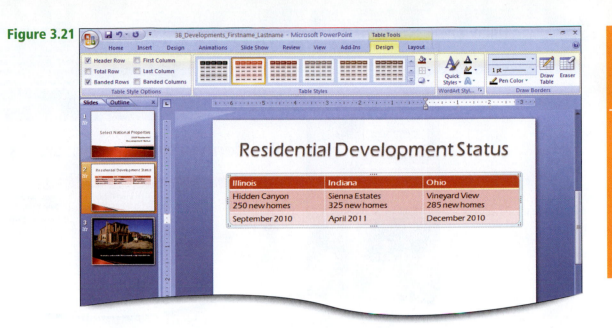

Alert! Did you add an extra row to the table?

Recall that when the insertion point is positioned in the last cell of the table, pressing Tab inserts a new blank row. If you inadvertently inserted a blank row in the table, on the Quick Access Toolbar, click Undo.

10 Save 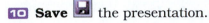 the presentation.

Activity 3.10 Modifying the Layout of a Table

You can modify the layout of a table by inserting or deleting rows and columns, changing the alignment of the text in a cell, adjusting the height and width of the entire table or selected rows and columns, and by merging multiple cells into one cell.

1 Click in any cell in the first column, and then click the **Layout tab**. In the **Rows & Columns group**, click the **Insert Left** button.

A new first column is inserted and the width of the columns is adjusted so that all four columns are the same width.

2 Click in the first cell in the *second row*, and then type **Development** Click in the first cell in the third row, type **Projected Completion** and then compare your table with Figure 3.22.

Figure 3.22

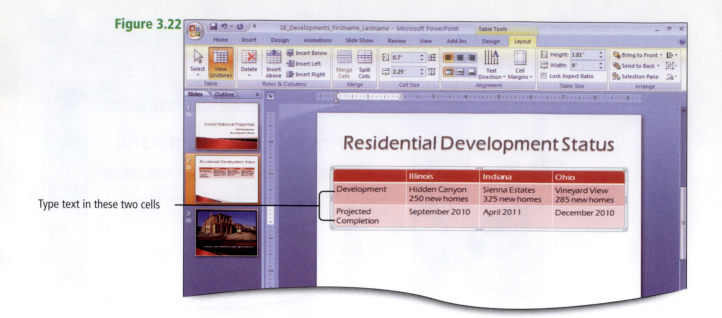

Type text in these two cells

3 With the insertion point positioned in the third row, on the **Layout tab**, in the **Rows & Columns group**, click the **Insert Above** button to insert a new third row. In the first cell type **Percent Sold** and then press ⌷Tab⌷. Type the remaining three entries, pressing ⌷Tab⌷ to move from cell to cell: **75% 50%** and **65%**

More Knowledge

Deleting Rows and Columns

To delete a row or column from a table, click in the row or column that you want to delete. Click the Layout tab, and in the Rows & Columns group, click Delete. In the displayed list, click Delete Columns or Delete Rows.

4 At the center of the lower border surrounding the table, point to the four dots—the sizing handle—to display the ⌷↕⌷ pointer, as shown in Figure 3.23.

When you drag the pointer down, an outline of the table displays, indicating the new size of the table.

Figure 3.23

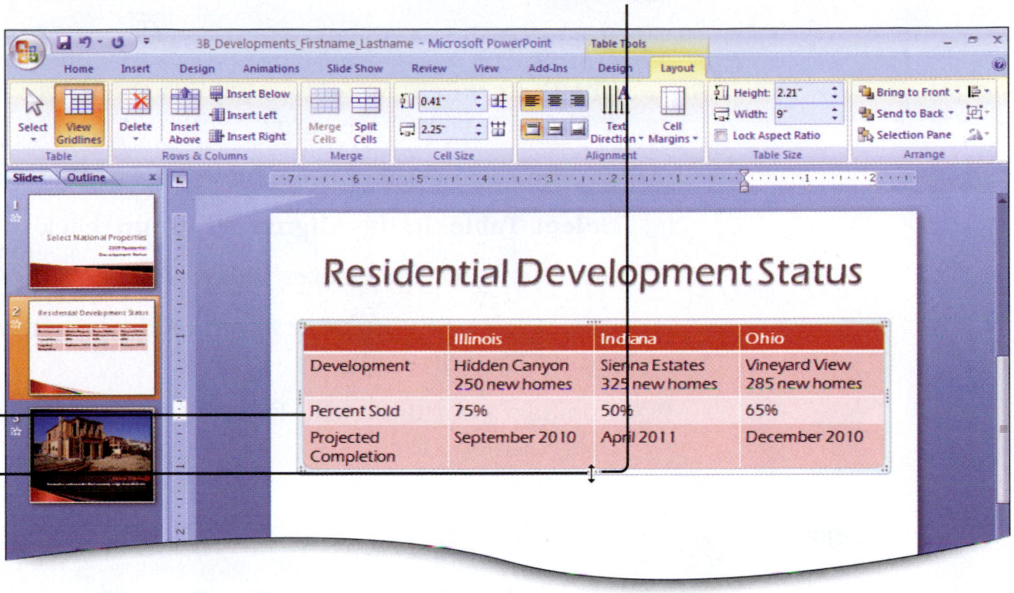

Sizing handle

Inserted row

Vertical Resize pointer

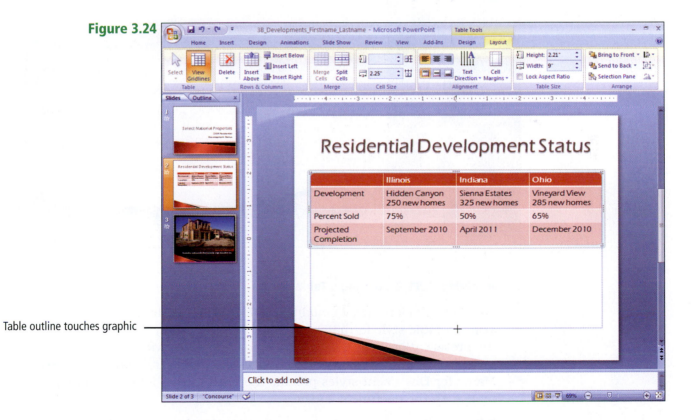

5 Drag down until the lower left corner of the table outline touches the graphic in the lower left corner of the slide as shown in Figure 3.24, and then release the mouse button to size the table.

Figure 3.24

Table outline touches graphic

6 Click in the first cell of the table. On the **Layout tab**, in the **Cell Size group**, click the **Distribute Rows** ⊞ button.

The Distribute Rows option adjusts the height of the rows in the table so that they are equal.

7 On the **Layout tab**, in the **Table group**, click **Select**, and then click **Select Table**. In the **Alignment group**, click the **Center** button ☰, and then click the **Center Vertically** button ⊟.

All of the text in the table is centered horizontally and vertically within the cells.

8 Compare your table with Figure 3.25, and then **Save** 💾 your presentation.

Figure 3.25

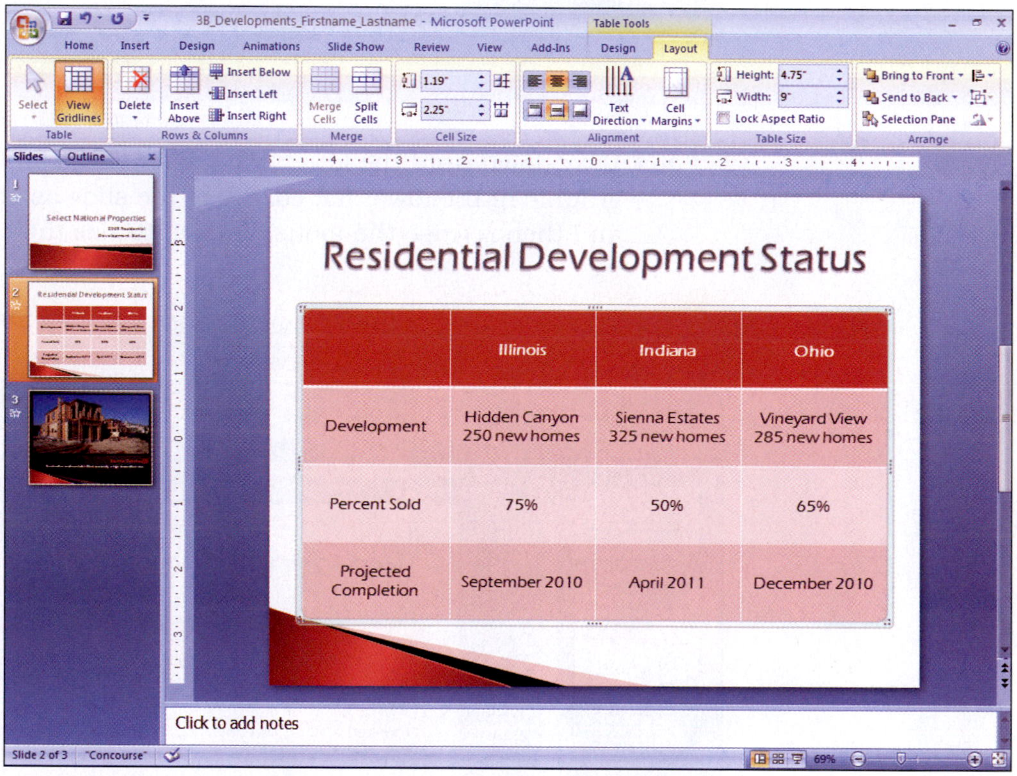

Activity 3.11 Modifying a Table Design

The most efficient way to modify the design of a table is to apply a *table style*. A table style formats the entire table so that it is consistent with the presentation theme. There are color categories within the table styles—Best Match for Document, Light, Medium, and Dark. The Best Match for Document styles provide the best choices for coordinating the table with the document theme.

1 Click in any cell in the table. Click the **Design tab**, and then in the **Table Styles group**, click the **More** button ▼. In the displayed **Table Styles gallery**, point to several of the styles to Live Preview the style.

2 Under **Best Match for Document**, click the second button—
Themed Style 1 – Accent 1—to apply the style to the table.

3 On the **Design tab**, in the **Table Style Options group**, click to clear
the **Banded Rows** check box. Notice that each row except the header
row displays in the same color.

The check boxes in the Table Style Options group control where
Table Style formatting is applied.

4 Click again to select the **Banded Rows** check box.

5 Move the pointer outside of the table so that is positioned to the left
of the first row in the table to display the ➡ pointer, as shown in
Figure 3.26.

Figure 3.26

Right-pointing Row Select arrow

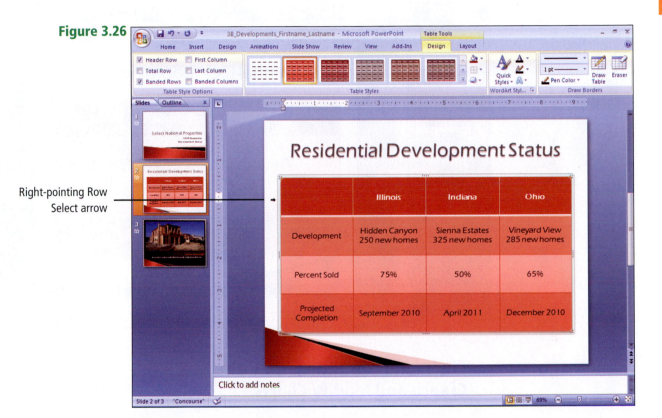

6 With the ➡ pointer pointing to the first row in the table, click the
mouse button to select the entire row so that you can apply formatting to the selection. Move the pointer into the selected row, and
then right-click to display the Mini toolbar and shortcut menu. On
the Mini toolbar, change the **Font Size** to **28**.

More Knowledge

Selecting Columns

To select an entire column, position the pointer above the column that you
want to select to display the ⬇ pointer, and then click to select the column.

7 Verify that the first row is still selected. Click the **Design tab**, and then in the **Table Styles group**, click the **Effects** button. Point to **Cell Bevel**, and then under **Bevel**, click the first bevel—**Circle**.

The Bevel effect is applied to the first row in the table.

8 Click in a blank area of the slide, and then compare your slide with Figure 3.27. **Save** the presentation.

Figure 3.27

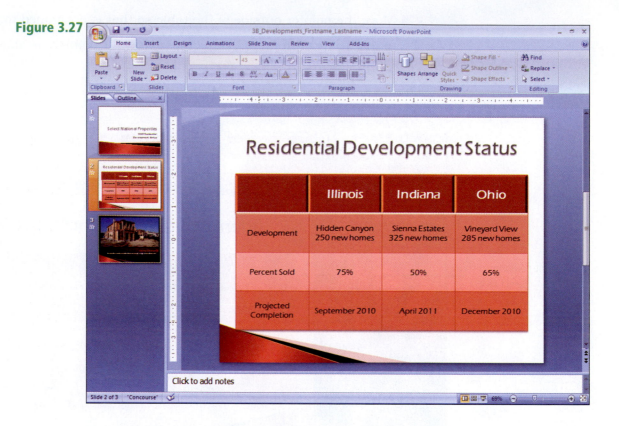

Objective 4
Create and Modify Charts

A *chart* is a graphic representation of numeric data and is often easier to understand than a table of numbers. Chart types frequently used in presentations include bar and column charts, pie charts, and line charts. When you create a chart in PowerPoint, the chart data is stored in an Excel worksheet that is incorporated in the PowerPoint file.

Activity 3.12 Creating a Column Chart and Applying a Chart Style

A *column chart* is useful for illustrating comparisons among related numbers. In this activity you will create a column chart that compares the quarterly 2009 revenue generated by the Residential Development Sector of Select National Properties.

1 Display **Slide 3**, and then add a **New Slide** with the **Title and Content** layout. In the title placeholder, type **2009 Revenue** and then **Center** the title.

2 In the content placeholder, click the **Insert Chart** button to display the **Insert Chart** dialog box. Drag the scroll box to view the types of charts that you can insert in your presentation, and then on the left side of the dialog box, if necessary, click Column.

3 Point to the first chart to display the ScreenTip *Clustered Column*, and then if necessary, click to select it. Compare your screen with Figure 3.28.

Figure 3.28

Clustered Column chart

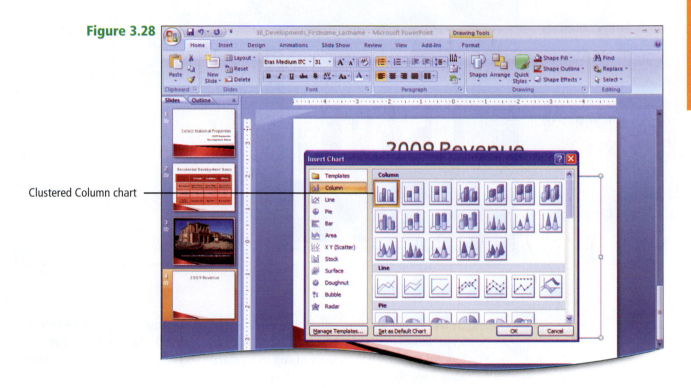

4 Click **OK**, and then compare your screen with Figure 3.29.

On the left side of your screen, the PowerPoint window displays a column chart. On the right side of your screen, a Microsoft Office Excel worksheet displays containing vertical columns and horizontal rows. Recall that the intersection of a column and a row forms a small rectangular box referred to as a cell. A cell is identified by the intersecting column letter and row number, which forms the **cell reference**.

The worksheet contains sample data in a data range outlined in blue, from which the chart in the PowerPoint window is generated. You can include additional data by dragging the lower right corner of the data range, and you can replace the sample data to update the chart. The column headings—*Series 1*, *Series 2*, and *Series 3* display in the chart **legend** and the row headings—*Category 1*, *Category 2*, *Category 3*, and *Category 4*—display as **category labels**. The legend identifies the patterns or colors that are assigned to the categories in the chart. The category labels display along the bottom of the chart to identify the categories of data.

Figure 3.29

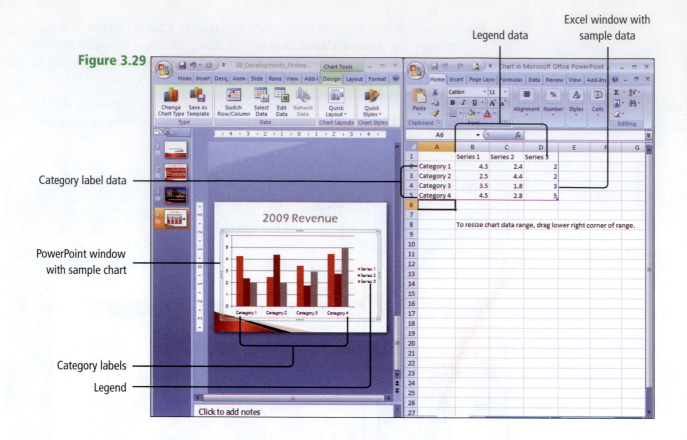

Excel window with sample data

Legend data

Category label data

PowerPoint window with sample chart

2009 Revenue

Category labels

Legend

To resize chart data range, drag lower right corner of range.

5   In the Excel window, click in cell **B1**, which contains the text *Series 1*. Type **Illinois** and then press Tab to move to cell **C1**. Notice that the legend in the PowerPoint chart is updated to reflect the change in the Excel worksheet.

6   In cell **C1**, which contains the text *Series 2*, type **Indiana** and then press Tab to move to cell **D1**, which contains the text *Series 3*. Type **Ohio** and then press Tab. Notice that cell **A2**, which contains the text *Category 1*, is selected.

The blue box outlining the range of cells defines the area in which you are entering data. When you press tab in the rightmost cell, the first cell in the next row becomes the active cell. Compare your worksheet with Figure 3.30.

Type these column headings

Figure 3.30

Cell A2 selected

Legend updated to reflect Excel data

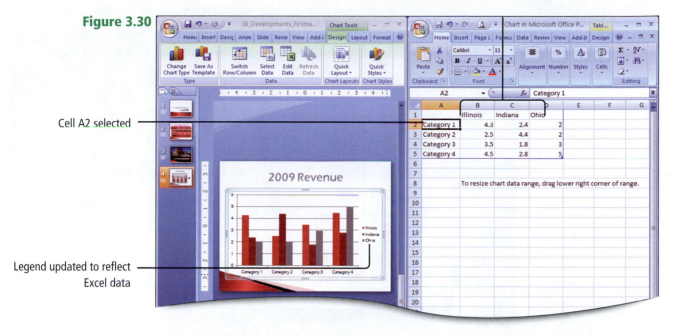

7 Beginning in cell **A2**, type the following data, pressing Tab to move from cell to cell.

	Illinois	Indiana	Ohio
Qtr 1	857300	453228	639852
Qtr 2	1235750	563214	741258
Qtr 3	987653	852147	632145
Qtr 4	789000	674982	

8 In cell **D5**, which contains the value 5, type 753951 and then press Enter so that cell D6 becomes the active cell.

Pressing Enter in the last cell of the blue outlined area maintains the existing data range. Pressing Tab expands the chart data range by including the next row.

9 Compare your worksheet and your chart with Figure 3.31. If you have made any typing errors, click in the cell that you want to change, and then retype the data.

Alert!

Did you press Tab after the last entry?

If you pressed Tab after entering the data in cell D5, you expanded the chart range. In the Excel window, click Undo.

Each of the twelve cells containing the numeric data that you entered is a ***data point***—a value that originates in a worksheet cell. Each data point is represented in the chart by a ***data marker***—a column, bar, area, dot, pie slice, or other symbol in a chart that represents a single data point. Related data points form a ***data series***; for example, there is a data series for *Illinois*, *Indiana*, and *Ohio*. Each data series has a unique color or pattern represented in the chart legend.

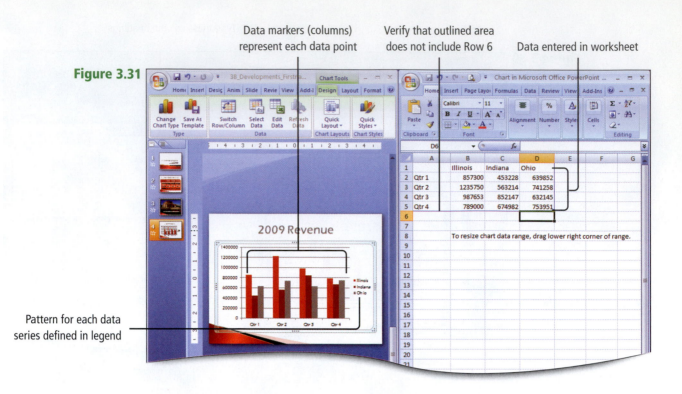

Figure 3.31

Data markers (columns) represent each data point

Verify that outlined area does not include Row 6

Data entered in worksheet

Pattern for each data series defined in legend

10 In the **Excel window**, click the **Office** button 📊, and then click **Close**.

You are not prompted to save the Excel worksheet because the worksheet data is a part of the PowerPoint presentation. When you save the presentation, the Excel data is saved with it.

More Knowledge

Editing the Chart Data After Closing Excel

You can redisplay the Excel worksheet and make changes to the data after you have closed Excel. In PowerPoint, click the chart to select it, and then on the Design tab in the Data group, click Edit Data to redisplay the Excel worksheet.

11 If necessary, click on the chart so that it is selected. Click the **Design tab**, and then in the **Chart Styles group**, click the **More** button ▼.

The chart styles are numbered sequentially and ScreenTips display the style numbers.

12 In the displayed **Chart Styles gallery**, use the ScreenTips to locate **Style 20**. Click **Style 20** to apply the style to the chart.

13 **Save** 💾 the presentation.

Activity 3.13 Deleting Chart Data and Changing the Chart Type

To analyze and compare annual data over a three-year period, an additional chart must be inserted. Recall that there are a number of different types of charts that you can insert in a PowerPoint presentation. Once a chart has been created, you can easily change the chart type. In this Activity, you will create a column chart and then change it to a line chart.

1 With **Slide 4** displayed, add a **New Slide** with the **Title and Content** layout. In the title placeholder, type **Three-Year Projection** and then

Center  the title.

2 In the content placeholder, click the **Insert Chart** button. In the displayed **Insert Chart** dialog box, click the first **Column** chart—**Clustered Column**—and then click **OK**.

3 In the displayed Excel worksheet, click in cell **B1**, which contains the text *Series 1*. Type **Illinois** and then press Tab. Type **Indiana** and then press Tab. Type **Ohio** and then press Tab.

4 Beginning in cell **A2**, type the following data, pressing Tab to move from cell to cell. If you make any typing errors, click in the cell that you want to change, and then retype the data.

	Illinois	Indiana	Ohio
2009	3156951	4238714	2289746
2010	3786521	4095372	2589674
2011	3569782	3679850	3226915

5 In the Excel window, position the pointer over **row heading 5** so that the pointer displays as shown in Figure 3.32.

Figure 3.32

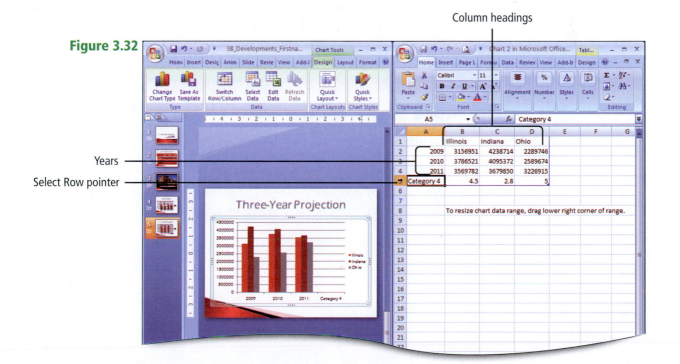

6 With the ➡ pointer displayed, click the right mouse button to select the row and display the shortcut menu as shown in Figure 3.33.

Figure 3.33

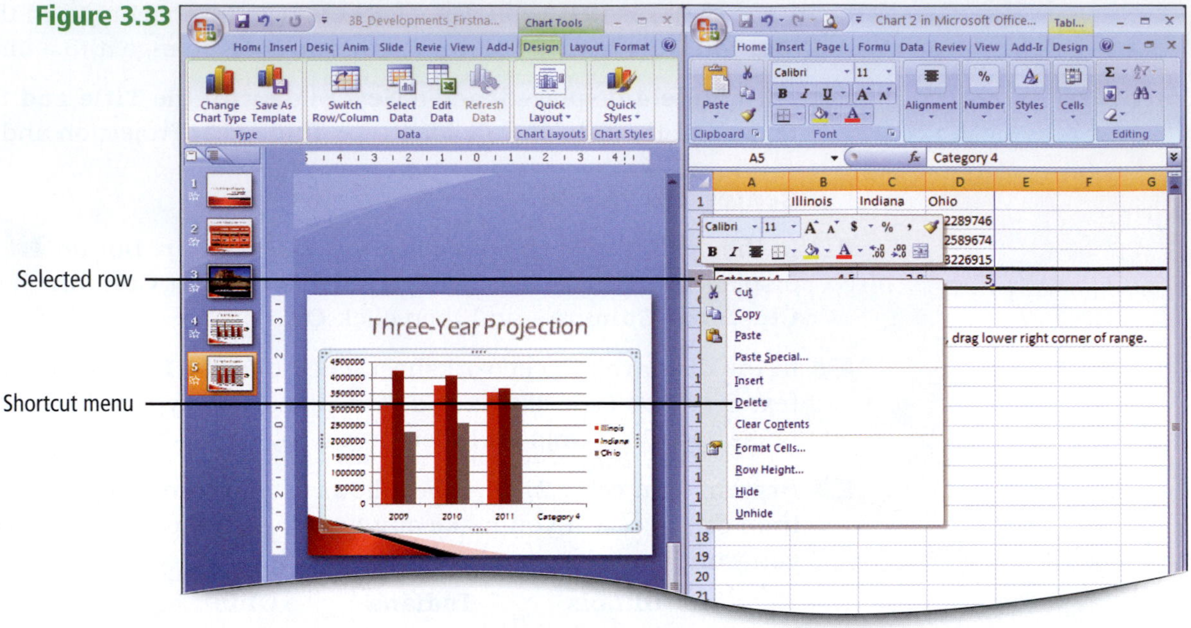

Selected row

Shortcut menu

7 From the shortcut menu, click **Delete** to delete the extra row from the worksheet.

The sample data in the worksheet contains four columns and four rows and the blue outline defining the chart data range is resized. You must delete columns and rows that you do not want to include in the chart. Alternatively, you can resize the data range. You can add additional rows and columns by typing column and row headings and then entering additional data. When data is typed in cells adjacent to the chart range, the range is resized to include the new data.

More Knowledge

Deleting Columns

To delete a worksheet column, position the pointer over the column letter that you want to select so that the ⬇ pointer displays. Right-click to select the column and display the shortcut menu. Click Delete.

8 **Close** ☒ the Excel window.

9 If necessary, click the chart to select it, and then click the **Design tab**. In the **Type group**, click **Change Chart Type**. Under **Line**, click the fourth chart type—**Line with Markers**—and then click **OK**.

The column chart is converted to a *line chart*. A line chart is ideal for this data because line charts are used to show trends over time.

10 In the **Chart Styles group**, click the **More** button ⯆. In the displayed **Chart Styles gallery**, click **Style 26**, and then compare your slide with Figure 3.34.

Figure 3.34

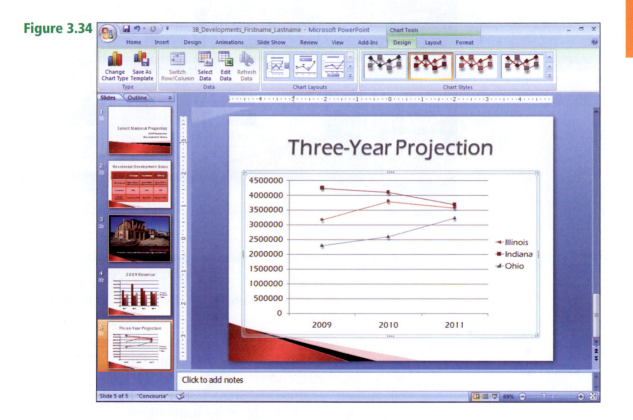

11 **Save** 🖫 the presentation.

Activity 3.14 Animating a Chart

1 Display **Slide 4**, and then click the column chart to select it.

2 Click the **Animations tab**, and then in the **Animations group**, click the **Animate arrow** to display the Animate list as shown in Figure 3.35.

Animate arrow

Figure 3.35

Animate list

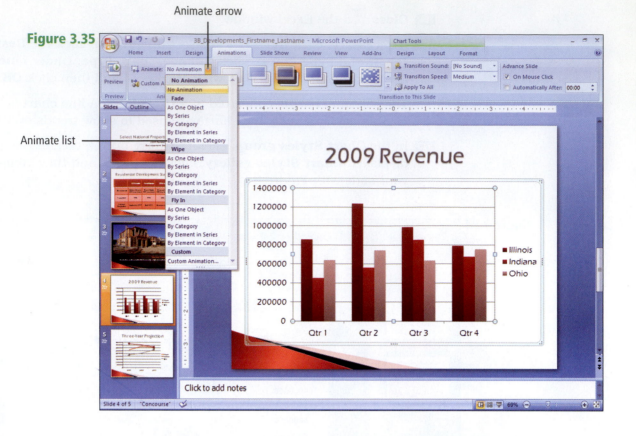

3 Point to several of the **Animate** options to Live Preview the animation effects. Then, under **Wipe**, click **By Category**.

In this chart, the *By Category* option animates the column data markers by Qtr.

4 Click the **Slide Show tab**. In the **Start Slide Show group**, click **From Current Slide** to view the animation on Slide 4. Press Spacebar to display the legend and labels. Press Spacebar again to display the Qtr 1 data. Continue to press Spacebar to advance through the remaining animation effects. After the animations for Slide 4 are complete, press Esc to end the slide show and return to the presentation.

5 Create a **Header and Footer** for the **Notes and Handouts**. Include the **Date and time updated automatically**, the **Page number**, and a **Footer** with the file name **3B_Developments_Firstname_Lastname**

6 Check your *Chapter Assignment Sheet* or *Course Syllabus* or consult your instructor to determine if you are to submit your assignments on paper or electronically. To submit electronically, go to Step 8, and then follow the instructions provided by your instructor.

7 **Print Preview** your presentation, and then print **Handouts, (6 slides per page)**.

8 **Save** the changes to your presentation, and then **Close** the presentation.

End You have completed Project 3B

There's More You Can Do!

From My Computer, navigate to the student files that accompany this textbook. In the folder **02_theres_more_you_can_do_pg1_36**, locate and open the folder for this chapter. Open and print the instructions for this project, which are provided to you in Adobe PDF format.

Try IT!—Compress Pictures

In this Try IT! exercise, you will compress pictures in a presentation in order to reduce file size.

Content-Based Assessments

Summary

In this chapter, you formatted a presentation by applying background styles, inserting pictures on slide backgrounds, and by changing the theme fonts. You enhanced your presentation by applying animation effects and by changing effect and timing options. You practiced creating tables to present information in an organized manner and you used charts to visually represent data.

Key Terms

Animation effects 172

Background style 164

Body font 171

Category labels 191

Cell 182

Cell reference 191

Chart 190

Column chart 190

**Custom animation
  list** 174

Data marker 193

Data point 193

Data series 193

Effect options 175

Entrance effects 172

Font theme 171

Headings font 171

Legend 191

Line chart 197

Table 182

Table style 188

Content-Based Assessments

Matching

Match each term in the second column with its correct definition in the first column. Write the letter of the term on the blank line in front of the correct definition.

_____ **1.** A slide background fill variation that combines theme colors in different intensities.

_____ **2.** A theme that determines the font applied to two types of slide text—headings and body.

_____ **3.** The font applied to slide titles.

_____ **4.** The font applied to all slide text except titles.

_____ **5.** Effects used to introduce individual slide elements so that the slide can progress one element at a time.

_____ **6.** Animations that bring a slide element onto the screen.

_____ **7.** A list that indicates the animation effects applied to slide items.

_____ **8.** Animation options that include changing the direction of an effect and playing a sound when an animation takes place.

_____ **9.** A format for information that organizes and presents text and data in columns and rows.

_____ **10.** The intersection of a column and row.

_____ **11.** Formatting applied to an entire table so that it is consistent with the presentation theme.

_____ **12.** A graphic representation of numeric data.

_____ **13.** A type of chart used to compare data.

_____ **14.** A combination of the column letter and row number identifying a cell.

_____ **15.** A chart element that identifies the patterns or colors that are assigned to the categories in the chart.

A Animation effects

B Background style

C Body font

D Cell

E Cell reference

F Chart

G Column chart

H Custom animation list

I Effect options

J Entrance effects

K Font theme

L Headings font

M Legend

N Table

O Table style

Content-Based Assessments

Fill in the Blank

Write the correct word in the space provided.

1. To help an audience understand numeric data and trends, insert a(n) _____ or a(n) _____ on a slide.

2. The charts most commonly used in PowerPoint presentations are _____, _____, _____, and _____.

3. When the background graphics interfere with slide content, you can _____ the background graphics.

4. When you insert a picture on a slide background, it is a good idea to choose a picture that has a(n) _____ area in which you can overlay a text box or title.

5. When you apply a new font theme to the presentation, the text on every slide is updated with the new _____ and _____ fonts.

6. Animation effects focus the audience's attention, providing the speaker with an opportunity to emphasize an important point using the slide element as an effective _____ _____.

7. The most efficient method of animating a SmartArt graphic is to use one of the choices in the _____ _____.

8. When you are delivering a presentation, you display the shortcut menu, and then point to _____ to view a list of the slides in the presentation.

9. You can modify the layout of a table by inserting or deleting _____ and _____.

10. The document matching styles provide the best choices for coordinating the table with the presentation _____.

11. When you create a chart in PowerPoint, the chart data is stored in a(n) _____ worksheet.

12. In a chart, categories of data are identified by _____ _____.

13. A chart value that originates in a worksheet cell is a(n) _____ _____.

14. A group of related data points is a(n) _____ _____.

15. A column, bar, area, dot, pie slice, or other symbol in a chart that represents a single data point is a(n) _____ _____.

Content-Based Assessments

Skills Review

Project 3C — Seniors

In this project, you will apply the skills you practiced from the Objectives in Project 3A.

Objectives: 1. *Customize Slide Backgrounds and Themes;* **2.** *Animate a Slide Show.*

In the following Skills Review, you will edit a presentation created by Marla Rodriguez, the Marketing Director for Select National Properties, which describes a new real estate development in Illinois. Your completed presentation will look similar to the one shown in Figure 3.36.

> **For Project 3C, you will need the following files:**
>
> p3C_Seniors
> p3C_Walkway
>
> **You will save your presentation as**
> **3C_Seniors_Firstname_Lastname**

Figure 3.36

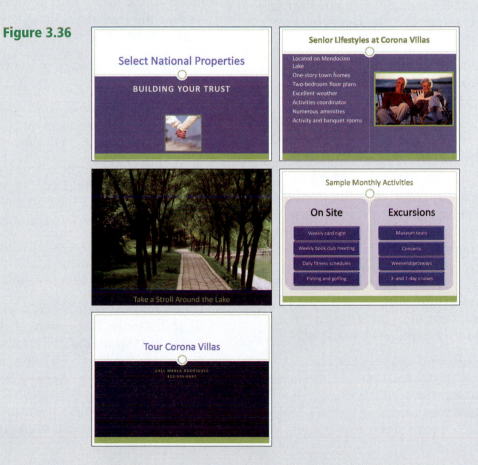

(Project 3C–Seniors continues on the next page)

(Project 3C—Seniors continued)

1. **Start** PowerPoint. From your student files, **Open** the file **p3C_Seniors**. From the **Office** menu, click **Save As**, and then navigate to your **PowerPoint Chapter 3** folder. In the **File name** box, type **3C_Seniors_ Firstname_Lastname** and then click **Save** to save your presentation.

2. Click the **Design tab**, and then in the **Themes group**, click the **More** button to display the Themes gallery. Under **Built-In**, in the first row, click **Civic**. In the **Themes group**, click the **Colors** button, and then click **Office** to change the theme color for the entire presentation. In the **Background group**, click the **Background Styles** button to display the Background Styles gallery. In the second row, right-click **Style 7**. From the displayed shortcut menu, click **Apply to Selected Slides** to apply the style to **Slide 1**.

3. Display **Slide 2**. On the **Design tab**, in the **Background group**, click the **Background Styles** button to display the Background Styles gallery. In the last row, right-click **Style 11**, and then click **Apply to Selected Slides** to apply the style to **Slide 2**.

4. With **Slide 2** displayed, click the **Home tab**. In the **Slides group**, click the **New Slide arrow**, and then click the **Title Only** layout to create a new Slide 3. In the title placeholder, type **Take a Stroll Around the Lake** Click the **Design tab**, and then in the **Background group**, click to select the **Hide Background Graphics** check box so that the background graphics do not display.

5. In the **Background group**, click the **Background Styles** button, and then click **Format Background**. In the displayed **Format Background** dialog box, if necessary, on the left side of the dialog box,

click **Fill**. On the right side of the dialog box, under **Fill**, click the **Picture or texture fill** option button.

6. Under **Insert from**, click the **File** button. In the displayed **Insert Picture** dialog box, navigate to the location where your student files are located, and then click **p3C_Walkway**. Click **Insert**, and then under **Stretch options**, if necessary, change the **Left**, **Right**, **Top** and **Bottom Offsets** to **0%** and then click **Close** to close the **Format Background** dialog box.

7. If necessary, click in the title placeholder. Click the **Format tab**, and then in the **Shape Styles group**, click the **Shape Fill** button. In the last row, click the fourth color—**Dark Blue, Text 2, Darker 50%** so that the text displays against the background.

8. Point to the outer edge of the placeholder to display the ⊕ pointer, and then drag the placeholder down so that its bottom edge aligns with the bottom of the slide. Point to the center, right sizing handle to display the ↔ pointer. Drag to the right so that the right side of the place-holder touches the right edge of the slide. Point to the center, left sizing handle to display the ↔ pointer. Drag to the left so that the left side of the placeholder touches the left edge of the slide.

9. Display **Slide 5**, and then select the subtitle text. On the **Home tab**, click the **Font Color button arrow**. Under **Theme Colors**, in the first row, click the seventh color—**Olive Green, Accent 3**. Click the **Design tab**. In the **Background group**, click the **Background Styles** button, and then click **Format Background**. In

(Project 3C—Seniors continues on the next page)

Skills Review

(Project 3C–Seniors continued)

the **Format Background** dialog box, if necessary, click the **Solid Fill** option button, and then click the **Color** button. Under **Theme Colors**, in the last row, click the fourth color—**Dark Blue, Text 2, Darker 50%**. Click **Close**.

10. Display **Slide 1**. On the **Design tab**, in the **Themes group**, click the **Fonts** button. Click the first font theme—**Office**, and then scroll through the slides in the presentation, noticing that the font changes have been applied to every slide.

11. Click the **Animations tab**, and then in the **Transition To This Slide group**, click the **More** button. Under **Wipes**, click **Box Out**. Click the **Transition Speed arrow**, and then click **Medium**. Click the **Apply To All** button.

12. Display **Slide 2**, and then click the bulleted list placeholder. In the **Animations group**, click the **Custom Animation** button. At the top of the displayed **Custom Animation** task pane, click the **Add Effect** button, and then point to **Entrance**. Click **More Effects** to display the **Add Entrance Effect** dialog box.

13. At the bottom of the **Add Entrance Effect** dialog box, if necessary, click to select the **Preview Effect** check box. Under **Basic**, click **Blinds**, and then click **OK**. In the **Custom Animation** list, click the **item 1 arrow**, and then click **Effect Options** to display the **Blinds** dialog box.

14. In the **Blinds dialog box**, if necessary, click the **Effect tab**. Under **Enhancements**, click the **After animation arrow**. In the row of colors, click the **fifth color**, and then click **OK** to apply the effect option.

15. Click to select the picture. In the **Custom Animation** task pane, click the **Add Effect**

button, point to **Entrance**, and then click **More Effects**. In the displayed **Add Entrance Effect** dialog box, under **Basic**, click **Dissolve In**, and then click **OK**.

16. Near the top of the **Custom Animation** task pane, under **Modify: Dissolve In**, click the **Start arrow**, and then click **After Previous** to display the picture immediately after the last bulleted item displays. In the **Custom Animation task pane**, under **Modify: Dissolve In**, click the **Speed arrow**, and then click **Fast**.

17. Display **Slide 3**, and then click in the title placeholder. In the **Custom Animation** task pane, click **Add Effect**, and then point to **Entrance**. Click **More Effects**. Under **Basic**, click **Fly In**, and then click **OK**. In the **Custom Animation task pane**, click the **Start arrow**, and then click **After Previous** to display the title immediately after the slide transition. If necessary, click the **Direction arrow**, and then click **From Bottom**. **Close** the task pane.

18. Display **Slide 4**, and then select the **SmartArt graphic**. On the **Animations tab**, in the **Animations group**, click the **Animate arrow** to display the Animate list. Under **Wipe**, click **By level at once**.

19. Click the **Slide Show tab**. In the **Start Slide Show group**, click **From Beginning**, and then view your presentation, clicking the mouse button to advance through the slides. Notice the animation that is applied to each slide, and then when the black slide displays, click the mouse button one more time to display the presentation in Normal view.

20. Create a **Header and Footer** for the **Notes and Handouts**. Include only the **Date and time updated automatically**, the **Page**

(Project 3C–Seniors continues on the next page)

Skills Review

(Project 3C–Seniors continued)

number, and a **Footer** with the file name
3C_Seniors_Firstname_Lastname

21. Check your *Chapter Assignment Sheet* or
    Course Syllabus or consult your instructor
    to determine if you are to submit your
    assignments on paper or electronically. To
    submit electronically, go to Step 23, and

then follow the instructions provided by
your instructor.

22. **Print Preview** your presentation, and then
    print **Handouts, (6 slides per page)**.

23. **Save** the changes to your presentation,
    and then **Close** the presentation.

End **You have completed Project 3C**

PowerPoint
chapter three

Skills Review

Project 3D — Commercial Developments

In this project, you will apply the skills you practiced from the Objectives in Project 3B.

Objectives: 3. *Create and Modify Tables;* **4.** *Create and Modify Charts.*

In the following Skills Review, you will add a table and two charts to a presentation that Shaun Walker, President of Select National Properties, is creating to apprise investors of the status of several new commercial developments. Your completed presentation will look similar to the one shown in Figure 3.37.

For Project 3D, you will need the following file:

p3D_Commercial_Developments

You will save your presentation as 3D_Commercial_Developments_Firstname_Lastname

Figure 3.37

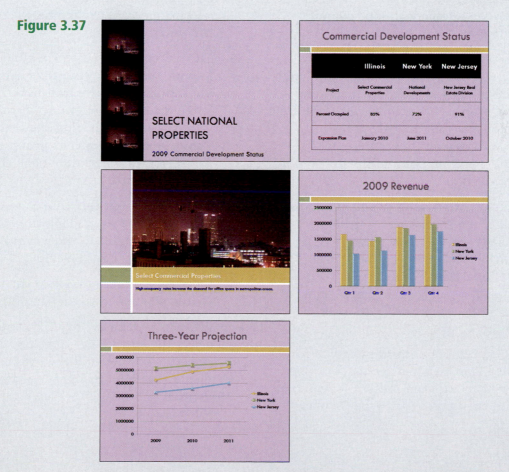

(Project 3D–Commercial Developments continues on the next page)

(Project 3D–Commercial Developments continued)

1. **Start** PowerPoint and from your student files, open **p3D_Commercial_Developments**. **Save** the presentation in your **PowerPoint Chapter 3** folder as 3D_Commercial_Developments_ Firstname_Lastname

2. With **Slide 1** displayed, on the **Home tab**, in the **Slides group**, click the **New Slide** button to insert a slide with the **Title and Content** layout. In the title placeholder, type **Commercial Development Status** and then **Center** the title.

3. In the content placeholder, click the **Insert Table** button. In the displayed **Insert Table** dialog box, in the **Number of columns box**, type **4** and then press [Tab]. In the **Number of rows** box, type **2**. Click **OK** to create a table with four columns and two rows.

4. Click in the second cell of the first row— the first cell will remain blank. Type **Illinois** and then press [Tab]. With the insertion point positioned in the third cell of the first row, type **New York** and then press [Tab]. Type **New Jersey** and then press [Tab] to move the insertion point to the first cell in the second row.

5. With the insertion point positioned in the first cell of the second row, type **Project** and then press [Tab]. Type **Select Commercial Properties** and then press [Tab]. Type **National Developments** and then press [Tab]. Type **New Jersey Real Estate Division** and then press [Tab] to insert a new blank row.

6. In the first cell of the third row, type **Expansion Plan** and then press [Tab]. Type **January 2010** and then press [Tab] Type **June 2011** and then press [Tab]. Type **October 2010**

7. With the insertion point positioned in the third row, click the **Layout tab**. In the **Rows & Columns group**, click the **Insert Above** button to insert a new third row. In the first cell of the newly inserted row, type **Percent Occupied** and then press [Tab]. Type the remaining three entries, pressing [Tab] to move from cell to cell: **85% 72%** and **91%**

8. If necessary, on the **View tab**, in the **Show/Hide group**, click to select the Ruler check box so that the Ruler displays. At the center of the lower border surrounding the table, point to the four dots—the sizing handle—to display the [↕] pointer. Drag down so that the bottom edge of the table is aligned at approximately **3 inches below zero on the vertical ruler**.

9. Click in the first cell of the table. On the **Layout tab**, in the **Cell Size group**, click the **Distribute Rows** button so that the four rows are equal in height. In the **Table group**, click **Select**, and then click **Select Table**. In the **Alignment group**, click the **Center** button, and then click the **Center Vertically** button.

10. Click the **Design tab**, and then in the **Table Styles group**, click the **More** button. Under **Light**, in the second row, click the first style—**Light Style 2**.

11. Move the pointer outside of the table so that is positioned to the left of the first row to display the [→] pointer. Click to select the entire row. Move the pointer into the selected row, and then right-click to display the Mini toolbar and shortcut menu. On the Mini toolbar, change the **Font Size** to **28**.

(Project 3D–Commercial Developments continues on the next page)

Content-Based Assessments

(Project 3D—Commercial Developments continued)

12. With the first row still selected, click the **Design tab**. In the **Table Styles group**, click the **Effects** button. Point to **Cell Bevel**, and then under **Bevel**, click the first bevel—**Circle**.

13. Display **Slide 3**, and then insert a **New Slide** with the **Title and Content Layout**. In the title placeholder type **2009 Revenue** and then **Center** the title. In the content placeholder, click the **Insert Chart** button. In the displayed **Insert Chart** dialog box, point to the first chart to display the ScreenTip *Clustered Column*, and then if necessary, click to select it. Click **OK**.

14. In the **Excel** window, click in cell **B1**, which contains the word *Series 1*. Type **Illinois** and then press Tab to move to cell **C1** containing the word *Series 2*. Type **New York** and then press Tab to move to cell **D1**. Type **New Jersey**

15. Click in cell **A2**, and then type the data from the following table, pressing Tab to move from cell to cell. Be sure that you press Enter after the last entry—1753840—not Tab.

	Illinois	New York	New Jersey
Qtr 1	1657305	1453230	1039855
Qtr 2	1434850	1563360	1141290
Qtr 3	1887640	1852175	1632785
Qtr 4	2286730	1974930	1753840

16. **Close** the Excel window. If necessary, click to select the chart. In the **Chart Tools**, click the **Design tab**, and then in the **Chart Styles group**, click the **More** button. In the displayed **Chart Styles gallery**, click **Style 26**. On the **Animations tab**, in the **Animations group**, click the **Animate**

arrow to display the Animate list. Under **Wipe**, click **As One Object**.

17. With **Slide 4** displayed, insert a **New Slide** with the **Title and Content Layout**. In the title placeholder type **Three-Year Projection** and then **Center** the title. In the content placeholder, click the **Insert Chart** button. In the displayed **Create Chart** dialog box, under **Line**, click **Line with Markers**, and then click **OK**.

18. In the displayed **Excel** worksheet, click in cell **B1**. Type **Illinois** and then press Tab. Type **New York** and then press Tab. Type **New Jersey** and then press Tab.

19. Beginning in cell **A2**, enter the projected revenue for each state and each year as shown in the following table. If you make any typing errors, click in the cell that you want to change, and then retype the data.

	Illinois	New York	New Jersey
2009	4236950	5138726	3289728
2010	4896525	5395318	3589622
2011	5289862	5569857	4026935

20. Position the pointer over **row heading 5** to display the ➡ pointer. Click the right mouse button to select the row. From the displayed shortcut menu, click **Delete** to delete the extra row from the worksheet.

21. **Close** the Excel window. Click the **Design tab**. In the **Chart Styles group**, click the **More** button. In the displayed **Chart Styles gallery**, click **Style 26**.

22. Create a **Header and Footer** for the **Notes and Handouts**. Include only the **Date and**

(Project 3D—Commercial Developments continues on the next page)

Skills Review

(Project 3D–Commercial Developments continued)

time updated automatically, the **Page number**, and a **Footer** with the file name 3D_Commercial_Developments_Firstname_Lastname

23. Check your *Chapter Assignment Sheet* or *Course Syllabus* or consult your instructor to determine if you are to submit your assignments on paper or electronically. To submit electronically, go to Step 25, and then follow the instructions provided by your instructor.

24. **Print Preview** your presentation, and then print **Handouts, (6 slides per page)**.

25. **Save** the changes to your presentation, and then **Close** the presentation.

End **You have completed Project 3D**

Mastering PowerPoint

Project 3E — Civic Center

In this project, you will apply the skills you practiced from the Objectives in Project 3A.

Objectives: 1. *Customize Slide Backgrounds and Themes;* **2.** *Animate a Slide Show.*

In the following Mastering PowerPoint project, you will edit a presentation that Shaun Walker, President of Select National Properties plans to show at a Farrington City Council meeting regarding the renovation of City Hall. Your completed presentation will look similar to Figure 3.38.

> **For Project 3E, you will need the following files:**
>
> p3E_Civic_Center
> p3E_City_Hall

**You will save your presentation as
3E_Civic_Center_Firstname_Lastname**

Figure 3.38

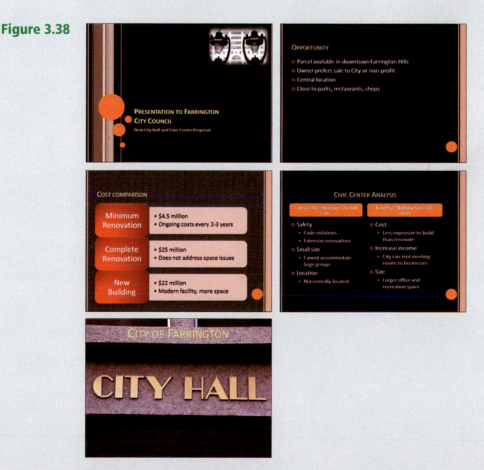

(Project 3E–Civic Center continues on the next page)

Content-Based Assessments

Mastering PowerPoint

(Project 3E–Civic Center continued)

1. **Start** PowerPoint. From your student files, **Open** the file **p3E_Civic_Center**. **Save** the presentation in your **PowerPoint Chapter 3** folder as **3E_Civic_Center_ Firstname_ Lastname**

2. Apply the **Oriel Theme** to the presentation, and then change the presentation **Background** to the solid black **Style 4** for all of the slides in the presentation. Change the **Fonts** theme to the **Office** theme, which includes the *Cambria* and *Calibri* fonts. Display **Slide 3**, and then change the **Background** to **Style 12** using the **Apply to Selected Slides** option.

3. Display **Slide 4**, and then insert a **New Slide** with the **Title Only** layout. In the title placeholder, type **City of Farrington** and then **Center** the title. On the **Design tab**, in the **Background group**, click to select the **Hide Background Graphics** check box so that the background graphics do not display.

4. Change the **Background Style** by inserting a picture on the background using the **Format Background** dialog box. Under **Fill**, click the **Picture or texture fill** option button. From your student files, insert the file **p3E_City_Hall**, and then verify that the **Stretch options Offsets** are set to **0%**. **Close** the **Format Background** dialog box.

5. Select the title text, and then change the **Font Size** to **54**. Drag the title placeholder up and slightly to the right so that the top of the placeholder aligns with the top edge of the slide and the words *City of Farrington* are centered over *City Hall*.

6. Display **Slide 2**, and then click the bulleted list placeholder. Display the **Custom Animation** task pane, and then display the **Add Entrance Effect** dialog box.

Under **Subtle**, click **Expand**, and then click **OK** to apply the animation to the bulleted list.

7. In the **Custom Animation** list, click the **item 1 arrow**, and then click **Effect Options** to display the **Expand** dialog box. In the **Effect tab** of the **Expand dialog box**, under **Enhancements**, click the **After animation arrow**. In the row of colors, click the **third color**, and then click **OK** to apply the effect option.

8. Display **Slide 3**, and then select the **SmartArt graphic**. Display the **Animate** list, and then under **Fade**, click **As One Object**.

9. Display **Slide 5**, and then click in the title placeholder. In the **Custom Animation** task pane, click **Add Effect**, and then point to **Entrance**. Click **More Effects**. Under **Basic**, apply the **Fly In**, effect. In the **Custom Animation task pane**, click the **Start arrow**, and then click **After Previous** so that the title displays immediately after the slide transition. Click the **Direction arrow**, and then click **From Top**. **Close** the task pane.

10. Under **Wipes**, apply the **Split Horizontal In** transition to all the slides in the presentation. View the slide show from the beginning, clicking the mouse button to advance through the slides. Notice the animation that is applied to each slide, and then when the black slide displays, click the mouse button one more time to display the presentation in Normal view.

11. Create a **Header and Footer** for the **Notes and Handouts**. Include only the **Date and time updated automatically**, the **Page number**, and a **Footer** with the file name **3E_Civic_Center_ Firstname_Lastname**

(Project 3E–Civic Center continues on the next page)

Mastering PowerPoint

(Project 3E–Civic Center continued)

12. Check your *Chapter Assignment Sheet* or *Course Syllabus* or consult your instructor to determine if you are to submit your assignments on paper or electronically. To submit electronically, go to Step 14, and then follow the instructions provided by your instructor.

13. **Print Preview** your presentation, and then print **Handouts, (6 slides per page)**.

14. **Save** the changes to your presentation, and then **Close** the presentation.

End **You have completed Project 3E** ———————————————

PowerPoint

chapterthree

Mastering PowerPoint

Project 3F — Forest Glen

In this project, you will apply the skills you practiced from the Objectives in Project 3B.

Objectives: 3. *Create and Modify Tables;* **4.** *Create and Modify Charts.*

In the following Mastering PowerPoint project, you will edit a presentation that the Marketing Department will use to showcase the Forest Glen Lifestyle Center. Your completed presentation will look similar to Figure 3.39.

> **For Project 3F, you will need the following file:**
>
> p3F_Forest_Glen

You will save your presentation as
3F_Forest_Glen_Firstname_Lastname

Figure 3.39

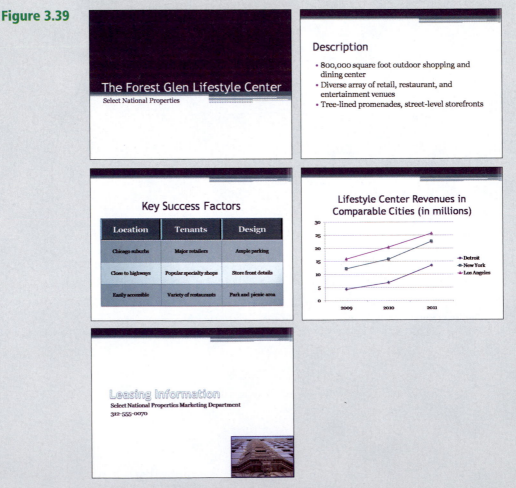

(Project 3F–Forest Glen continues on the next page)

Mastering PowerPoint

(Project 3F–Forest Glen continued)

1. **Start** PowerPoint. From your student files, **Open** the file **p3F_Forest_Glen**. **Save** the file in your **PowerPoint Chapter 3** folder as **3F_Forest_Glen_Firstname_Lastname**

2. Display **Slide 2**, and then insert a **New Slide** with the **Title and Content** layout. In the title placeholder, type **Key Success Factors** and then **Center** the title. In the content placeholder, insert a table with **3 columns** and **4 rows**. Type the following information in the table.

Location	Tenants	Design
Chicago suburbs	Major retailers	Ample parking
Close to highways	Popular specialty shops	Store front details
Easily accessible	Variety of restaurants	Park and picnic area

3. If necessary, display the Ruler. Size the table so that the bottom edge of the table is aligned at approximately **3 inches below zero on the vertical ruler**. On the **Layout tab**, in the **Cell Size group**, click the **Distribute Rows** button so that the four rows are equal in height. Select the table, and then **Center** the text horizontally and vertically in the cells.

4. Apply a **Best Match for Document** table style—**Themed Style 1 – Accent 2**, and in the **Table Style Options**, apply the **Header Row** and **Banded Row** options.

5. Select the first row of the table, change the **Font Size** to **28**, and then apply a **Cell Bevel** effect to the first row—**Circle**.

6. Insert a new slide with the **Title and Content Layout**. In the title placeholder, type **Lifestyle Center Revenues in Comparable Cities (in millions)** and then **Center** the title.

7. In the content placeholder, insert a **Clustered Column** chart, and then replace the data in the Excel window with the data below. Be sure to delete the extra row of data in **Row 5** in the Excel window.

	Detroit	New York	Los Angeles
2009	4.3	12.2	15.9
2010	6.9	15.8	20.4
2011	13.5	22.6	25.7

8. **Close** the Excel window. Select the chart, and then on the **Design tab**, in the **Type group**, click the **Change Chart Type** button. Under **Line**, click **Line with Markers**, and then apply chart **Style 26**.

9. Create a **Header and Footer** for the **Notes and Handouts**. Include only the **Date and time updated automatically**, the **Page number**, and a **Footer** with the file name **3F_Forest_Glen_Firstname_Lastname**

10. Check your *Chapter Assignment Sheet* or *Course Syllabus* or consult your instructor to determine if you are to submit your assignments on paper or electronically. To submit electronically, go to Step 12, and then follow the instructions provided by your instructor.

11. **Print Preview** your presentation, and then print **Handouts, (6 slides per page)**.

12. **Save** the changes to your presentation, and then **Close** the presentation.

End **You have completed Project 3F**

Mastering PowerPoint

Project 3G — Restaurants

In this project, you will apply the skills you practiced from the Objectives in Projects 3A and 3B.

Objectives: 1. *Customize Slide Backgrounds and Themes;* **2.** *Animate a Slide Show;* **3.** *Create and Modify Tables;* **4.** *Create and Modify Charts.*

In the following Mastering PowerPoint project, you will edit a presentation that the president of Select National Properties will make to the National Restaurant Owners Association proposing new restaurant construction in the city of Monroe Heights. Your completed presentation will look similar to Figure 3.40.

For Project 3G, you will need the following files:

New blank PowerPoint presentation
p3G_Tables

You will save your presentation as
3G_Restaurants_Firstname_Lastname

Figure 3.40

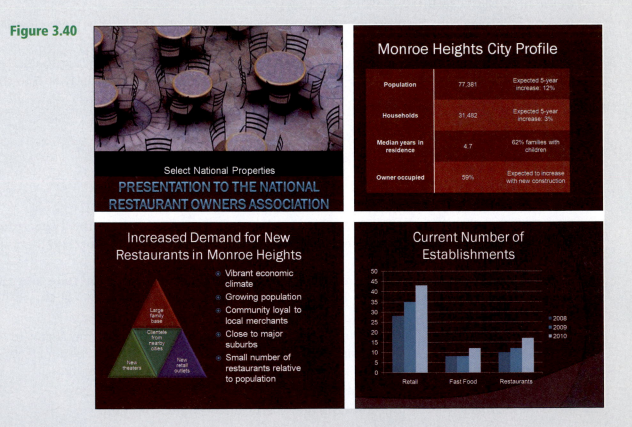

(Project 3G–Restaurants continues on the next page)

Content-Based Assessments

Mastering PowerPoint

(Project 3G—Restaurants continued)

1. **Start** PowerPoint and begin a new blank presentation. In the title placeholder, type **Presentation to the National Restaurant Owners Association** and then in the subtitle placeholder, type **Select National Properties**. **Save** the presentation in your **PowerPoint Chapter 3** folder as **3G_Restaurants_Firstname_Lastname**

2. Apply the **Technic** theme to the presentation, and then change the **Theme Colors** to **Solstice**. Hide the background graphics, and then display the **Format Background** dialog box. Use the **Picture or Texture fill option** to insert the **p3G_Tables** picture on the slide background. Verify that the **Stretch options Offsets** are set to **0%**.

3. Click in the title placeholder, and then on the **Format tab**, click the **Shape Fill** button, and then in the first row of colors, apply the **Brown, Background 2** fill to the title placeholder. In the **Size group**, change the **Height** to **1.5** and the **Width** to **10** and then **Center** the text. Move the title placeholder so that its lower edge aligns with the lower edge of the slide and the left and right edges of the slide and placeholder also align.

4. Click in the subtitle placeholder, and then change the **Shape Fill** color to **Black, Background 1**. Adjust the **Height** to **1.0** and the **Width** to **10** and then **Center** the text and change the **Font Size** to **28**. Drag the subtitle placeholder down so that its lower edge aligns with the top edge of the title placeholder and the left and right edges of the slide and placeholder also align.

5. Insert a **New Slide** with the **Title and Content** layout. Hide the background graphics on this slide.

6. In the title placeholder, type **Monroe Heights City Profile** and then **Center** the title. In the content placeholder, insert a table with **3 columns** and **4 rows**. Type the following table text.

Population	77,381	Expected 5-year increase: 12%
Households	31,482	Expected 5-year increase: 3%
Median years in residence	4.7	62% families with children
Owner occupied	59%	Expected to increase with new construction

7. If necessary, display the Ruler, and then adjust the size of the table so that its lower edge aligns at approximately **3 inches below zero on the vertical ruler**. Select the table, and then **Center** the text horizontally and vertically in the cells. Click **Distribute Rows** so that all of the rows are the same height.

8. Change the table **Design** by changing the **Table Style Options** so that only the **Banded Rows** and **First Column** check boxes are selected. In the **Tables Styles gallery**, under **Dark**, apply **Dark Style 1 – Accent 5**.

9. Add a slide with the **Two Content** layout. In the title placeholder, type **Increased Demand for New Restaurants in Monroe Heights** and then **Center** the title.

10. On **Slide 3**, hide the background graphics. In the placeholder on the left, insert a **SmartArt** graphic. In the **Choose a Smart Graphic** dialog box, click **Pyramid**, click the last pyramid graphic—**Segmented Pyramid**, and then click **OK**.

(Project 3G—Restaurants continues on the next page)

PowerPoint
chapterthree

Mastering PowerPoint

(Project 3G–Restaurants continued)

11. In the top triangle shape, type **Large family base** and then click in the center triangle. Type **Clientele from nearby cities** and then click in the lower left triangle. Type **New theaters** and then click in the lower right triangle. Type **New retail outlets**

12. On the **SmartArt Tools**, click the **Design tab**, and then click **Change Colors**. Under **Colorful**, click the last color set—**Colorful Range – Accent Colors 5 to 6.** In the **SmartArt Styles group**, under **3-D**, apply the fourth effect—**Powder.**

13. In the placeholder on the right, type the following bullet points.

Vibrant economic climate

Growing population

Community loyal to local merchants

Close to major suburbs

Small number of restaurants relative to population

14. Insert a **New Slide** with the **Title and Content** layout. In the title placeholder, type **Current Number of Establishments** and then **Center** the title.

15. In the content placeholder, insert a **Clustered Column** chart. In the **Excel** worksheet, type the following data, deleting extra columns and rows as necessary.

	2008	2009	2010
Retail	28	35	43
Fast Food	8	8	12
Restaurants	10	12	17

16. **Close** Excel, and then apply **Style 3** to the chart. Use the **Animate** list to apply the **Wipe By Category** animation.

17. Apply the **Wipe Down** transition, and then change the **Transition Speed** to **Medium**. Apply the transition setting to all of the slides in the presentation.

18. Display **Slide 3**, and then select the **SmartArt graphic**. Use the **Animate list** to apply the **Fade As One Object** animation. Click the bulleted list placeholder, and then use the **Custom Animation** task pane to apply the **Blinds Entrance Effect**. View the slide show from the beginning.

19. Create a **Header and Footer** for the **Notes and Handouts**. Include only the **Date and time updated automatically**, the **Page number**, and a **Footer** with the file name 3G_Restaurants_ Firstname_Lastname

20. Check your *Chapter Assignment Sheet* or *Course Syllabus* or consult your instructor to determine if you are to submit your assignments on paper or electronically. To submit electronically, go to Step 22, and then follow the instructions provided by your instructor.

21. **Print Preview** your presentation, and then print **Handouts, (4 slides per page)**.

22. **Save** the changes to your presentation, and then **Close** the presentation.

End **You have completed Project 3G**

Mastering PowerPoint

Project 3H—Town Centers

In this project, you will apply the skills you practiced from the Objectives in Projects 3A and 3B.

Objectives: 1. *Customize Slide Backgrounds and Themes;* **2.** *Animate a Slide Show;* **4.** *Create and Modify Charts.*

In the following Mastering PowerPoint Assessment, you will edit a presentation that Randall Thomas, Select National Properties Chief Executive Officer, has created to explain the growth of mixed-use town centers in large cities. Your completed presentation will look similar to Figure 3.41.

For Project 3H, you will need the following files:

New blank PowerPoint presentation
p3H_Definition

You will save your presentation as
3H_Town_Centers_Firstname_Lastname

Figure 3.41

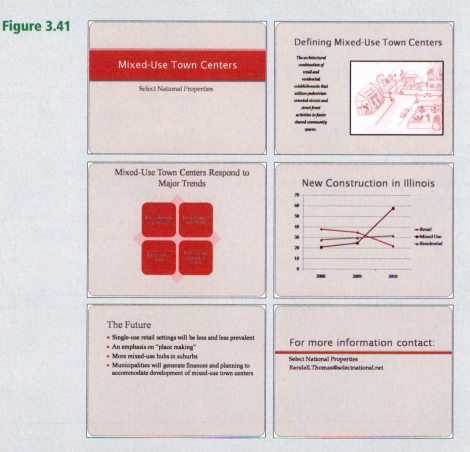

(Project 3H–Town Centers continues on the next page)

Mastering PowerPoint

(Project 3H–Town Centers continued)

1. **Start** PowerPoint and begin a new blank presentation. In the title placeholder, type **Mixed-Use Town Centers** In the subtitle placeholder, type **Select National Properties** and then **Save** the file in your **PowerPoint Chapter 3** folder as 3H_Town_Centers_Firstname_ Lastname

2. Apply the **Equity** theme to the presentation, and then apply **Background Style 2**. Apply the **Apex Fonts Theme** which consists of the *Lucida Sans* and *Book Antiqua* fonts.

3. From your student files, insert all of the slides from the **p3H_Definition** file. (**Hint:** click the **New Slide arrow**, and then click **Reuse Slides**). Display **Slide 2**, and then click in the text on the left side of the slide. Apply the **Compress Entrance Effect**. **Start** the effect **After Previous**, and change the **Speed** to **Medium**.

4. With **Slide 2** still displayed, move the picture so that its lower edge aligns at **2.5 inches below zero**.

5. Display **Slide 3**. Select the SmartArt graphic, and then use the **Animate** list to apply the **Wipe**, **One by one** animation. Apply the **Wipe Left** transition, and then set the **Transition Speed** to **Fast**. Apply the transition settings to all of the slides in the presentation.

6. With **Slide 3** still displayed, insert a **New Slide** with the **Title and Content** layout.

In the title placeholder, type **New Construction in Illinois** and then **Center** the title. In the content placeholder, insert a **Line with Markers** chart, and then enter the following data in the **Excel** worksheet:

	Retail	Mixed Use	Residential
2008	38	21	28
2009	35	25	30
2010	22	58	32

7. Delete the unused row, and then **Close** Excel. Apply **Chart Style 18**, and then view the slide show from the beginning of the presentation.

8. Create a **Header and Footer** for the **Notes and Handouts**. Include only the **Date and time updated automatically**, the **Page number**, and a **Footer** with the file name 3H_Town_Centers_Firstname_Lastname

9. Check your *Chapter Assignment Sheet* or *Course Syllabus* or consult your instructor to determine if you are to submit your assignments on paper or electronically. To submit electronically, go to Step 11, and then follow the instructions provided by your instructor.

10. **Print Preview** your presentation, and then print **Handouts, (6 slides per page)**.

11. **Save** the changes to your presentation, and then **Close** the presentation.

End **You have completed Project 3H**

Mastering PowerPoint

Project 3I—Clients

In this project, you will apply the skills you practiced from all the Objectives in Projects 3A and 3B.

Objectives: 1. *Customize Slide Backgrounds and Themes;* **2.** *Animate a Slide Show;* **3.** *Create and Modify Tables;* **4.** *Create and Modify Charts.*

In the following Mastering PowerPoint Assessment, you will edit a presentation that Randall Thomas, Select National Properties Chief Executive Officer will present to a group of prospective clients. Your completed presentation will look similar to Figure 3.42.

> **For Project 3I, you will need the following files:**
>
> p3I_Clients
> p3I_Building

**You will save your presentation as
3I_Clients_Firstname_Lastname**

Figure 3.42

Mastering PowerPoint

(Project 3I–Clients continued)

1. **Start** PowerPoint. From your student files, **Open** the file **p3I_Clients**. **Save** the file in your **PowerPoint Chapter 3** folder as 3I_Clients_Firstname_Lastname

2. Apply **Background Style 8** to all of the slides in the presentation, and then change the **Fonts Theme** to **Equity**. Apply the **Split Vertical Out** transition to all of the slides in the presentation.

3. Display **Slide 3**, and then in the content placeholder, insert a **SmartArt** graphic. In the **Choose a SmartArt Graphic** dialog box, insert the **Process** type graphic—**Funnel**. On the **Design tab**, in the **Create Graphic group**, click the **Text Pane** button to display the text pane. Type the following text in each of the four bullet points:

   Integrity

   Trust

   Loyalty

   Success

4. **Close** the text pane. Apply the **Fade As one object** animation to the SmartArt graphic.

5. With **Slide 3** displayed, insert a **New Slide** with the **Title Slide** layout. In the title placeholder, type **Quality** and then in the subtitle placeholder, type **Large enough to meet all your needs; small enough to give your project the attention it deserves. Center** the title and subtitle text.

6. With **Slide 4** still displayed, hide the background graphics, and then on the **Background**, insert a picture from your student files—**p3I_Building**. Before closing the **Format Background** dialog box, verify that the **Stretch options Offsets** are set to **0%**.

7. Drag the title placeholder up so that the top edge of the placeholder aligns with the top edge of the slide and the word *Quality* is centered at the intersection of the two buildings. Select **Quality**, and then change the **Font Color** to **Black, Background 1**.

8. Select the subtitle placeholder, and then change the **Shape Fill** color to **Black, Background 1**. Size the placeholder so that it extends from the left edge to the right edge of the slide, and then drag the placeholder down so that its lower edge aligns with the lower edge of the slide.

9. Display **Slide 6**, and then in the content placeholder, insert a **Clustered Column** chart. In the **Excel** worksheet, enter the following data.

	2009	2010	2011
Commercial	318	402	435
Housing	122	257	305
Non-profit	216	268	322

10. Delete the unused row in the worksheet, and then **Close** Excel. Apply chart **Style 42**, and then from the **Animate** list, apply the **Fade By Category** animation.

(Project 3I–Clients continues on the next page)

(Project 3I–Clients continued)

11. Display **Slide 7**, and then in the content placeholder, insert a **Table** with **3 columns** and **4 rows**. Type the following text in the table.

Service	Number	Location
Development	Over 15 million square feet	Throughout Midwest
Property Management	Over 40 properties	Illinois and Indiana
Current Construction	5 million square feet	Illinois and Maine

12. If necessary, display the Ruler. Size the table so that its lower edge aligns at approximately **1 inch below zero on the vertical ruler**. Distribute the rows, and then **Center** the text horizontally and vertically. In the **Tables Styles gallery**, apply **Dark Style 1 – Accent 1**. Select the entire table, and then change the **Font Size** to **28**. With the table still selected, apply the **Circle, Cell Bevel** effect.

13. Display **Slide 8**, and then select the title placeholder. Display the **Custom Animation** task pane, and then apply the **Blinds Entrance Effect**. **Start** the animation **After Previous**, and then change the **Speed** to **Fast**. Apply the same animation effect and settings to the subtitle, and then view the slide show from the beginning.

14. Create a **Header and Footer** for the **Notes and Handouts**. Include only the **Date and time updated automatically**, the **Page number,** and a **Footer** with the file name 3I_Clients_Firstname_Lastname

15. Check your *Chapter Assignment Sheet* or *Course Syllabus* or consult your instructor to determine if you are to submit your assignments on paper or electronically. To submit electronically, go to Step 17, and then follow the instructions provided by your instructor.

16. **Print Preview** your presentation, and then print **Handouts, (4 slides per page)**.

17. **Save** the changes to your presentation, and then **Close** the presentation.

End **You have completed Project 3I** —————————————————————————

Content-Based Assessments

Business Running Case

Project 3J — Business Running Case

In this project, you will apply the skills you practiced in Projects 3A and 3B.

From My Computer, navigate to the student files that accompany this textbook. In the folder **03_business_running_case_pg37_86**, locate and open the folder for this chapter. Open and print the instructions for this project, which are provided to you in Adobe PDF format. Follow the instructions and use the skills you have gained thus far to assist Jennifer Nelson in meeting the challenges of owning and running her business.

End **You have completed Project 3J**

Rubric

The following outcomes-based assessments are *open-ended assessments*. That is, there is no specific correct result; your result will depend on your approach to the information provided. Make *professional quality* your goal. Use the following scoring rubric to guide you in *how* to approach the problem and then to evaluate *how well* your approach solves the problem.

The *criteria*—Software Mastery, Content, Format and Layout, and Process—represent the knowledge and skills you have gained that you can apply to solving the problem. The *levels of performance*—Professional Quality, Approaching Professional Quality, or Needs Quality Improvements—help you and your instructor evaluate your result.

	Your completed project is of Professional Quality if you:	Your completed project is Approaching Professional Quality if you:	Your completed project Needs Quality Improvements if you:
1-Software Mastery	Choose and apply the most appropriate skills, tools, and features and identify efficient methods to solve the problem.	Choose and apply some appropriate skills, tools, and features, but not in the most efficient manner.	Choose inappropriate skills, tools, or features, or are inefficient in solving the problem.
2-Content	Construct a solution that is clear and well organized, contains content that is accurate, appropriate to the audience and purpose, and is complete. Provide a solution that contains no errors of spelling, grammar, or style.	Construct a solution in which some components are unclear, poorly organized, inconsistent, or incomplete. Misjudge the needs of the audience. Have some errors in spelling, grammar, or style, but the errors do not detract from comprehension.	Construct a solution that is unclear, incomplete, or poorly organized, containing some inaccurate or inappropriate content; and contains many errors of spelling, grammar, or style. Do not solve the problem.
3-Format and Layout	Format and arrange all elements to communicate information and ideas, clarify function, illustrate relationships, and indicate relative importance.	Apply appropriate format and layout features to some elements, but not others. Overuse features, causing minor distraction.	Apply format and layout that does not communicate information or ideas clearly. Do not use format and layout features to clarify function, illustrate relationships, or indicate relative importance. Use available features excessively, causing distraction.
4-Process	Use an organized approach that integrates planning, development, self-assessment, revision, and reflection.	Demonstrate an organized approach in some areas, but not others; or, use an insufficient process of organization throughout.	Do not use an organized approach to solve the problem.

Outcomes-Based Assessments

Problem Solving

Project 3K — Coral Ridge

In this project, you will construct a solution by applying any combination of the Objectives found in Projects 3A and 3B.

For Project 3K, you will need the following file:

New blank PowerPoint presentation

**You will save your presentation as
3K_Coral_Ridge_Firstname_Lastname**

Select National Properties has developed a new housing development in the suburbs of Chicago. Randall Thomas, CEO, will be making a presentation on the new community to prospective home buyers. The development—Coral Ridge—consists of 55 homes with two different floor plans. The first floor plan—The Oakmont—includes 1,700 square feet and has 3 bedrooms and 2 baths. There is a fireplace in the family room and the kitchen and bathrooms have tile countertops. The second floor plan—The Seneca—has 1,925 square feet with 4 bedrooms and 2 baths. There are fireplaces in the master bedroom and in the family room, and the bathrooms and kitchens have granite countertops. The community has an excellent school district and is accessible by major highways.

Create a presentation with six slides that describes the community and the development. Apply a design template of your choice, change the background style on at least one slide, and include a picture on the background of one slide. Using the information in the preceding paragraph, insert a slide with a table that compares the two floor plans. Apply slide transitions and animation. Add the file name to the Notes and Handouts footer and check the presentation for spelling errors. Save the presentation as **3K_Coral_Ridge_Firstname_Lastname** and submit it as directed.

Note: You can find many appropriate images available to Office users. To access these images, click the Insert tab, and then from the Illustrations group, click the Clip Art button. In the Clip Art task pane, type a key word—such as *construction*—in the *Search for* box. You can specify the image type (clip art or photographs) and where to search. The largest variety of photographs can be found by including Web Collections in the *Search in* box. You can also use images from earlier projects in this chapter, or images from your personal collection.

End **You have completed Project 3K**

Outcomes-Based Assessments

Problem Solving

Project 3L — Land Development

In this project, you will construct a solution by applying any combination of the Objectives found in Projects 3A and 3B.

For Project 3L, you will need the following file:

New blank PowerPoint presentation

You will save your presentation as
3L_Land_Development_Firstname_Lastname

Select National Properties owns several land parcels in the growing community of Lake Monahan. The Chief Financial Officer, Morgan Bannon-Navarre, is creating a presentation for the members of the Lake Monahan Real Estate Association that describes the available parcels located in three areas of the city: North, South, and Central. Create a presentation with four to six slides describing the community and the parcels using the following information.

The City of Lake Monahan is a vacation destination for many out-of-state families. The lake provides opportunities for water sports, fishing, and boating. Select National Properties invested in the city by purchasing several land parcels approximately 15 years ago and is now ready to develop and sell the parcels.

In your presentation, insert one slide with a picture on the slide background that depicts the lake. (See the note at the end of project 3K for ideas on locating images). Insert a slide titled **Available Parcels** and use the data below to create a table describing the parcels.

	North	South	Central
Parcels	10	15	18
Size	.75 acres	1.2 acres	1.05 acres
Price	$45,000	$68,000	$52,000

Insert a slide with the title **Average Parcel Price** and then insert an appropriate chart using the following data.

	North	South	Central
2008	$22,300	$55,675	$41,375
2009	$32,500	$62,420	$45,850
2010	$45,000	$68,000	$52,000

Use formatting and animation techniques that you learned in this chapter to create a professional presentation. Add the file name to the Notes and Handouts footer and check for spelling errors. Save the presentation as **3L_Land_Development_Firstname_Lastname** and submit it as directed.

End **You have completed Project 3L**

Problem Solving

Project 3M — Renovation

In this project, you will construct a solution by applying any combination of the Objectives found in Projects 3A and 3B.

For Project 3M, you will need the following files:

New blank PowerPoint presentation
p3M_Scaffold
p3M_Scaffold2

You will save your presentation as
3M_Renovation_Firstname_Lastname

Select National Properties' Vice President of Construction, Michael Wentworth, is presenting the status of The Lincoln Plaza—a large renovation project—to the project investors. Use the following information to create a presentation with at least four slides, including a table and a chart.

The Lincoln Plaza consists of three 10-story buildings on the perimeter of a large courtyard. The renovation is taking place in three overlapping phases: Exteriors which are 75 percent complete with an expected completion date of September 2009; Interior Infrastructure which is 55 percent complete with an expected completion date of June 2010; and Courtyard Enhancements which is 35 percent complete with an expected completion date of December 2010. The cost of each phase in millions is estimated as follows:

	Exterior	Interior	Courtyard
Labor	22.6	33.8	5.25
Materials	36.9	48.7	12.6

Apply an appropriate design and background style, and change the Fonts Theme. Format the background of one slide using one of the pictures provided with your student files—p3M_Scaffold or p3M_Scaffold2. Apply chart and table styles and slide transitions and animation. Add the file name to the Notes and Handouts footer and check for spelling errors. Save the presentation as **3M_Renovation_Firstname_Lastname** and submit it as directed.

End **You have completed Project 3M** ———————

Problem Solving

Project 3N—High School

In this project, you will construct a solution by applying any combination of the Objectives found in Projects 3A and 3B.

> **For Project 3N, you will need the following file:**
>
> New blank PowerPoint presentation

**You will save your presentation as
3N_High_School_Firstname_Lastname**

Select National Properties has been chosen as one of three contractors bidding on the construction of a new high school in Monroe Heights. Company President Shaun Walker is making a presentation to the Monroe Heights School Board regarding the company's proposal. Create a presentation that includes one or two slides with information about the company, one slide with a table, one slide with a chart, and two slides that include slide backgrounds with pictures of school facilities. (See the note at the end of project 3K for ideas on locating images). Use the following information for your presentation.

Select National Properties is a diversified real estate company which develops, builds, manages, and acquires a wide variety of properties nationwide. Among the company's portfolio of properties are shopping malls, mixed-use town center developments, high-rise office buildings, office parks, industrial buildings and warehouses, multifamily housing developments, educational facilities, and hospitals. Residential developments are mainly located in and around the company's hometown, Chicago; commercial and public buildings in the portfolio are located nationwide. The company is well respected for its focus on quality and commitment to the environment and economic development of the areas where it operates. Use the information below to create a slide with a table using columns 1, 2, and 3 and a slide with a chart using columns 1 and 4.

	Description	Completion	Estimate
Buildings	45 classrooms	January 2010	$18.0 million
Network	Wireless access	July 2010	$0.5 million
Pool	Outdoor Olympic size with bleachers	December 2010	$1.5 million
Exteriors	Parking, landscape	July 2010	$5.0 million

Apply an appropriate design and background style and change the Fonts Theme. Apply chart and table styles and slide transitions and animation. Add the the file name to the Notes and Handouts footer and check for spelling errors. Save the presentation as **3N_High_School_Firstname_Lastname** and submit it as directed.

End **You have completed Project 3N**

Problem Solving

Project 3O — Recruiting

In this project, you will construct a solution by applying any combination of the Objectives found in Projects 3A and 3B.

> **For Project 3O, you will need the following file:**
>
> New blank PowerPoint presentation
>
> **You will save your presentation as**
> **3O_Recruiting_Firstname_Lastname**

To serve the growing national needs of the company, the Board of Directors for Select National Properties has decided to open an office in Austin, Texas. Nancy Chung, Human Resources Director, will be recruiting college graduates for professional opportunities in the new location. Use the following information to create a presentation that she can show at several colleges she is visiting.

Select National Properties is a diversified real estate company which develops, builds, manages, and acquires a wide variety of properties nationwide. The mission of Select National Properties is to be a leader in the real estate development business through a commitment to integrity, high ethical standards, and operational expertise. Among the company's portfolio of properties are shopping malls, mixed-use town center developments, high-rise office buildings, office parks, industrial buildings and warehouses, multifamily housing developments, educational facilities, and hospitals. Residential developments are mainly located in and around the company's hometown, Chicago; commercial and public buildings in the portfolio are located nationwide. The company is well respected for its focus on quality and commitment to the environment and economic development of the areas where it operates.

(Project 3O–Recruiting continues on the next page)

Problem Solving

(Project 3O—Recruiting continued)

The following table includes information about the sales growth of Select National Properties in millions over the past 10 years.

Sector	2000	2005	2010
Residential	125	158	209
Commercial	167	219	282
Land	95	132	191

The following table summarizes the types of positions for which Nancy is recruiting.

Position	Description	Starting Salary
Civil Engineer	Applies knowledge of design, construction procedures, zoning and building codes, and building materials to render structural designs.	$45,000
Project Manager	Prepares and reviews facilities plans, construction contract bid documents, and specifications for projects. Monitors project progress and costs.	$53,000
Accountant	Performs professional accounting work, including auditing, analyzing, and verifying fiscal records and reports.	$38,000

Create a presentation that includes at least six slides, including background information on the company, and a table and a chart using the preceding information. Apply an appropriate design and background style and change the Fonts Theme. Apply chart and table styles, and slide transitions and animation. Add the file name to the Notes and Handouts footer and check for spelling errors. Save the presentation as **3O_Recruiting_Firstname_Lastname** and submit it as directed.

End **You have completed Project 3O** ——————————

Outcomes-Based Assessments

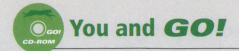 **You and *GO!***

Project 3P — You and *GO!*

In this project, you will construct a solution by applying any combination of the skills you practiced from the Objectives in Projects 3A and 3B.

From My Computer, navigate to the student files that accompany this textbook. In the folder **04_you_and_go_pg87_102**, locate and open the folder for this chapter. Open and print the instructions for this project, which are provided to you in Adobe PDF format. Follow the instructions to create a presentation about the registration process at your school.

End **You have completed Project 3P** ———————

GO! with Help

Project 3Q — *GO!* with Help

There are a number of different types of charts that you can create in PowerPoint. Use Microsoft Office PowerPoint Help to learn about the different types of charts in PowerPoint.

1 **Start** PowerPoint. At the far right end of the Ribbon, click the **Microsoft Office PowerPoint Help** button.

2 In the **Type words to search for** box, type **Chart Types** and then press Enter.

3 Click the **Available chart types** link, and then read the information on each type of chart. When you are through, **Close** the Help window, and then **Close** PowerPoint.

End **You have completed Project 3Q** ———————

Group Business Running Case

Project 3R — Group Business Running Case

In this project, you will apply all the Objectives found in Projects 3A and 3B.

Your instructor may assign this group case project to your class. If your instructor assigns this project, he or she will provide you with information and instructions to work as part of a group. The group will apply the skills gained thus far to help the Bell Orchid Hotel Group achieve its business goals.

End **You have completed Project 3R** ——————————————

Glossary

Animation effects A command that introduces individual slide elements so that the slide can be displayed one element at a time.

Background style A slide background fill variation that combines theme colors in different intensities.

Black slide A slide that displays at the end of a slide presentation indicating the end of the slide show.

Body font A font that is applied to all slide text except titles.

Bulleted levels Outline levels identified by a symbol.

Category labels A chart element that display along the bottom of the chart to identify the categories of data.

Cell The intersection of a column and row.

Cell reference A combination of the column letter and row number identifying a cell.

Chart A graphic representation of numeric data.

Clip Art Drawings, movies, sounds, or photographic images that are included with Microsoft Office or downloaded from the Web.

Column chart A type of chart used to compare data.

Contextual tabs Specialized tools for working with a selected object and that appear as additional tabs in the Ribbon.

Contextual tools Tools that enable you to perform specific commands related to the selected object, and display one or more contextual tabs that contain related groups of commands that you will need when working with the type of object that is selected.

Copy A command that duplicates a selection and places it on the Clipboard.

Crosshair pointer The pointer that indicates that you can draw a shape.

Custom animation list A list that indicates the animation effect applied to slide items.

Cut A command that removes selected text or graphics from your presentation and moves the selection to the Clipboard.

Data marker A column, bar, area, dot, pie slice, or other symbol in a chart that represents a single data point.

Data point A chart value that originates in a worksheet cell.

Data series A group of related data points.

Deselect The action of canceling a selection.

Drag-and-drop The action of moving a selection by dragging it to a new location.

Dragging The technique of holding down the left mouse button and moving over an area of text in order to select it.

Editing The process of adding, deleting, or changing the contents of a slide.

Effect options Animation options that include changing the direction of an effect and playing a sound when an animation takes place.

Entrance effects Animations that bring a slide element onto the screen.

Fill color The inside color of text or an object.

Font A set of characters with the same design and shape.

Font styles Font formatting that emphasizes text, including bold, italic, and underline.

Font theme A theme that determines the font applied to two types of slide text—headings and body.

Footer Text that displays at the bottom of every slide or that prints at the bottom of a sheet of slide handouts or notes pages.

Format Painter A feature that copies formatting from one selection of text to another, thus ensuring formatting consistency in your presentation.

Formatting Changing the appearance of the text, layout, and design of a slide.

Gallery A visual representation of a command's options.

Gradient fill A color combination in which one color fades into another.

Guides Vertical and horizontal lines that display in the rulers to give you a visual indication of where the crosshair pointer is positioned so that you can draw a shape.

Header Text that displays at the top of every slide or that prints at the top of a sheet of slide handouts or notes pages.

Headings font The font that is applied to slide titles.

Insertion point A blinking vertical line that indicates where text will be inserted.

Layout The placement and arrangement of the text and graphic elements on a slide.

Legend A chart element that identifies the patterns or colors that are assigned to the categories in the chart.

Line chart A type of chart that show trends over time.

Live preview A technology that shows the results of applying an editing or formatting change as you move your pointer over the results presented in the gallery.

Mini toolbar A small toolbar containing frequently used formatting commands, and sometimes accompanied by a shortcut menu of other frequently used commands, which displays as a result of right-clicking a selection or of selecting text.

Normal view The view in which the PowerPoint window is divided into three areas: the Slides/Outline pane, the Slide pane, and the Notes pane.

Notes pages Printouts that contain the slide image in the top half of the page and speaker's notes in the lower half of the page.

Office Clipboard A temporary storage area maintained by your Microsoft Office program.

Paste The action of placing text or objects that have been copied or moved from one location to another location.

Placeholder A slide element that reserves a portion of a slide and serves as a container for text, graphics, and other slide elements.

Points A unit of measure to describe the size of a font.

Presentation graphics software A program used to effectively present information to an audience.

Print Preview A feature that displays your presentation as it will print based on the options that you select.

Shape Style A combination of formatting effects that includes 3-D, glow, and bevel effects and shadows.

Shapes Drawing objects including lines, arrows, stars and banners, and ovals and rectangles that are used to help convey a message by showing process and by containing text.

Shortcut menu A context-sensitive menu that displays commands and options relevant to the selected object.

Sizing handles White circles or squares that surround an image and are used to size the image.

Slide handouts Printed images of more than one slide on a sheet of paper.

Slide Sorter View A view useful for rearranging slides in which all of the slides in the presentation display as thumbnails.

SmartArt graphic A designer-quality visual representation of your information that you can create by choosing from among many different layouts to effectively community your message or ideas.

SmartArt Styles Combinations of formatting effects that are applied to diagrams.

Synonyms Words with the same meaning as a selected word.

Table A format for information that organizes and presents text and data in columns and rows.

Table style Formatting applied to an entire table so that it is consistent with the presentation theme.

Task pane A window within a Microsoft Office application that allows you to enter options for completing a command.

Template The horizontal placement of text within a placeholder.

Text Alignment A model on which a presentation is based that may include text, graphics, and color schemes.

Text box An object that is used to position text anywhere on the slide.

Thesaurus A research tool that provides a list of synonyms.

Thumbnails Miniature images of each slide.

Toggle button Buttons that are clicked once to turn them on and then clicked again to turn them off.

Transitions The way that a slide appears or disappears during an onscreen slide show.

WordArt A feature that applies combinations of decorative formatting to text, including shadows, reflections, and 3-D effects, as well as changing the line and fill color of text.

Index

 The CD symbol represents Index entries found on the CD (See CD file name for page numbers).

A

alignment
    objects, 101–104
    text, 23–24
animation, 162
    effect and timing options, setting, 175–178
    effective use of, 179
    entrance effects, 172–174
    removing, 175
    to SmartArt graphic, 179–180
animation effects, 8

B

backgrounds
    fill color, applying, 170–171
    formatting with picture, 166–170
    hiding graphics, 165–166
    style, 164–165
black slide, 8–9
Blinds, 176–177
bullet points, creating from SmartArt graphic, 123
bulleted levels, 14
Bullets button arrow, 85

C

category labels, 191
CD, packaging presentation for, **CD 3–4**
cell, table, 185–188
cell reference, 191
charts, 162
    animating, 197–198
    column, creating, and applying chart style, 190–194
    deleting columns, 196–197
    deleting data and changing type, 195–196
    editing data after closing Excel, 194
clip art, 40–42
closing, 31
color, changing, 31
columns
    chart, creating, 190–192
    deleting, 186, 196
    layout, modifying, 185–186
    selecting, 189
command, repeating, 84
Command tab, 5
compressing pictures, **CD 5–6**
contextual tab, 41
contextual tools, 41
contrast, creating, 115
copying text, 109–111
crosshair pointer, 96
Cycle graphic, 115

D

data marker, 193
data point, 193
data series, 193
deleting
    animation, 175
    columns, 196–197
    data and changing type, 195–196
    rows or columns, 186, 196
    shapes containing text, 119
demoting text, 15

designing presentation, 80
    bulleted list, changing to numbered list, 85
    bulleted list style, modifying, 85–87
    Format Painter, 89–90
    placeholder text and repeat key, 82–84
    WordArt styles, applying to text, 87–89
dragging, 15
duplicating objects, 101–104

E

editing data after closing Excel, 194
editing text
    slides, 11–12
    using thesaurus, 18
effect options, 175
Excel, editing data after closing, 194
existing presentation, inserting slides from, 36–37

F

file names, 10
folder, 9–11
Format Painter, 89–90
formatting
    font and font size, changing, 20–22
    font styles, applying, 22–23
    slide layout, modifying, 24–25
    text, clearing, 114
    text alignment and line spacing, 23–24
    text box, 96
    theme, changing, 25–27

G

gallery, 12
gradient fill, 99
graphics
    adding and removing shapes in diagram, 118–119
    changing diagram type and size, 120–122
    deleting shapes containing text, 119
grayscale, 31
Group buttons, 5
guides, 96

H

headers and footers, 27–29
Help, 45–46
Hierarchy graphic, 115
Home tab
    Drawing group, 98
    Font group, 21, 22, 99
    Paragraph group, 23–24, 85
    Slides group, 24

I

Insert tab, 116
inserting slide, 12–14
insertion point, 93
Internet file transfer programs, 10

L

landscape orientation, slides, **CD 1–2**
layout, 12

legend, 191
line spacing, 23–24
List graphic, 115
list levels, increasing and decreasing, 14–16
Live Preview, 21

M

Matrix graphic, 115
Microsoft Office PowerPoint Help button, 46
Mini toolbar, 15, 21
   Bold button, 23
moving
   images, 42–44
   slides, 39
   text, 109–111
multiple selections, copying with Office Clipboard, 112–113

N

Next Slide button, 8
notes pages, 27–29
Notes pane, 5, 19

O

Office button, 5
   New, 34
   Save As, 35
Office Clipboard
   multiple selections, copying, 112–113
   single items, copying, 114
Office Theme, 26
opening presentation, 6–8
orientation and size, slide, CD 1–2

P

packaging presentation for CD, CD 3–4
Paste Options button, 110
pictures, 39, 90
   changing size and shape of picture, 92–93
   clip art, 40–42
   compressing, CD 5–6
   duplicating and aligning objects, 101–104
   inserting using Content Layout, 91
   moving and sizing images, 42–44
   style, applying, 44–45
   styles, applying, 99–101
   text box, inserting and positioning, 93–96
placeholders, 13
points, 20
portrait orientation, slides, CD 1–2
PowerPoint 2007
   animation, 162
      effect and timing options, setting, 175–178
      effective use of, 179
      entrance effects, 172–174
      removing effects, 175
      to SmartArt graphic, 179–180
   backgrounds
      fill color, applying, 170–171
      formatting with picture, 166–170
      hiding graphics, 165–166
      style, 164–165
   charts, 162
      animating, 197–198
      column, creating, and applying chart style, 190–194
      deleting columns, 196–197
      deleting data and changing type, 195–196
      editing data after closing Excel, 194
   closing, 31
   creating folders and saving presentation, 9–11
   designing presentation, 80
      bulleted list, changing to numbered list, 85
      bulleted list style, modifying, 85–87

      Format Painter, 89–90
      placeholder text and repeat key, 82–84
      WordArt styles, applying to text, 87–89
   editing text
      slides, 11–12
      using thesaurus, 18
   formatting presentation
      font and font size, changing, 20–22
      font styles, applying, 22–23
      slide layout, modifying, 24–25
      text alignment and line spacing, 23–24
      theme, changing, 25–27
   graphics
      adding and removing shapes in diagram, 118–119
      changing diagram type and size, 120–122
      deleting shapes containing text, 119
   headers and footers, 27–29
   Help, 45–46
   inserting new slide, 12–14
   inserting slides from existing presentation, 36–37
   list levels, increasing and decreasing, 14–16
   new, creating, 33–36
   opening presentation, 6–8
   pictures, adding to presentation, 39
      clip art, 40–42
      moving and sizing images, 42–44
      style, applying, 44–45
   pictures and shapes, 90
      changing size and shape of picture, 92–93
      duplicating and aligning objects, 101–104
      inserting using Content Layout, 91
      styles, applying, 99–101
      text box, inserting and positioning, 93–96
   previewing and printing presentation, 29–31
   shapes
      inserting, sizing, and positioning, 96–98
      text, adding, 98–99
   Slide Sorter view
      moving slides, 39
      selecting and deleting slides, 38–39
   slide transitions, 105–107
   SmartArt graphic
      bullet points, creating from, 123
      color and style, 123–124
      creating by using content layout, 115–118
   speaker's notes, 19–20
   spell-checking, 16–17
   starting, 2, 4
   tables, 162
      columns, selecting, 189
      creating, 182–185
      design, modifying, 188–190
      layout, modifying, 185–188
   text
      changes, undoing and redoing, 114
      contrast, creating, 115
      formatting, clearing, 114
      moving and copying, 109–111
      multiple selections, copying with Office Clipboard, 112–113
   themes, 171–172
   viewing slide show, 8–9
   window parts, identifying, 4–6
presentation
   packaging for CD, CD 3–4
   pictures, compressing, CD 5–6
presentation graphics software, 4
previewing presentation, 29–31
Previous Slide button, 8
printing presentation, 29–31
Print Preview, 29
Process graphic, 115
promoting text, 15
Pyramid graphic, 115

Q

Quick Access Toolbar (QAT), 5
    Repeat button, 84
    Save button, 12
Quick Style, 101

R

Redo button, 114
Relationship graphic, 115
Repeat button, 84
Reuse Slides task pane, 36–37
Ribbon, 5
    Home tab, 12, 21, 22
    Paragraph group, 14
    Review, 17, 18
    SmartArt Tools group, 117
row
    adding to table, 185
    deleting, 186
    layout, modifying, 185–186

S

saving presentation, 9–11
screen elements, 5–6
ScreenTip, 24
selecting columns, 189
Shape Style, 90, 101
shapes, 90
    changing size and shape of picture, 92–93
    duplicating and aligning objects, 101–104
    inserting, sizing, and positioning, 96–98
    inserting using Content Layout, 91
    styles, applying, 99–101
    text, adding, 98–99
    text, deleting, 119
    text box, inserting and positioning, 93–96
shortcut menu, 16
single items, copying with Office Clipboard, 114
sizing handles, 42
sizing images, 42–44
slide
    orientation and size, setting, ● CD 1–2
    transitions, 105–107
slide handouts
    headers and footers, 27–29
Slide pane, 5
Slide Sorter button, 38
Slide Sorter view
    moving slides, 39
    selecting and deleting slides, 38–39

Slides/Outline pane, 6, 7
SmartArt graphic
    bullet points, creating from, 123
    color and style, 123–124
    creating by using content layout, 115–118
SmartArt Styles, 123–124
SmartArt Tools group, 117
speaker's notes, 19–20
spell-checking, 16–17
starting, 2, 4
Status bar, 6
style, applying to picture, 44–45
style, table, 188–189
symbols, using as bullet characters, 87
synonyms, 18

T

table, 162
    columns, selecting, 189
    creating, 182–185
    design, modifying, 188–190
    layout, modifying, 185–188
table style, 188–189
task pane, 36–37
templates, finding, 34
text
    alignment, 23–24
    changes, undoing and redoing, 114
    contrast, creating, 115
    deleting shapes containing, 119
    formatting, clearing, 114
    moving and copying, 109–111
    multiple selections, copying with Office Clipboard, 112–113
text box, inserting and positioning, 93–96
Text Fill button arrow, 88
themes
    font, 171–172
    formatting, 25–27
Title bar, 6
toggle buttons, 23
transitions, 8, 105–107

V

View buttons, 6

W

window, parts of, 4–6

SINGLE PC LICENSE AGREEMENT AND LIMITED WARRANTY